OPTIONS TRADING FOR THE CONSERVATIVE INVESTOR

OPTIONS TRADING FOR THE CONSERVATIVE INVESTOR

INCREASING PROFITS WITHOUT INCREASING YOUR RISK

Michael C. Thomsett

Vice President, Publisher: Tim Moore
Associate Publisher and Director of Marketing: Amy Neidlinger
Executive Editor: Jim Boyd
Editorial Assistant: Pamela Boland
Operations Manager: Gina Kanouse
Senior Marketing Manager: Julie Phifer
Publicity Manager: Laura Czaja
Assistant Marketing Manager: Megan Colvin
Cover Designer: Alan Clements
Managing Editor: Kristy Hart
Project Editors: Julie Anderson and Jovana San Nicolas-Shirley
Copy Editor: Karen Gill
Proofreader: Dan Knott
Indexer: Michael C. Thomsett
Senior Compositor: Gloria Schurick
Manufacturing Buyer: Dan Uhrig

© 2010 by Pearson Education, Inc.
Publishing as FT Press
Upper Saddle River, New Jersey 07458

FT Press offers excellent discounts on this book when ordered in quantity for bulk purchases or special sales. For more information, please contact U.S. Corporate and Government Sales, 1-800-382-3419, corpsales@pearsontechgroup.com. For sales outside the U.S., please contact International Sales at international@pearson.com.

Printed in the United States of America

Second Printing August 2010

ISBN-10: 0-13-704200-0
ISBN-13: 978-0-13-704200-5

Pearson Education LTD.
Pearson Education Australia PTY, Limited.
Pearson Education Singapore, Pte. Ltd.
Pearson Education North Asia, Ltd.
Pearson Education Canada, Ltd.
Pearson Educación de Mexico, S.A. de C.V.
Pearson Education—Japan
Pearson Education Malaysia, Pte. Ltd.

Library of Congress Cataloging-in-Publication Data

Thomsett, Michael C.

  Options trading for the conservative investor : increasing profits without increasing your risk / Michael C. Thomsett. — 2nd ed.

    p. cm.

  Includes bibliographical references and index.

  ISBN 978-0-13-704200-5 (hardback : alk. paper) 1. Stock options. 2. Options (Finance) 3. Investments. 4. Risk management. I. Title.

  HG6042.T462 2010

  332.63'2283—dc22

                                    2009036159

CONTENTS

ACKNOWLEDGMENTS xi

ABOUT THE AUTHOR xii

PREFACE xiii

CHAPTER 1: SETTING THE GROUND RULES 1

The Ground Rules 2

A Model Portfolio 4

CHAPTER 2: OPTION BASICS 7

The Workings of Option
Contracts .8

Long and Short 13

Calls and Call Strategies 17

Puts and Put Strategies 22

Listed Options and LEAPS
Options 28

Coordinating Strategies with
Portfolio Goals 32

Option and Stock Volatility:
The Central Element of Risk 35

Trading Costs in the Option
Analysis 46

Tax Rules for Options:
An Overview 47

The Importance of Professional
Advice and Tax Planning 48

CHAPTER 3: OPTIONS IN CONTEXT 51

The Nature of Risk and Reward . . .52

Perceptions about Options 60

Short Positions: Naked or
Covered 63

Margin Requirements and
Trading Restrictions 68

Return Calculations: Seeking
Valid Comparisons 70

Long-Term Goals as a
Guiding Force 80

Exercise as a Desirable Outcome . .82

CHAPTER 4: MANAGING PROFITS
AND LOSSES 85

Your Conservative Dilemma 87

Managing Profits with Options . . .89

Overcoming the Profit-Taking
Problem 92

Managing the Inertia Problem 99

Taxes and Profits 102

CHAPTER 5: OPTIONS AS CASH
GENERATORS 107

The Covered Call Concept 108

Examples: Ten Stocks and
Covered Calls 110

Smart Conservative Ground
Rules 115

A Conservative Approach 121

Tax Ramifications of
Covered Calls 125

Rolling Forward and Up:
Exercise Avoidance 130

The Exercise Acceptance
Strategy .131

CHAPTER 6: ALTERNATIVES TO STOCK
PURCHASE 133

Leverage and Options 134

The Long-Call Contingent-
Purchase Strategy 137

The Covered Long Call 140

Short Puts and Contingent
Purchase 144

Rescue Strategy Using Calls 148

Rescue Strategy Using Puts 154

Covered Calls for
Contingent Sale 155

CHAPTER 7: OPTION STRATEGIES IN DOWN
MARKETS 157

Thinking Outside the
Market Box 158

The Long Put:
The Overlooked Option 161

Short Puts: A Variety of
Strategies 165

Comparing Rates of Return for
Dissimilar Strike Prices 170

Using Calls in Down Markets 172

Evaluating Your Stock Positions ..175

Stock Positions and Risk
Evaluation 180

Options and Downside Risk 182

Option Planning with
Loss Carryover 185

CHAPTER 8: COMBINATION CONSERVATIVE
TECHNIQUES 189

Spread Techniques 190

Straddle Techniques 192

Long or Short Positions 194

Theory Versus Practice 196

Tax Problems with Combination
    Strategies .199

The Ultimate High-Return
    Strategy .200

Examples of the Strategy in
    Practice 202

Outcome Scenarios 211

The Augmented Strategy:
    A Short Straddle 213

Rescue Strategies 218

CHAPTER 9: STOCK SELECTION AND THE
        OPTION CONTRACT 221

Remembering Your Conservative
    Profile as a Priority 223

Dangers and Pitfalls in Using
    Options 224

Temptation to Select Most
    Volatile Stocks 226

Creating Sensible Conservative
    Standards .228

Maintaining Fundamental
    Clarity 232

The Importance of Taxes in the
Option Equation 235

Option Volatility to
Judge Stocks 236

APPENDIX: OPTION TRADING STRATEGIES . .239

GLOSSARY 243

INDEX 249

ACKNOWLEDGMENTS

Many thanks to Michael Panzner, Rudy Morando, Harry Domash, and Steve Kursh, all of whom added to this project with their suggestions. Also, I am most grateful to my editor, Jim Boyd, for his steady hand and guidance.

ABOUT THE AUTHOR

Michael C. Thomsett has published more than 70 books on investing and business topics, including *Stock Profits: Getting to the Core* (FT Press, 2004) and many other books concerning options and stock market investing. His best-selling book *Getting Started in Options* (John Wiley & Sons, 2009) is in its 8th edition and has sold more than 250,000 copies. He has written many other books published by John Wiley & Sons, Amacom Books, and Dearborn. Thomsett lives in Nashville, Tennessee.

PREFACE

The Elusive Goal: Low Risk and High Yield

There is good news about the market. Recent stock market trends have been troubling for just about everyone invested in stocks. The traditional approach of buy-and-hold and the trusted technique of value investing based on a study of the fundamentals seemed to fall apart beginning in 2008. Does this mean that buy-and-hold is dead? Not at all. The cyclical nature of the market simply went through a strong bear cycle, but the strength of the American stock market has shown time and again that downward movements are temporary and are always followed by record-breaking upward-moving markets.

In the meantime, however, you may have seen most of your retirement savings and personal portfolio disappear. The staggering losses in even the best-known value investments brought into question the basic "safe" philosophy of the market. To protect yourself in this kind of volatile and uncertain environment, you need strategies to hedge losses; create extra sources of income; and most of all, reduce risk while increasing net yield.

Is it even possible to match low risk with high yield in the volatile markets that have dominated recent years? Most experts question the idea that risk-averse investors can outperform the market averages. However, this book challenges the conventional wisdom by demonstrating how conservative investors can exploit a narrow band of potential strategies, dramatically increase yields, and, at the same time, manage risks within their self-defined risk limitations.

To some conservative investors, options are too exotic and too risky. If a range of strategies is too much trouble or contains too many pitfalls, it is not worth pursuing. But a basic premise in this book is that a *conservative* investor is not necessarily someone who does not want to expand beyond a well-understood and short list of investment possibilities. Being a conservative investor does not necessarily mean that you are unwilling to examine new ideas, expand your portfolio, or take acceptable risks. It just means that you are not interested in speculation or in exposing yourself to the possibilities of high risk.

Investors tend to be aware of the potential for high returns without also acknowledging that such strategies are usually accompanied by unavoidable high risks. This is where the inexperienced suffer losses in the market. The lack of experience that attracts the novice to speculation in options and other high-risk strategies has caused much grief in the market. When you look back at the dot-com years, you see that many first-time investors made quick paper profits, only to lose it all in a sudden reversal of fortunes. But conservative investors know that putting all capital in a single industry is ill advised, especially if companies are chosen that have never reported a net profit, whose stock has risen more than $200 per share in a few months, or whose actual core business is only vaguely defined.

Given these observations, conservative investors naturally seek methods for using their capital that achieve some specific goals, including the following:

- Preserving spending power after both inflation and taxes
- Avoiding unacceptable market, liquidity, and diversification risks
- Protecting profits without loss of invested positions, hedging the portfolio against the possibility of loss

These goals are typical for conservative investors and actually serve moderate investors just as well. They involve strategies for avoiding loss. As a *conservative* investor, you are not averse to risk in any and every form; essentially, you are averse to unexpected surprises. This is perhaps the most important distinguishing characteristic between you and other investors. The majority of novice investors are surprised when they lose money in the market, but, in retrospect, should they have been surprised? In most situations, novices operate on certain assumptions concerning potential profits but are unaware of the related risk or the degree of risk exposure. Otherwise, their investment decisions probably would have been different.

With this in mind, this book offers a more realistic definition of *conservative* investors: those who are experienced enough to be aware of both yield and risk and who make decisions based on that level of awareness. Conservative investors are not as likely as other investors to be taken by surprise when they lose money in the market. Another aspect of this expanded definition distinguishes between risk profile and the willingness to use creative and alternative strategies. Conservative investors are not close-minded and do not reject exotic instruments like options merely because of their reputation as high-risk. Instead, well-informed conservative investors are likely to examine claims about high-yield potential with an open mind. You may be skeptical and, at the same time, willing to listen to the suggestion that the combination is at least possible. A limited number of strategies do, in fact, offer the potential for various conservative applications to meet the three goals common to conservative investors: preserving capital, avoiding unacceptable risk, and protecting paper profits. For example, this book includes 12 overall strategies (see the Appendix, "Option Trading Strategies"), qualified in terms of risk levels.

This book does not suggest that you have to become an expert in a broad range of complex or exotic options strategies. Instead, it proposes a rather limited number of strategies appropriate for conservative investors. This approach respects the risk limitations in the conservative strategy while showing how experienced stock market investors can expand their yield levels significantly, protect existing positions, and come through market down cycles intact.

1

SETTING THE GROUND RULES

In any discussion of an investment strategy, you begin with a series of assumptions. Your assumptions tie in to your conservative profile: You have prequalified the stock of a limited number of companies; you believe these stocks will rise in value over time; fundamentals are essential in stock selection; you would be happy to buy more shares; and a finite number of companies meet your standards. We have identified ten companies that make up a "model portfolio" to illustrate the options strategies in this book. These serve as examples of companies meeting a few basic criteria for picking companies and their stocks, as candidates for conservative options trading.

This book explains how conservative investors can employ options strategies to (a) enhance current income without increasing market risks; (b) protect long positions through options used for insurance; and (c) create a form of contingency to survive in volatile market conditions.

The Ground Rules

Because you are a *conservative* investor, the arguments in this book are based on a series of underlying assumptions. Always keep these ground rules in mind, because they relate to your risk profile and to your investing philosophy. Five underlying assumptions are used in this book.

1. **You will limit options activities to stocks you have prequalified.** This is a necessary starting point as long as your portfolio—and the stocks you use for options strategies—includes stocks you believe in as long-term-hold stocks, and you consider these stocks permanent parts of your portfolio (as long as the fundamentals remain strong). This is an important attribute because it is not conservative to buy stocks solely to use for options strategies. A conservative approach to options must include the premise that your activities will be limited to the strongest possible stocks you can find.

2. **You believe that your stocks will rise in value.** A conservative investor naturally expects stocks to rise in value; otherwise, why keep them? But this seemingly obvious point has relevance in the underlying assumptions of this book. Many of the discussions of strategies are premised on a belief that over the long term, the subject stock's market value will rise. Many options strategies work best when stocks do not rise, so for example, covered call writing (a very conservative strategy) is most profitable when stock values remain steady or even fall slightly. This

means that you may need to time a strategy to produce profits resulting from short-term stability in prices, hoping for longer-term growth. So a second underlying assumption is in line with the conservative approach. This means you want to accumulate shares of value investments; you expect prices to rise over time; and you will change a hold to a sell when the fundamentals change. However, at the same time, some options strategies are designed to take advantage of short-term price volatility. When marketwide volatility affects short-term prices in your stocks, you have an opportunity to pick up discounted shares, take profits (without having to sell stock), or average down your overall basis. Of course, the proposal that you should average down is conservative only if the basic stock selection assumptions remain valid. You will want to employ such a strategy only for stocks in which you have a strong belief as long-term value investments.

3. **You accept the premise that fundamental analysis of stocks is an essential first step in the process of examining option opportunities.** Options have no fundamental attributes. These are intangible contractual instruments, and they have no value on their own; thus, you can only judge the tangible value of stock as a means for selecting appropriate options strategies. Many first-time options traders make the mistake of overlooking this basic reality. They select options (and stocks) based on the immediate return potential, but they ignore the real market risks of the underlying stocks. This violates the conservative tenet that stocks should be chosen for their fundamental strength and growth potential.

4. **In the event of a temporary downward movement in a stock's price, you would be happy to buy more shares.** Some investors may be unwilling to pick up more shares of a particular stock, even when the opportunity to buy discounted shares is presented. In this book, several strategies are introduced proposing that additional shares may be purchased (or exposed to contingent purchase) using options. If this is not the case in a particular situation, those suggestions should be passed over. You may have a strict formula for diversification or asset allocation that

you use to limit risks in any particular stocks, for example, so strategies aimed at increasing your holdings in one stock may contradict your portfolio management standards in such an instance. Strategies proposing that you set up situations in which more shares may be picked up work *only* if that suggestion conforms to your overall portfolio plan.

5. **You believe that an adequate number of available stocks meet your criteria.** Some investors become convinced that their short list of stocks is the only list available to them. Thus, if they were to sell shares of stock from their portfolio, they would be unable to reinvest profits in equally acceptable stocks. If you do not believe this, you are probably aware that dozens of stocks meet your fundamental criteria, in terms of price level, PE ratio, volatility, dividend payment history, and a range of other analytical tests. Accordingly, if a particular stock is sold from your portfolio, a number of other stocks that you could and would purchase upon sale of stocks you currently own also conform to your criteria.

Incidentally, this practice makes sense whether you trade options or not. The fundamentals can change for any company, so if a hold stock changes to a sell, you need to reinvest funds. As a matter of basic portfolio management, every investor needs a secondary list of stocks that would be used to replace sold stocks from the current portfolio. The need for maintaining this list relates to options trading because some strategies result in selling shares of stock. In those cases, you want to reinvest capital in a new issue on your list of qualified stocks.

A Model Portfolio

In the examples used in the following chapters, these five underlying assumptions demonstrate how options work within the conservative framework. These criteria are applied to a model portfolio of ten stocks, which are used in various combinations throughout. This helps to tie together the various examples and range of possible outcomes. This model portfolio is by no means a recommendation of stocks you should own. It was selected to include stocks with some common attributes. Many have increased dividends every year for the past ten years and reported low volatility in trading. Others have exhibited rising market value in recent years. All these stocks have available both listed options and long-term options (LEAPS), enabling you to look at a variety of scenarios for each conservative strategy.

Employing a single portfolio throughout the book is helpful in another way. Not every strategy works well for each stock in the model portfolio, so you can walk through the selection process to demonstrate how a particular strategic decision is made. Although your portfolio may contain a number of excellent value investments, some strategies simply do not work at all times or in all cases. You can compare the different potentials for strategies across a range of stocks by following the model portfolio throughout the explanations in each chapter.

The values of each stock, current bid, and asked value of every option used in this book are based on the closing prices reported by the Chicago Board of Exchange (CBOE) on April 18, 2009. Table 1-1 summarizes this model portfolio.

Table 1-1 Model Portfolio

Stock Name	Trading Symbol	Closing Price *
Caterpillar	CAT	32.29
IBM	IBM	101.27
Johnson & Johnson	JNJ	53.05
Coca-Cola	KO	45.02
McDonald's	MCD	56.09
3M	MMM	53.81
Altria	MO	16.99
United Parcel Service	UPS	54.65
Wal-Mart	WMT	50.20
Exxon Mobil	XOM	66.75

* Closing prices as of April 18, 2009

Is this a "conservative" portfolio? That is a matter of opinion—and one that depends on the timing of purchase, long-term goals, and your personal opinion about the fundamentals for each corporation. These ten stocks provide a cross section of stocks that illustrate where strategies work well and where they do not work at all. The actual definition of a conservative portfolio is (and should be) always evolving based on changes in the market, in a stock's market price and volatility, and, of course, in emerging information concerning fundamental strength or weakness of a particular company.

Is this information out of date? The data gathered on the closing date—April 18, 2009—is old, but it would be impossible to perpetually update 10 stocks and still meet the publication date of this book. However, all the information is relative. The values of options for a particular stock will probably be consistent from one period to the next—assuming the proximity between closing price and option strike price is about the same, and that months to go until expiration are the same as well. Although these relationships can and do vary based on ever-changing perceptions about a particular company, the data is valid for the purpose of illustrating strategies. The use of some measurement in time is necessary, and all these stocks were selected and summarized on the same date. Given all these qualifications, these closing prices (and the option values used in this book) are fair and reasonable. As of that same date, April 18, 2009, there were about 2,500 stocks that had options available to trade—a lot of choices for conservative investors.

2

OPTION BASICS

The biggest hurdle in the options market is terminology. This chapter explains the basic concepts and defines option terms; introduces call and put strategies; explains how long and short positions work in both types of option contracts; and provides an overview of the options market.

T ypically, books about options start by showing how you can leverage a small amount of capital to make fantastic profits, often in the triple digits. Such books tend to quickly become overly technical and complex, so that you end up with two problems. First, you are exposed to the proposition that you can get rich by speculating in options; second, the discussion becomes obscure as the details emerge.

This is not an approach that works for conservative investors. One basic assumption in this book is that, as a conservative investor, you want to know exactly how options might or might not work in your portfolio, and you want the information to be presented clearly and logically. Because this involves a fairly narrow range of possible strategies—only those appropriate in a conservative portfolio—a lot of the more exotic potential of options is avoided.

Even the most experienced investor struggles with terminology and the meaning of key concepts, so this chapter covers the important matters that you need to master, including explanations of calls and puts in either long or short positions; how option contracts work; expiration of options; strike prices; and time, extrinsic, and intrinsic value. In discussing the range of possible strategies, the purpose is not to recommend any particular approach but to explore and review all the possibilities. As a conservative investor, you will find only a small portion of these strategies to be of interest; but you can also benefit from knowing about *all* the potential uses of calls and puts.

The Workings of Option Contracts

In this section, you find a review of the option contract rules. The mechanics of expiration, strike price, and time, extrinsic, and intrinsic value affect all decisions related to how you should or should not employ options and how risks increase or decrease as you employ a particular strategy.

Option Attributes to Determine Value

Collectively, the attributes of the option contract determine its value. This value relates not only to how high or low the value is today, but also to how the option gains or loses value as a strategic tool in your stock portfolio. Option contracts refer to 100 shares, so each contract allows the buyer to control 100 shares of the underlying stock. Every option relates specifically to that one stock and cannot be transferred. The premium is the cost (to the buyer) or value (to the seller) of the option contract. This cost/value is expressed as the value per 100 shares, usually without dollar signs. For example, if an option's current premium is 6, it is worth $600, and if the current premium is 4.75, it is worth $475.

Some strategies make options useful for protecting paper profits, maximizing short-term income with little or no market risk, or hedging other positions. If the option premium is too high (for long-position strategies) or too low (for short-position strategies), a particular option strategy cannot be justified.

Expiration limits the lifetime of the option. The potential profit period for the option speculator is the flip side of the advantage the short seller enjoys. Just as a short seller of stock sells and has an open position, the short seller is an options trader who initiates a position by selling the option. The short option position can be closed in one of three ways. First, it may expire worthless, in which case the entire premium received by the seller is profit. Second, it may be closed by buying back at any time, with the difference between the initial sales price and final purchase price representing profit or loss. Third, it may be exercised by the buyer, and the short seller may be obligated to complete the exercise transaction. When a call is exercised, the seller is required to deliver 100 shares of stock at the strike price. When a put is exercised, the seller is required to take delivery of 100 shares at the strike price—shares are "assigned" to the seller.

Intrinsic, Extrinsic, and Time Value Premium

An option premium has three components: intrinsic value, extrinsic value, and time value. The intrinsic value is equal to the number of points that an option is in the money (ITM). This concept is explained in greater detail later in this chapter; for now, it is important to understand the meaning of intrinsic value related to the stock price. The strike price is the price at which an option can be exercised; for example, if a call option has a strike price of 45, it provides the buyer the right (but not the requirement) to buy 100 shares at $45 per share. The money rules for this example are as follows.

1. If a 45 call is held on stock currently valued at $47 per share, the option is 2 points ITM.

2. If the stock is valued at $45 per share, there is no intrinsic value. This condition—when strike price and stock market value are identical—is called at the money (ATM).

3. If the stock is valued below the strike price, there is no intrinsic value. For example, if the strike price is 45 and the stock is selling at $44 per share, the condition is 1 point out of the money (OTM).

The opposite direction applies to puts. In-the-money intrinsic value refers to the number of points the stock is below the strike price of the option. For example, if the strike price of a put is 40 and the stock is currently selling at $37 per share, the put option contains 3 points of intrinsic value. If the stock is lower than the call's strike price or higher than the put's strike price, there is no intrinsic value.

Time value and extrinsic value are the portions of the option premium above and beyond intrinsic value. The longer the time to expiration date, the higher the time value. This value decays over time in a predictable manner, accelerating as expiration nears. Extrinsic value is the key to identifying option strategy opportunities; it is the volatility premium of the options beyond both intrinsic and time value premium. There is also a relationship between extrinsic value and the proximity between strike price of the option and current value of the underlying stock. A study of option values demonstrates how this relationship works.

Long-Term Options and Their Advantages

The LEAPS (Long-term Equity AnticiPation Security) option is a long-term contract. In comparison, the standard listed option lasts only about 9 months maximum. When various strategies are viewed comparing LEAPS options to listed options, that longer expiration makes a lot of difference to both long and short strategies. There is a far higher time value in a long-term LEAPS option, which may exist for up to 30 months. In the stock market, that is a long time, and everyone knows that many changes can occur over 30 months. So, if you purchase options, you must expect to pay more for the longer life of the LEAPS option, because you also buy far greater time. For the short seller, the longer period translates to higher income, because as a seller, you *receive* the premium when you open the short position. For that higher premium income, you also have to accept a longer exposure period. However, although the dollar amount of the premium is greater, the annualized return for selling short is normally less than for shorter-term options.

The expiration and, more specifically, the time between opening an option position and the expiration date, determines the extrinsic value and affects the decisions made by speculators on the long side and investors on the short side.

Strike Price of Options

The strike price is the second feature that determines the option's value. The strike price is fixed and, in the event of exercise, determines the cost or benefit to every option position, whether long or short. The proximity of current market value to the strike price of the option also determines the current premium value and the potential for future gain or loss, as well as the likelihood of exercise. For example, if a call's strike price is 30 (meaning it would be exercised at $30 per share) and the current market value of the stock is $34, the call is 4 points ITM. It is quite likely that this option will be exercised in this condition, especially as expiration approaches. If the stock's price declines to $28 per share, the call would be 2 points OTM; and if the price stops at the strike price of $30 per share, it is ATM.

These definitions are opposite for puts. When the market value of a put is *lower* than the strike price, the put is ITM; and when the stock's value is higher, it is OTM. These definitions are important because the actual time value, extrinsic value, and intrinsic value are affected by the relationship of the stock's market price to the option's strike price. This relationship also determines the short side's exposure to exercise. The actual timing of exercise is uncertain; it can occur any time the option is ITM. When an option is ITM, changes in the option's premium track stock price movement point for point, so changes in the option's value are more dramatic when a stock's market value changes in the in-the-money range.

Extrinsic value premium is the intangible portion of the premium value. Extrinsic value varies depending on the volatility of the underlying stock. In comparison, time value inevitably declines as expiration approaches. For the option buyer, time is the enemy. Even when the long option is ITM, time value declines as expiration approaches. So, if a speculator pays a lot for time value, it takes substantial price movement to offset that intangible feature. For example, a buyer pays 7 points ($700) for a call that consists entirely of time value premium. By the point of expiration, if the stock has moved 7 points above the strike price, that call is worth only $700, because all the time value will have evaporated. In this situation, the buyer breaks even. (Actually, the buyer loses money due to the trading expense on both sides of the transaction.)

The Time Advantage for Short Sellers

For the option seller, time is an advantage. The higher the time value premium when the short position is opened, the greater that advantage. Referring to the previous example, if you were to sell a call with 7 points of time value, you could close the position at a profit as long as the premium value was lower than the original 7 points. For example, if the stock were 5 points higher than the strike price near expiration, you could close the position and avoid exercise—and make a $200 profit ($700 received when the short position was opened, minus $500 paid to close the position—not considering trading fees).

The intrinsic value of the option premium is equal to the number of points the option is ITM. For example, if your 40 option is held on stock currently valued at $43 per share, the option contains 3 points of intrinsic value. If that call is currently valued at 5 ($500), it consists of $300 intrinsic value and $200 time and extrinsic value. As another example, if your put has a strike price of 30 and the stock is now valued at 29, the put has 1 point—$100—of intrinsic value because the stock's value is 1 point below the put's strike price. If the current value of the put is 4 points, it consists of $100 intrinsic value and $300 time and extrinsic value.

Long and Short

The decision to go long (buy options) or short (sell options) involves analyzing opposite sides of the risk spectrum. The interesting feature of options is that strategies cover the entire range of risk, often with only a subtle change. Long options are disadvantageous in the sense that time works against the buyer; time value disappears as expiration approaches. Given the certainty that time value evaporates by expiration, it is difficult to overcome that obstacle and produce profits consistently. The less time until expiration, the more difficult it is to profit from buying options; and the longer the time until expiration, the more the speculator has to pay to pick up those contracts. Long options can insure paper profits, but the more popular application of long options is to leverage capital and speculate.

There are circumstances in which you, even as a conservative investor, will want to go long in options. For example, following a large price decline in the market in a short time span, prices of strong stocks are likely to rebound; but not being sure where the market bottom is, you may tend to be the most fearful when the greatest opportunities are present. In these cases, buying calls allows you to control shares of stock, limit potential losses, and expose yourself to impressive gains—as long as prices rebound in a timely manner. This is a speculative move, but even the most conservative investor may see market declines as buying opportunities, especially if a small amount of capital is at risk.

This does not mean that going long with options *is* conservative or even advisable. But every investor holding a portfolio for the long term knows how market cycles work. Options present occasional opportunities to take advantage of price swings. When overall market prices fall suddenly, conventional wisdom identifies the occurrence as a buying opportunity; realistically, such price movements make investors fearful, and it is unlikely that many people will willingly place more capital at risk—especially because the paper position of the portfolio is at a loss. So, buying options can represent a limited risk for potentially rewarding profits—an opportunity to buy *more* shares of stocks you continue to think of as long-term hold issues.

Taking Profits without Selling Stock

The same argument applies when stock prices rise quickly. Sudden price run-ups are of concern to you as a long-term conservative investor. The dilemma is that you do not want to sell shares and take profits because you want to hold the stock as a long-term investment; at the same time, you expect a price correction. In this situation, you can use long puts to offset price decline. You create a choice using long puts. First, if and when the price decline occurs, you can sell puts at a profit; the short-term profit from puts offsets the price decline in stock. The second choice is to exercise the puts and dispose of the stock at the strike price (which would be higher than current market value). You would take this path if your opinion of the company were to change, so that your hold position moved to a sell position along with the decline in stock value.

You are likely to stick with the conservative path: As long as you want to hold the stock for the long term, you are willing to ignore short-term price volatility. Even so, few investors can ignore dramatic price movement in their portfolio. When prices plummet or soar—especially as part of a marketwide trend as witnessed in 2008 and not for any fundamental reasons—the change in price levels may be only temporary. The tendency for some investors is to panic and sell at the low or to buy at a price peak. In other words, rather than following the wisdom "buy low, sell high," investors often react to short-term trends and "buy high, sell low." It helps to ignore short-term trends and to resist the human tendencies toward panic or greed; and as a conservative investor, you are more likely to equip yourself with a cooler head during volatile times.

Even so, you can retain your conservative standards and, at the same time, use options to exploit the market roller coaster. There are risks involved, but the alternative is to take no action but a wait-and-see approach. Options can help you deal with price volatility on the upside or the downside for fairly low risk and without losing sight of your long-term investment goals.

The question of speculative versus conservative is not easily addressed. Yes, using options to play market prices is speculative; but at times, you can take advantage of that volatility without selling off shares from your portfolio. The same observation applies on the short side of options, where risks are far different and market strategies can vary.

Buyer and Seller Positions Compared

When you short options, you do not have the rights that buyers enjoy. Buyers pay for the right to decide if and when to exercise or whether to sell their long positions. When you are short, you receive payment when you open the position, but someone else decides whether to exercise. Time value works to your advantage in the short position, so you can control the risks while creating a short-term income stream. Risk levels depend on the specific strategy you employ.

The highest risk use of options is the uncovered call. When you sell a call, you receive a premium, but you also accept a potentially unlimited risk. If the stock's market value were to rise many points and the call were exercised, you would have to pay the difference between the strike price and current market value at the time of exercise. For example, let's say you sold a call with a strike price of 40 and you received a premium of 8 ($800). That reduces your risk exposure to as much as $48 per share (strike price of 40 plus 8 points you received for selling the call)—but without considered trading costs. However, what if the stock's market value rises to $74 per share before expiration, and the call is exercised? In that event, you must deliver shares and pay $3,400 upon notice of assignment ($74 per share current market value, minus $40 per share strike price). Your loss would be $2,600 ($3,400 payment minus $800 you received for selling the call).

The uncovered call is the highest risk strategy; in comparison, the covered call is the lowest risk strategy. If you own 100 shares, you can deliver those shares to satisfy exercise, no matter what the market price is. Upon exercise, you keep the premium you were paid. The greatest argument against covered call writing is the chance of lost appreciation. In the previous example, had you merely held onto your 100 shares, their value would have increased to $74 per share. Because you wrote a 40 call, you would be required to sell them for $40 per share. As a counter to this argument, a couple of points have to be remembered. First, the frequency of large price increases should be studied in comparison to the certainty of option premium you earn for selling calls. Second, as long as exercise creates a profit in the call as well as capital gain in the stock, you earn a profit. For example, let's say your original basis in the stock was $32 per share and the stock is currently valued at $38 per share. You sell a 40 call and receive a premium of 8 ($800). Upon exercise, your profit is $600 capital gain on the stock plus $800 profit on the short call (plus any dividends you received during the holding period). That is an overall 43.75 percent return ($1,400 ÷ $3,200). Including stock profits with option profits is not entirely accurate because the two are separate transactions. However, in picking a strike price for covered call writing, you need to evaluate the outcome in the event of exercise. Your selection of one strike over another certainty affects your total profit on the exercised covered call.

The capital gain created when a covered call is exercised may produce impressive levels of profit as long as the basis in stock was far lower. However, for the purpose of comparing option returns under different outcome scenarios, capital gains are not normally included as part of the analysis. If you owned stock and simply sold it without writing options, you would earn the capital gains, so stock and option profits in covered call examples are not tied together as part of the comparison. In the previous scenario, the option-only return, you received $800 for selling a call when the stock was at $38 per share. This is a 21.1 percent return ($800 ÷ $3,800). To make this comparable to other option returns, you also need to annualize this return, meaning the yield is recalculated as if the position remained open for exactly one full year.

Understanding Short Seller Risks

The short call may be high risk or highly conservative. In comparison, the short put has varying risk levels depending on the purpose of going short, your willingness to accept exercise, and the amount of premium paid to you at the time you open the short position.

The decision to employ options in either long or short positions defines risk profile; the definition of conservative is rarely fixed or inflexible. It is more likely to define an overall level of attitude about specific strategies while acknowledging that strategies may be appropriate in different circumstances. It is all a matter of timing a decision based on the current status of the market, your portfolio, and your personal decision to take action or to wait out volatile market conditions.

Calls and Call Strategies

As a starting point in any discussion of option strategies, two matters have to be remembered. If you buy a call or a put option, you have the *right* to take certain actions in the future, but you do not have an *obligation*. Second, if you sell a call or a put, the premium you receive as part of an opening transaction is yours to keep, whether the option is later closed, expires, or is exercised. These two points are crucial in developing an understanding of how options trading works.

Options are contracts that grant specific rights to the buyer and impose specific obligations on the seller. If you think of options as intangible contractual rights (rather than as tangible items such as shares of stock, for example), the entire discussion of how to use options is easier. It may be worrisome for you as a conservative investor to consider trading in an intangible product, but when you relate it to other types of investments, you can appreciate both the logic and the need for options. For example, in a real estate lease option, you have two parts: a lease specifying monthly rent and other terms, and an option. The option fixes the price of the property. If you decide to exercise that option before it expires, you can buy the property at the specified contractual price even if property values are significantly higher.

Stock market options are the same, but they involve stock instead of real estate. Every option refers to 100 shares of stock, and options come in two types: calls and puts. When you buy a call, you acquire the right to buy 100 shares of stock at a specific price (the strike price) before the option expires. All options have fixed expiration dates, so the time element of options is a crucial feature to consider when comparing option values. For the buyer, a relatively small risk of capital potentially fixes the price of 100 shares of stock for several months. If and when that buyer decides to buy the stock, the call can be exercised to acquire 100 shares at a price below current market value. That is the essence of the call.

Is the Strategy Appropriate?

For your conservative portfolio, buying calls is not an appropriate fit in most applications. Buying calls is the best known and most popular option strategy, but it is usually a purely speculative move. If you are convinced that a stock's market value is sure to rise before the expiration of an option, you can buy calls as an alternative to outright purchase of shares. This strategy would be appropriate in the following circumstances.

- You are concerned with short-term price volatility, and you do not want to commit funds to buy shares, but you still want to fix the price of stock at the option's strike price value.
- You want to buy shares, but you do not have funds available at the moment, so buying a relatively cheap call is a sensible alternative (given the chance that you could lose the money).
- You are aware of the risk of loss, and you want to proceed with buying a call anyway.

So, as with any general rule, there are exceptions. You retain your status as a conservative investor even though circumstances may arise in which you would want to buy a call. It is not a conservative strategy, but all investment decisions should be driven by circumstances and not by hard-and-fast rules. Although the general rules you set for yourself guide your portfolio decisions, special circumstances and momentary opportunities or limitations can bring about exceptions.

Option Terms and Their Meaning

Every call contains a series of terms. These are the type of option, the strike price, the underlying stock, and the expiration date.

The type of option is either a call or a put. The two have to be distinguished because they are opposites. If you placed a buy order for an option without specifying whether it was a call or a put, that order could not be filled. All the terms have to be specified in an order.

The strike price is the price of stock that may be acquired if and when the option is exercised. This strike price remains unchanged until the option expires, except in cases of stock splits. You have the choice, as a buyer, of either selling the option to close the position or exercising the option. Upon exercise of a call, you buy shares at the strike price. You "call away" the 100 shares of stock from the seller. If you exercise a put, you have the right to sell 100 shares, or to "put shares of stock" to the buyer and dispose of stock at a fixed price.

The underlying stock is the company on which the option is traded. The company cannot be changed; it is as fixed as the strike price. Options are not available on all stocks, but they can be found for the majority of large-cap stocks listed on American stock exchanges.

The expiration date is a fixed date in the future specifying when the option expires. This term is critical because after the expiration date, the option no longer exists. As a buyer, you know that the time value premium evaporates if your option is not exercised or sold *before* the expiration date.

These four terms collectively define and distinguish every option. None of the terms can be modified or exchanged after you open an option, and the terms determine the option's value (the premium you pay when you open the option).

If you accept the beginning argument—that buying options is not normally appropriate for you as a conservative investor, but special situations can bring about an exception to that rule—it is always possible that going long could be a useful strategy. It makes sense to keep the long position in reserve as one of many possible ideas. It's a mistake to simply reject a possible strategy because it is not a good fit with your overall investing theme. However, remember that, for the most part, you will not be willing to speculate by buying options.

The Cost of Trading

Augmenting the complexity of buying is the trading expense involved. This applies to both sides of the transaction. You are charged a fee when you open the position and another fee when you close it. In any calculation of risk and potential profit or loss, the cost of trading therefore must be included. If you deal with single-option contracts, you limit your exposure to loss. But at the same time, the per-option cost of trading is quite high. With this in mind, option traders often execute transactions using multiple option contracts. This reduces the cost of trading and results in a lower per-option cost. But remembering that buying options is a high-risk venture, using multiple contracts just to reduce per-option trading costs does not reduce overall risk; it increases it, because you must put more capital at risk. For the option buyer, trading costs make the proposition even less likely to turn out profitably.

As a call buyer, the odds are against you. A second possibility is far more interesting and potentially more profitable: selling calls. If you are familiar with selling short, using stock, you know that the sequence of events is opposite from when you go long. You have to borrow shares of stock to sell, and opening the short position exposes you to the possibility of loss. If the stock's market value rises, you lose money. So, short sellers expect the price of stock to fall. Eventually, they close the position by entering a closing purchase transaction. Short sellers have to make enough profit to offset the cost of borrowing stock, trading fees, and the point spread between original selling price and final purchase price.

Selling stock is high risk without a doubt. If the stock's value rises, you lose money, and short sellers are continually exposed to that market risk. Two observations about going short on calls: First, the transaction is far cheaper and easier than shorting stock; second, the strategy can be either high risk or conservative.

In, At, or Out of the Money

Selling a call is easier than selling short shares of stock, because you do not have to borrow calls to go short. You simply enter a sell order, and the premium (the value of the call) is placed into your account the following day. When you sell a call in this manner, you are in the same market posture as the short seller of stock, but at less risk. You are hoping that the price of stock will fall so that your short call will *lose* value. That means you will be able to either close the position profitably with a closing purchase transaction or wait for the call to expire worthless. As long as the market value of the underlying stock remains at the strike price (ATM) or below the strike price of the call (OTM), exercise will not occur. When the stock's market value is higher than the call's strike price (ITM), you are at risk of exercise. The proximity of the stock's current market value to the strike price is summarized in Figure 2-1.

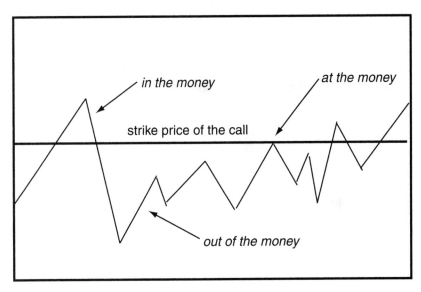

Figure 2-1 Strike price and stock price

In the figure, observe that the option's strike price remains level, but the status of the option relies on stock price movement. This illustrates how a call functions. Whenever the stock's price is higher than the call's strike price, the call is ITM, and whenever the stock's price is below strike price, the call is OTM.

The same logic applies to a put, but the terms are reversed. Referring again to Figure 2-1, if the stock's price were higher than the strike price of the put, it would be OTM, and if the stock's price moved below the strike price, the put would be ITM.

The relationship between strike price and stock price is critical for anyone who opens a short position in options. The short-call position can be one of the highest risk positions you can assume. However, it can also be one of the most conservative positions. This riddle is explained by whether or not you own 100 shares of stock when you sell a call. If you go short with calls and you do not own the stock, risks are theoretically unlimited because the market value of stock can rise indefinitely. This uncovered call strategy is clearly inappropriate for your conservative portfolio. However, when you own 100 shares, those shares are available in the event the call is exercised; so in the right circumstances, call selling is highly profitable *and* conservative. Chapter 3, "Options in Context," compares short calls in these contradictory risk profiles, and Chapter 5, "Options as Cash Generators," provides in-depth explanations of covered call-writing strategies, the ultimate conservative use of options.

Puts and Put Strategies

The put is the opposite of the call. If you buy a put, you acquire the right (but not the obligation) to *sell* 100 shares of the underlying stock. If you exercise a put, you sell 100 shares at that strike price, even if the current market value of stock is far below that level. Like the call, the put expires at a specific date in the future.

As a put buyer, three outcomes are possible.

1. ***The put is sold.*** You can sell the put at any time prior to expiration. For example, if the underlying stock's market value falls below the strike price, the value of your long put increases, and the put can be sold at a profit. Because time value declines over the holding period, it is a highly speculative strategy to buy puts

purely for short-term profits. It is unlikely that you can earn profits by consistently buying long puts without some other reasoning behind that decision. For example, if you believe that stocks in your portfolio are overbought and you want to protect paper profits, long puts can be used as a form of insurance to protect your stock positions.

2. *The put expires worthless.* If you take no action before the expiration date, the long put becomes worthless, and the entire premium you paid would be a loss. When you buy puts, you profit only if and when the market value of the underlying stock declines; if the value remains at or above the strike price, your put does not appreciate. Even if the stock does fall a few points, the put loses time value as expiration approaches; so to profit, you need the stock to decline enough points to offset your original cost and to replace time value with intrinsic value, all before expiration date.

3. *You exercise the put.* If the stock's current market value is far lower than the put's strike price, you have the right to sell 100 shares at the higher strike price. If you own shares of stock and you bought the put for downside protection, exercise can work as a sensible exit strategy. For example, you may have purchased shares originally when the stock looked like a viable long-term hold, but the financial picture has since changed. If you own one put per 100 shares, exercising the put and selling shares enables you to keep paper profits while escaping from the long position in stock.

The Overlooked Value of Puts

The put's strategic potential is easily overlooked by investors and speculators. More attention is paid to calls. There are good reasons for this. Short calls can be covered by ownership of 100 shares of stock per call, but puts cannot be covered in the same way. The put is more exotic and alien to the mindset of many investors. Most people are used to betting on the potential for stocks to rise in value, but they are not as willing to consider the possibility of price declines. This is ironic considering the unavoidable cyclical nature of investing. Prices rise, but they also fall, so using puts as well as calls to speculate on price movement or to protect paper profits presents a number of interesting strategic possibilities. In markets like 2008, when 28 out of 30 Dow Industrial stocks lost value, puts would have offered far greater value than calls as speculative trades.

Where do puts fit for the conservative investor? Several possible applications of puts are worth considering on both the long and short sides. The best known is the use of long puts for insurance. If you buy one put for every 100 shares of stock, you protect your paper profits; in the event of a decline in the stock's market value, the put's premium value increases. So, once the stock's price goes below the put's strike price, loss of stock value is replaced dollar for dollar in higher put premium value.

This protection of paper profits—a form of insurance—is a conservative strategy. You pay a premium for the put because you fear that stock prices have risen too quickly, but you do not want to take profits in the stock. You can use puts in this situation to keep the stock while protecting profits and, perhaps, even taking profits without needing to sell stock. This insurance does not have to be expensive. Just as you can select insurance based on varying levels of deductible and copayment dollar values, you can select puts based on their cost and level of protection. For example, if you want to protect all your paper profits, you buy puts with strike prices close to current market value; that means you pay a premium with a high level of time value. If you are willing to carry some of the risk, you could buy puts at lower strike prices; these would be far cheaper but would provide less protection. For example, if you originally purchased 100 shares of stock at $42 per share, and today's market price is $52, you have 10 points of paper profits. If you buy a 50 put, you protect 8 of those 10 points, but the put is expensive. If you buy a 45 put, you cover only 3 points of paper profits, but the put is far cheaper.

The Insurance Cost of Puts

The put has a limited life, so your protection extends only to expiration date. Using puts for insurance therefore requires periodic replacement of the put. Again, this compares to insurance like health, homeowners, or life policies, where periodic premium payments are required. As with all insurance, the value of paying a premium depends on the premium cost and the protection it provides.

Buying puts can provide benefits beyond mere speculation. Selling puts—going short—presents an entirely different risk profile than the long strategy, but it is not necessarily high risk. Shorting puts may, in fact, be a viable strategy in your conservative portfolio.

A short call can be covered simply by owning 100 shares of stock. That relationship eliminates the market risk and converts a high-risk strategy to a conservative one. But short puts can be covered only by also buying long puts that expire later. There is an important difference, however, between short calls and short puts. Although an uncovered call presents tremendous risks, the uncovered short put has only a limited risk. The stock can only fall to zero value in the worst case, so the potential risk is finite. On a practical level, a stock's likely market value has a floor somewhere higher than zero, and this level is subjective. You can define the price floor as technical support level, book value per share, or based on recent trading patterns. The point is that the real risk is the difference in points between the put's strike price and the lowest likely trading price per share. Most people consider the technical support level to be that price.

If you accept that a specific price-support level is also a lowest likely trading price, you can likewise accept the risk of going short with puts. That risk is further discounted by the value of the put premium you will be paid when you short the put. When you also consider that time value is involved, that net risk can be quite minor. Remember, *buying* puts is a long shot for the speculator due to time value premium. But for the seller, time value is a benefit; the further the time value falls, the higher your profit in shorting the put. You may review recent trading ranges of the stock to judge the safety or risk of selling puts.

Conservative Guidelines: Selling Puts

Is selling puts a conservative strategy? It can be in some circumstances. You have to assume several elements to conclude that short puts are appropriate in your conservative portfolio.

- **The strike price is a fair price for the stock.** Whenever you short a put, you have to accept the possibility that the put will be exercised. You have to accept the strike price as a price you are willing to pay for the stock.

- **The premium you receive justifies the exposure.** When you sell options, you are paid the premium. That premium and the length of time you remain exposed to possible exercise have to justify the decision.

- **The risk range is minimal.** When you consider the spread between the put's strike price and your estimated support price for the stock, minus the put premium, how many points remain? This is the most reliable method for judging whether to sell puts.

- **Ultimately, you would like to acquire shares of the stock.** Whenever you sell puts, you should also be willing to acquire shares in the company. If you really don't want to own the stock, you should not sell puts.

You have been watching a company for several months, and you like the fundamentals. The stock is currently valued at $62 per share. You decide that if the stock's value declines to $55, you will buy 100 shares. As an alternative, you also consider selling puts. You analyze the values and conclude that it would be a smart move. The lowest likely trading price, in your opinion, is about $46, or 9 points lower than your target acquisition price of $55 per share. The 55 put is currently valued at 6 ($600).

Here is the risk profile of these price relationships:

Strike price of the put	$55
Less: Support level estimate	$46
Gross risk margin	$ 9
Less: put premium	$ 6
Net risk per share	$ 3

Should you sell the 55 put? If the stock's value were to fall below $55 per share, the put would be exercised. Your risk exposure is really at the $49-per-share level (strike price of 55 minus 6 points of premium). The entire premium consists of time value, and your net risk is 3 points. The longer the short put remains open, the more the time value deteriorates. Given the minimal risk, this is a sensible strategy in a conservative portfolio. Were the margins higher, the risk of acquiring stock at potentially inflated values would not make sense.

Puts as a Form of Contingent Purchase

Short puts can be thought of as a form of contingent purchase. When you compare the risk of selling puts to the risk of buying shares outright, it makes sense. Consider the alternative given in the previous example. If you bought shares today, your cost would be $62 per share. If the stock's market value falls, you lose one dollar per share for each point of loss. If the stock falls to $49 per share, your long stock loss is $1,700. Compared to the alternative, selling a put, the risk of buying 100 shares is far greater. In this situation, you are better off selling the 55 put. Your net cost, after considering the premium you receive for selling the put, would be $49 per share, equal to the market value at that time.

This type of analysis—reviewing one decision against another—demonstrates how realistic comparisons can help to define your risk levels. If you begin with the assumption that selling puts short is high risk, you can never get beyond that conclusion. It is true that in some circumstances, shorting puts is extremely high risk. For example, if you short puts on stock you do not want to own, that contradicts your conservative standards. The analysis of any option-based strategy should include a preliminary but thorough analysis of the underlying stock and its fundamental strength or weakness as well as a study of its price volatility. If you shop for the richest option premium levels, you end up shorting puts on the highest-risk stocks, which you do not want to do. The previous example demonstrates, however, that in the right circumstances, using puts as a form of contingent purchase is a wise decision.

Listed Options and LEAPS Options

Traditionally, risk assessment for options is based on a short lifespan— 8 months or less for listed options. The ever-growing popularity of LEAPS—long-term options that last as long as 30 months—changes the analysis. Even for the long position, the risk of ever-declining time value takes on a different context when looking 2 or 2 ½ years ahead.

The availability of long-term options makes long positions more viable in many more situations. Longer-term options contain far greater time value, of course, because time value is just that: the value of time. So, compared to a 6- or 8-month time span, a 24- to 30-month option has far greater potential—for both long and short positions.

For example, it is practical to use LEAPS to leverage capital while retaining the choice of buying shares in the future and, at the same time, reducing the cost of buying options. Chapter 6, "Alternatives to Stock Purchase," explains how contingent purchase strategies work.

Using Long Calls in Volatile Markets

Let's assume that you have your eyes on several stocks, and you believe that all offer potential for growth over time. The problem is that the market has been volatile lately, and you're not sure whether the timing is good for picking up shares. For example, if you liked a particular stock in 2008 but you saw how poorly the market was acting, buying stock was a dangerous move. In these circumstances, LEAPS can provide a safe alternative. The not-uncommon situation of a volatile market makes it difficult even for conservative investors to time their decisions. The fundamentals work, and long-term prospects are strong; even so, you are not sure about the short-term prospects for a stock. Influencing your decision, annual cyclical change, outside economic forces, and market or sector trends affect the timing of your decision. In this environment, it could make sense to buy LEAPS calls instead of stock. As an initial risk analysis, you cannot lose more than the premium cost of the LEAPS call, so the initial market risk is lower. At the same time, in going long with calls, you would acquire the right (but not the obligation) to buy 100 shares of the underlying stock at any time before expiration. If the LEAPS call has 30 months to go, a lot can happen between now and then.

The risk is that the stock's market value will not rise, or even if it does, it may not rise enough to offset the cost of time value and to appreciate adequately to justify your investment. The solution allows you to reduce the cost of buying the LEAPS call by selling calls on the same stock. As long as those short calls expire *before* the long call, and as long as the short call's strike prices are higher than the strike price of the long call, there is no market risk. This is a form of covering the short call. For example, you buy a 50 call expiring in 30 months, and then you sell a 55 call expiring in 21 months. If the stock's market value rises and the short 55 call is exercised, you can satisfy the exercise with your long call, making $500 on the transaction (selling at 55, buying at 50). Or, if the short call expires, it can be replaced with another. A likely scenario in this "covered option" position is that the short call's time value will decline; it can be closed at a profit and replaced with another call. As long as you remember the rule—higher strike prices, earlier expiration—and the number of short positions does not exceed the number of long positions open at the same time, you can write as many covered short positions as you like, limited only by margin limits set by Federal law and your broker. It is even possible, based on ideal price movement of the underlying stock, that your premium income from selling short calls can repay the entire cost of the long-term long LEAPS position. There are no guarantees, but it is possible.

The basic long-short LEAPS strategy is summarized in Figure 2-2.

In the figure, you see that this strategy has two legs. First, you purchase a long call with a 50 strike price, and later, you sell a 55 call. To avoid an uncovered short position, the 55 call *must* expire at the same time as the long call, or before. If the short call outlasts the long call, you face a period in which that short call will be uncovered.

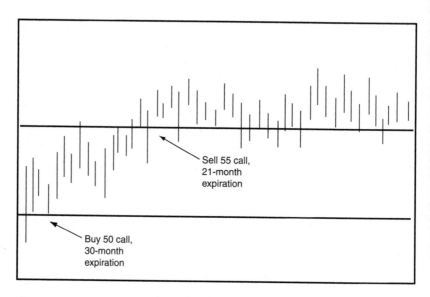

Figure 2-2 Long- and short-call strategy

This example shows that the ideal price movement in the underlying stock involves a minimum number of points. You want to acquire value in the long position so that you can exercise the long call later; at the same time, you do not want to see the short position rising in value because you want it to expire worthless (or you want to be able to close it out at a profit in the future). Remember, the goal in this strategy is twofold. First, you want to have the ability to exercise the long call and buy 100 shares of stock at the strike price. Second, you want to reduce the cost of the long position with a "covered" short position at a higher strike price. The quotation marks are placed around the word *covered* because this strategy is not the same as covering a short call with 100 shares of stock. The coverage refers to offsetting positions: one long and the other short. If the short position is exercised, you can use the long position to fulfill the obligation. This enables you to mitigate risk in terms of both cost and potential exercise.

The "contingent purchase" with "covered option" strategy is not complex, and it may be a smart fit for conservative portfolios. This question is explored in depth in Chapter 6. The point is that LEAPS options expand the strategic possibilities while also making it possible to reduce many forms of risk.

Using LEAPS Puts in a Covered Capacity

Long LEAPS puts can work in the same way. For example, you may purchase LEAPS puts for insurance on existing long stock positions and reduce your insurance cost by selling puts that expire sooner than the long put and have lower strike prices. This basic strategy—combining long puts and covering them with short puts—is summarized in Figure 2-3.

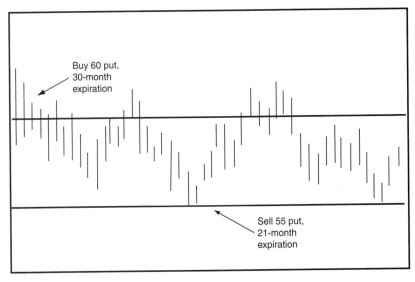

Figure 2-3 Long- and short-put strategy

This figure is the reverse of the contingent purchase previously shown. The difference is that puts are used instead of calls. This strategy assumes that the underlying stock's value is trending downward or trading in a narrow price range. The purpose in covering the put is to reduce the risk of exercise and resulting loss, and at the same time, to reduce the cost of buying the long put. This strategy has a limited risk. If the stock's price rises above the original strike price, the loss is limited to the net cost between the long and short put positions; and if the stock's price falls below the short put's strike price, exercise can be offset by the long put. (This means that instead of being required to buy 100 shares of stock, you would simply exercise your long put, so that you would pick up 5 points of profit, the difference between the long 60 put and the short 55 put.)

These strategies—covering long options with shorter-term short positions—work best when your estimate of likely price movement in the stock is correct. This, of course, is true for any market strategy you employ. The call strategy works best when the market price of the underlying stock rises over time, and the put strategy is preferable when the price declines. The wisdom of using either strategy is based on your ability to read intermediate-term volatility trends accurately. The strategies make long positions in options more practical than the purely speculative approach, but profitability is not ensured. The overall purpose of the long option strategy is to maximize the opportunity while identifying worst-case outcomes and setting up the strategies so that you will not lose or so that losses are minimal. In the case of calls, you may want to exercise the call to acquire stock far below market value; in the case of puts, you can insure existing long stock positions while mitigating the cost of carrying that insurance.

Coordinating Strategies with Portfolio Goals

Your ultimate purpose in using options should be to augment or protect your conservative goals. If your goals are best served by simply buying stock and not using options for any purpose, that is the policy that should overrule all other possibilities. However, some option strategies are compelling enough that they cannot be rejected without further study.

The conservative strategies worth considering must be coordinated with a broader overall strategy. The following basic conservative option strategies are explained in greater detail in Chapters 4, 5, and 6.

- **Using long puts to insure long stock positions.** Your conservative position in stocks, held for the long term, should not be affected by short-term price uncertainties. If you accept the precepts of both the Dow Theory and the random-walk hypothesis, you realize that short-term price movement is not reliable as an indicator of longer-term trends. As a conservative investor, you have probably based your portfolio decisions on fundamental indicators, and you monitor financial reports as they are released to spot emerging and changing trends. In theory, you can simply ignore short-term price movement without concern for temporary market volatility; many supporters of value investing suggest this approach. In practice, though, marketwide price gyrations are unsettling; they raise questions even among conservative investors. The 2008 market was a perfect example of extreme volatility and a strong bear market, bringing into question even the most conservative approach to investing. (See Chapter 4, "Managing Profits and Losses.")

The strategically timed purchase of puts can work as a timing mechanism at what you consider to be market tops. You want to continue holding stock as a long-term investment, so you are not inclined to take profits; but you are also concerned about losing paper profits in the short term, even though that concern is contradicted by your long-term investment goals. Buying puts makes sense for two reasons. First, if you are correct and the stock is overpriced at the moment, the long put will be profitable and those profits will offset the unavoidable price correction. Second, the fundamental indicators for the stock may change at the same time that the price gyration is occurring; in fact, the unexpected volatility may foreshadow weakness in the fundamentals. The change could also affect your opinion of the stock as a safe long-term investment, in which case you may want to dispose of shares. If the stock's market value is depressed by the time you decide to dispose of shares, you will have to sell at a loss off the high. However, if you bought puts for insurance at or near the price peak, you now have a choice. You can sell the put and realize a short-term profit while holding onto shares, or you can exercise the put and dispose of stock at the higher strike price. In this manner, you achieve two goals. First, you preserve your paper profits by selling at or near the price peak (the fixed put strike price). Second, you dispose of shares when your opinion of the company has changed.

In this example, the use of puts for insurance was perfectly in line with your conservative goals. You can never assume that conservative means you pick a portfolio and stay with it, no matter how the fundamentals change. On the contrary, you are probably continually monitoring financial strength, and you make changes in your portfolio to ensure that your fundamental standards are matched in the mix of stock you hold. Changes in price may precede a change in financial strength or operating results, so price changes may be reliable indicators for using puts to insure paper profits.

- **Covered call writing against long stock positions.** The best-known conservative options strategy is the traditional covered call. In this strategy, you write one call for every 100 shares owned. It is appropriate when the call, if exercised, would produce a capital gain in the stock that you would be happy to realize. In other words, if you are not willing to have stock exercised, you should not write the covered call. Assuming that you would accept exercise as one possible outcome, you can use techniques such as rolling out of one call and into another to maximize income. The properly selected covered call strategy produces consistent current income. In exchange for writing covered calls, you risk losing out on increased market value; when stock prices rise above strike price and calls are exercised, your shares can be called away. However, when you compare that risk to the regular and dependable creation of current income in a conservative market risk profile, it is apparent that covered call writing will beat market averages without increasing market risks. Covered call writing also discounts your basis in stock, so your profit cushion is further protected. (See Chapter 5.)

  The traditional covered call strategy makes sense and fits well with your conservative risk profile when all the required elements are present: You will accept exercise if it occurs; exercise will produce a good return on your investment; and overall, the strategy will produce short-term profits while enabling you to retain your long-term portfolio. In those instances where stock is called away, you can replace it with a different stock or use long calls for contingent purchase planning. (See the next bullet.)

- **Options for contingent purchase plans.** Of the three basic conservative option strategies, contingent purchase plans are the most complex. The various methods you can employ are good matches in a conservative portfolio as long as the overall standards are maintained and given priority. One common trap for options traders is to become intrigued with the potential profitability of a particular strategy and to lose sight of the more important portfolio goals. A contingent purchase is conservative because it provides alternatives to buying stock at a fixed price or, when price trends do not continue, to limiting losses with the use of long options. Those losses are limited in two ways. First, you can never lose more than the long premium you pay. Second, when employing LEAPS call or put options, you can cover the long-call position with short sales as long as the short calls expire earlier and are higher-strike calls or lower-strike put contracts. A contingent purchase is equally interesting when using short puts in place of long calls, and the most advanced strategy involves selling covered calls and uncovered puts at the same time. In Chapter 6, a detailed example of this more complex strategy demonstrates why this is a conservative strategy and how it consistently produces extra current income in your portfolio.

Option and Stock Volatility: The Central Element of Risk

The whole question of risk is central to the options decision and to maintaining the conservative structure and theme in your portfolio. The selection of options can be directly related to price volatility as one measurement of risk— perhaps the most important.

When you pick stocks, you decide whether to follow fundamental or technical indicators, or a combination of both. Conservative investors tend to lean toward the fundamentals, so you probably prefer financial statements to charts and price trends. However, with options, you face a different criterion for judging safety. Because options have no tangible value of their own, there are no fundamentals specifically related to options. The stock fundamentals are crucial for picking stocks, especially if you plan to write covered calls. However, for options, you need to compare volatility to determine safety and risk levels.

An option's premium level is one of many technical indicators for the volatility levels of stocks. The more volatile the stock's price, the greater the risk to buying the stock; and the more risk in the stock, the greater the profit potential (and risk) in the option. Several features contribute to volatility in options, including the time until expiration, the proximity of the stock market price to the strike price, and to some extent, the volatility of the market as a whole (as measured by index movements).

Critical Analysis of Volatility

As a conservative standard, you need to balance the volatility of the stock and option (as a measurement of risk levels) against premium income potential in the option (as a measurement of opportunity for profits). The two sides of the question—risk and opportunity—are related, of course, and cannot be reviewed separately. Options traders often are mistakenly attracted to higher premium options for covered call writing. Beginning with the standard of investing conservatively, it is a mistake to seek high-premium options to sell and then buy stock primarily to cover calls. This approach programs in high-risk portfolio selection.

It would be simple if option valuation could be fixed by formula. Logically, it would seem that premium levels should be fixed by the various factors involved. In fact, time value declines at a predictable rate as expiration nears; intrinsic value is, by definition, also predictable based on movement in the stock's price; and proximity of current stock value to strike price of the option affects valuation in an equally predictable manner. But these theoretical price standards for options are only starting points. Options do often sell at or near their calculated time-plus-intrinsic value levels, but the real buying and selling opportunities in options consist of variation in extrinsic value. This is the portion of option premium beyond intrinsic and time value representing volatility in the underlying stock. The variation in volatility always occurs because the market is chaotic, and the more chaotic trading in a particular stock, the greater the volatility (thus, extrinsic value) in its options. However, extrinsic value behavior is also affected by both time value and by proximity between the strike and current stock price. The longer the time to expiration, the less responsive the option premium is to changes, even ITM intrinsic value. There may be an offsetting change in extrinsic value for far-extending options. For example, an ITM long-term option may increase only two points even when the stock increases by three. In this case, intrinsic value, by definition, matches stock movement, but the offsetting point represents an adjustment in extrinsic value. In this regard, time affects extrinsic value behavior. You will also notice that when strike and current stock price are far apart either ATM or OTM, option price movement is less responsible to changes in the stock price. In this respect, extrinsic value is also affected by intrinsic value (or, in near-the-money situations, the *anticipation* of an option going ITM).

These observations make the point that extrinsic value, defined as the volatility factor of premium value, represents the nonintrinsic and nontime portion of the premium. However, even though volatility is the primary driver, extrinsic value is also influenced by both time and intrinsic value. These variables are not predictable, and they vary by stock, time, and overall market trends. They may also be affected by trader interest in a particular option. The tendency for extrinsic value to vary is identified as implied volatility.

Options traders, like all investors, affect prices by anticipating future volatility, and that is manifested in the volume of activity in particular options. Some events, such as current earnings reports or new announcements, can cause higher volatility in the immediate few days before the earnings deadline or immediately following an announcement. The term *implied* is a substitute for *anticipated*, and aberrations in option pricing are indeed caused by options traders' anticipation of future profit potential.

Free 20-Minute Delayed Quotes

Professional options traders employ many formulas to spot implied volatility and to select advantageously priced contracts. However, the selection does not have to be that difficult. If you study options on a comparative basis, you can pick higher than average premium levels with little trouble. For example, the CBOE (Chicago Board Options Exchange) website provides free option listings with 20-minute delay, so you can check various option listings side by side. For example, you can limit your search to (a) stocks you already own, (b) stocks with current market price within 5 points below option strike price, or (c) stocks with 6 months until expiration. These criteria provide comparable options, and the return on each is easy to calculate. Divide option premium by the current market value of the stock. (Don't use your original basis in the stock, because your basis in various issues will be different, making the comparison less valid.)

The point is that you do not have to involve complex formula studies or become well versed in the technical side of options. The process is similar to picking stocks on the basis of high/low pricing, dividend yield, and trading range. When you perform these analyses comparatively, you can spot bargains easily.

The Black-Scholes Model

Professional options traders, who use sophisticated methods for more speculative trading, are likely to use advanced volatility measurements such as the well-known Black-Scholes formula. For most investors, Black-Scholes is too complex to be of value; a more practical approach is simple modeling based on current option premium and time to expiration, evaluated with an understanding of the proximity between strike price and current value of the stock.

The Black-Scholes model was introduced in 1973 in a paper published in the *Journal of Political Economy*, titled "The Pricing of Options and Corporate Liabilities." At that time, options were fairly recent devices in the stock market, and the theory was devised to identify the theoretical value of options based on stock price, strike price, volatility, time to expiration, and short-term interest rates. However, the formula contains some flaws; for example, it is based on European-style exercise (exercise occurring only on or right before expiration). Listed options on U.S. exchanges can be closed or exercised at any time, so the assumptions in the formula can be inapplicable.

The Black-Scholes formula is as follows:

$$c = SN(d_1) - Xe^{-rT}(d_2)$$

$$p = Xe^{-rT}N(-d_2) = SN(-d_1)$$

where

$$d_1 = \frac{\ln (S / X) + (r + \sigma^2 / 2) T}{\sigma \sqrt{T}}$$

$$d_2 = \frac{\ln (S / X) + (r - \sigma^2 / 2) T}{\sigma \sqrt{T}} = d_1 - \sigma \sqrt{T}$$

c = Call (European style)
p = Put (European style)
S = Stock price
X = Strike price of the option
r = Risk-free interest rate
T = Time to expiration (in years)
σ= Volatility of the relative price change of the underlying stock price
$N(x)$ = The cumulative normal distribution function

Finding the fair value of options for your purposes does not necessarily require complex analysis. You can simply review options on stocks you already own and keep comparative analysis simple. Selecting stocks for covered call writing should be based on several initial assumptions. First, you must be willing to accept exercise as one of the possible outcomes. Exercise, if it does occur, creates a capital gain in the stock, and the rate of return on both stocks and options justifies the covered call position. If you meet all these tests with stocks in your portfolio, comparing current option prices in the same price and time range is a reliable method for seeking value.

You should also question whether it is necessary to seek out high-priced options. The rate of return on options could be high enough to justify covered call writing, especially if you are working with stock that has appreciated since your original purchase price. For example, if you bought stock at $34 per share and you're thinking of selling 35 calls, the capital gains margin is minimal; after trading costs, the stock transaction will probably be close to a wash with such a narrow margin. But if you bought stock at $34 per share and current market value is $74, selling a 75 call would create substantial profits. If exercised, you will earn a gross capital gain of $4,100 in addition to dividend income and option premium. This outcome is always possible with appreciated stock, so as long as the stock's fundamentals continue to work for you, writing covered calls is a winning idea. You will make a good return whether the option is exercised or not.

Identifying Your Market Opportunities

Considering the potential for gain with appreciated stock, covered call writing can be a way to utilize paper profits to create additional income. In this situation, you do not need to seek high volatility in option premium; the potential return can work well for you even when implied volatility is low or nonexistent. As a *general rule*, you should establish a minimum return to justify covered call writing. To meet that standard, you may need to adjust both strike price and expiration. For example, you might decide to write covered calls only if and when you can earn an annualized return of 10 percent or better.

Another factor to consider is the level of time value involved. The listed option is likely to have a lifespan of 8 months at the most, but if you study LEAPS calls as candidates for the covered call equation, you find that time value is far higher when expiration is 24 to 30 months out. You can sell calls between 5 and 10 points higher than current market value and earn significant returns. If the stock's price rises to strike price or above, you can roll out of the position to avoid exercise. You can accept exercise and earn current income from call premium, or you can close the short options at a profit due to reduced time value premium. Include LEAPS options in your study, but also compare outcomes on an annualized basis. LEAPS are also listed at the CBOE site: Go to Delayed Option Quotes from the home page and enter the stock symbol; all options and LEAPS options are shown. LEAPS vastly increase the profit potential because time value is significantly higher for long-term LEAPS contracts.

Table 2-1 shows a comparison of all ten stocks in the model portfolio. The premium levels available for options expiring in 1-month, 9-month, and 21-month increments are summarized. In each instance, the call selected is the closest out-of-the-money call based on current strike price that is available in all the indicated periods. The option premium is divided by the current stock price to arrive at the initial yield.

Table 2-1 Comparative Call Yields

Stock	Price	Strike	Premium 1-month	9-month	21-month
Caterpillar	32.29	35	1.26	4.70	7.00
%			3.9%	14.6	21.7
annualized			46.9%	19.5%	12.4%
IBM	101.27	110	1.03	7.90	13.43
%			1.0%	7.8%	13.3%
annualized			12.0%	10.4%	7.6%
Johnson & Johnson	53.05	55	0.60	3.60	6.20
%			1.1%	6.8%	11.7%
annualized			13.2%	9.1%	6.7%
Coca-Cola	45.02	50	0.05	2.11	2.45
%			0.001%	4.7%	5.4%
annualized			0.01%	6.3%	3.1%
McDonald's	56.09	60	0.35	3.50	5.20
%			0.006%	6.2%	3.0%
annualized			0.07%	8.3%	1.7%
3M	53.81	55	1.75	5.44	8.00
%			3.3%	10.1	14.9%
annualized			39.6%	13.5%	8.5%
Altria	16.99	20	0.02	0.60	1.32
%			0.001%	3.5%	7.8%
annualized			0.01%	4.7%	4.5%
United Parcel Service	54.65	60	0.45	3.60	6.00
%			0.008%	6.6%	11.0%
annualized			0.1%	8.8%	6.3%

continues

Table 2-1 Continued

Stock	Price	Strike	1-month	9-month	21-month
			Premium		
Wal-Mart	50.20	55	0.31	3.20	5.90
%			0.06%	6.4%	11.8%
annualized			0.7%	8.5%	6.7%
Exxon Mobil	66.75	70	0.95	6.01	10.00
%			1.4%	9.0%	15.0%
annualized			16.8%	12.0%	8.6%

This comparison between three different calls makes the point that the longer the call has to go until expiration, the higher the *dollar value*. To make the analysis accurate, however, these returns should be annualized, reflected as if the holding period was equal in each case, to one full year. Because you are dealing with 1-month, 9-month, and 21-month options, the outcome changes dramatically upon annualizing. For example, referring to the 3M calls:

1-month option:	$(3.3\% \div 1) \times 12 = 39.6\%$
9-month option:	$(10.1\% \div 9) \times 12 = 13.5\%$
21-month option:	$(14.9\% \div 21) \times 12 = 8.5\%$

This exercise demonstrates that the shorter-term sale is far more profitable than the longer-term sale. In most of the examples in the table (specifically, IBM, Coca-Cola, McDonalds, Altria, UPS, Wal-Mart, and Exxon Mobil), the one-month returns are quite minimal. This is due to the combined short duration of the calls and the proximity between current value and strike. Annualizing in all cases assumes that the options are held to the day of expiration, which makes the comparison valid among the three choices. In practice, exercise could occur any time the option is ITM, and the longer-term options expand the exposure for a longer time. The shorter-term call in this example is desirable not only because annualized return is higher, but also because there is a shorter term of exercise risk. So the 3M example demonstrates that the preannualized returns are inaccurate; after these are adjusted to a comparative,

12-month basis, the value of shorter-term options is apparent in the higher yields they produce.

In writing options, you also face a reinvestment risk. You may earn 39.6% percent on an annualized basis with a 1-month call, but it is not always possible to repeat that experience in each month that follows. So, although a study of current annualized returns is instructive when comparing two or more option choices, it does not mean that you will be able to continue that trend throughout an entire year. With this in mind, annualizing should be used solely for comparisons, and not as an estimate of the *likely* outcome from writing covered calls.

However, as long as one annualized return is more favorable than another, the analysis on an annualized basis is important—as long as you accept the possibility that shares of stock may be called away. In this example, a seemingly modest 3.3 percent return (on 3M) actually would yield 39.6 percent on an annualized basis. The validity of the strategy assumes that (a) you are willing to accept exercise as one possible outcome, (b) your basis in stock is far lower than current price levels, and (c) you like the rate of return that one or more of these options provide. The obvious offset between time and rate of return has to be considered; if you sell a shorter-term option, its time value declines more rapidly, and it can be closed or allowed to expire, to be replaced with another call, perhaps even with a higher strike price. Longer-term options take longer for time value to decline, and the longer period also represents more exposure to the risk of exercise. If the stock rises substantially within the option period, you must accept exercise or roll out of open short positions.

You also need to be careful to not fall into the trap of overlooking lower-priced stocks. Referring again to Table 2-1, five of the stocks (Caterpillar, IBM, Johnson & Johnson, 3M, and Exxon Mobil) yield double-digit annualized returns for the 1-month calls. As exercise approaches, time value falls away with accelerating speed, and these are the most attractive annualized returns on the chart. Remember, however, that these one-month annualized yields reflect proximity between strike and stock price, whereas the other five stocks are not as favorable on those terms.

This study reveals that it makes more sense to seek shorter-term covered calls because (a) time value dissipates more rapidly as expiration nears,

(b) the exposure to exercise is less than for longer-term calls, and (c) annualized yield is greater, so you can sell subsequent calls more often using faster expiration cycles. Given the problem of one-month expirations when the closest call increment is several points away, it often makes more sense to seek similar rates of return using 2-month or 3-month expirations rather than 1-month calls.

Although capital gains are normally excluded as part of the annualized return analysis, you must be aware of the spread between your original cost and the call's strike price. This is essential in judging whether the covered call strategy makes sense. Because exercise is one of the possible outcomes, you cannot ignore that possibility. The potential for exercise if you had purchased 3M at $30 per share would be viewed differently than if you had purchased it at $50 per share.

Limiting Your Strategies to Conservative Plays

Remember the basic premise for conservative options trading: The covered call strategy should be used only on stocks with sound fundamentals that you bought for their value, not used simply to write options with high implied volatility. You may view exercise as part of a plan to reinvest proceeds in stock with equal growth potential and strong fundamentals. However, if you can hold calls until expiration without threat of exercise, a new covered call can be written. The process can be repeated indefinitely, while you continue receiving dividends and avoiding exercise—hopefully while the stock's market value rises over time. That scenario—the existence of strong fundamental value in the stock, long-term growth, dividend income, and repetitive covered call writes—maximizes the covered call strategy.

Option volatility—for all the detailed and technical study that goes into it—is not necessarily the sole determining point for selection of options for conservative strategies. It is important, but more weight should be given to overall rates of return in various scenarios: exercise, expiration, and close of the short position. It is that overall return—based on your original basis in the stock—that provides the greatest flexibility. Remember, too, that out of respect for limitations you impose on yourself as a conservative investor, it may be preferable to select options and stocks with average price levels and to avoid high volatility altogether. If you accept the theory that high price volatility translates to higher market risk, it is ill advised to consider writing covered calls at all. Risk levels of the stock increasing since original purchase date could signal the need for reevaluation of the company. Should you sell that stock and find an alternative issue with safer volatility levels? You may be better off respecting your conservative stock standards based on fundamental analysis, writing options with "typical" pricing, and staying away from stocks and options with higher-than-average volatility.

The idea of avoiding stocks and options with higher-than-average implied volatility makes sense in your conservative portfolio. If you restrict your activity to long stock positions, you monitor your portfolio constantly. If and when the fundamentals change, you replace your hold position with a sell. Not only should that standard be retained, but the implied volatility in option premium can serve as a red flag, enabling you to check other indicators to decide whether you want to keep your long stock position.

Identifying Quality of Earnings

The last word in picking options is that quality of earnings mandates the quantifications of a stock.[1] The fundamentals apply only to the stock because options have no tangible value. So, when option-implied volatility changes from the norm, it happens for a reason. It is a symptom and perhaps a signal that the fundamental strength (the quality of earnings) of the stock has changed as well. Anticipation is the spark of the stock market, and more decisions are made in anticipation of future risk, profit, and other change than on any known fundamentals. In adhering to your conservative standards, then, a highly volatile option premium may be a more cautionary sign than a covered call opportunity.

---

1. *Quality of earnings* refers to the fundamental strength of the corporation and to its long-term growth potential. A high quality of earnings translates to greater prospects for long-term growth and fewer unpleasant earnings surprises. One definition of this term is "The amount of earnings attributable to higher sales or lower costs rather than artificial profits created by accounting anomalies such as inflation of inventory." (www.investopedia.com)

Trading Costs in the Option Analysis

Risk analysis often involves small margins, and it is easy to overlook all the elements that go into that margin of profit. Trading costs are especially troublesome when you deal in single-option trades. The per-contract cost is relatively high. Single-option examples are used throughout this book to keep those examples clear, but in practice, the trading costs affect your likely profits on both sides of the transaction. Trading fees vary widely, so you must shop around. You may discover that the brokerage you have been using to execute stock trades is not necessarily the best priced for option trades.

The problem with multiple-contract trades is the increased risk exposure. It does not make sense to involve 10 options just so that the per-contract trading price is lower. Is it practical to increase risk 10 times by using that many options? It might be in some situations, but reducing trading costs should not be the primary criterion for employing multiple option contracts. The determining factor is potential return and risk level compared to the ultimate conservative goals in your portfolio. For example, let's say you own 1,000 shares of stock. You might decide to write covered calls on as many as 300 shares, but you might not want to write calls on all 1,000 shares; in the event of exercise, you'd profit from option premium income, but you may also like to keep the remaining 700 shares. In this case, it would not make sense to write 10 calls just because you owned 1,000 shares. Yes, trading costs would be lower, but it may also violate your risk standards. In this case, you might not be willing to have all your shares called away, so you might decide to write calls on 30 percent of your holdings. The trading costs are only one factor to consider; your desire to retain the other 70 percent of your portfolio is more important. If all 10 calls were exercised and 1,000 shares were called away, you would regret the decision even though it worked out profitably. It could also have tax consequences you would prefer to avoid or defer.

Calculating the Net Profit or Loss

Based on the trading costs of the service you end up using, you must calculate that cost into your profit outcome. For example, based on the number of options you trade, let's say that your trading costs are a quarter point on either side of the transaction. You have to deduct a half point from estimated profit levels (or add a half point to target closing price levels) to cover the cost of trading—a quarter point to open a position and a quarter point to close.

In considering capital gains upon exercise, you also have to include the trading cost of having stock called away. So, if your selected covered call's strike price is too close to your original basis in the stock, you could make no profit (or even suffer a loss) if and when the call is exercised. There is no value in programming a net loss into a covered call position; it only makes sense in the conservative portfolio when the net outcome is going to be profitable overall, based on your original cost of the stock, dividend income, and call premium. While you do not consider capital gains as part of the return on an options strategy, the *level* of gain (or loss) will certainly affect your decision to open a short option against stock you own. If your basis in stock is 30 points below the call's strike price, exercise will result in 30 points of profit; but if your basis in stock is equal to the strike price, there will be no capital gain upon exercise. This reality should affect the decision to enter a covered call position.

Tax Rules for Options: An Overview

Tax rules for options are, for the most part, the same as for other investment activity. You are taxed on capital gains based on the holding period and most option income i9s treated as short-term.

Some important exceptions apply to taxes on option trades. The most complex relate to writing ITM calls. These rules are explained in detail in Chapter 5. Otherwise, the following tax rules apply.

- **Short-term capital gains.** If you hold an investment for less than 12 months, you are taxed on profits as short term.
- **Long-term capital gains.** If you own stock for 12 months or more, your maximum rate is reduced.
- **Wash sales.** The "wash sale rule" prevents you from taking a loss at the end of the tax year by selling stock and then repurchasing the same stock immediately. So, if you sell stock and repurchase

it within 30 days, it is treated as a wash sale. You are not allowed to claim a loss. In some instances, you can create a wash sale by replacing stock with a synthetic option position (one that acts like stock).

- **Capital gains for unexercised long options.** If you buy an option, it is taxed like other investments. The gain is taxed as short term if the option is held less than 12 months and taxed as long term if it is held one year or more.

- **Exercised long options.** If you exercise your option, the amount you pay in premium is not separate: it is taken into your basis in stock. For a call, your cost is added to the basis in the stock; for a put you exercise, your option cost lowers the gain on stock when you sell.

- **Short calls.** You pay tax not when you sell the call, but when it is closed (through expiration or a closing purchase). All profits on short calls are short term even when your holding period was longer than 12 months. If your short call is exercised, your premium adjusts your basis in the stock.

- **Taxes on short puts.** You pay tax when the short put is closed. If that occurs by way of a closing purchase order or expiration, it is a short-term gain or loss. If the short put is closed through exercise, your premium adjusts your basis in the stock.

Federal tax rules for option trades are exceptionally complex, and you will probably need an experienced tax advisor to help complete your tax return. Make certain that your advisor understands the federal rules. As explained in Chapter 5, the calculation of taxes for ITM short sales can be quite complex. In some cases, long-term capital gains on stocks can be reverted to short-term status as a consequence of selling an ITM call.

The Importance of Professional Advice and Tax Planning

With the potential tax consequences in mind, you need to consult with an experienced tax professional before writing calls to ensure that you don't create higher tax liabilities unintentionally. Be sure that you know the tax rules of a particular strategy before you proceed.

One possible planning strategy is the intentional creation of short-term profits. This is a way to close out positions with option premium and capital gains combined, without regard to tax consequences. This works when you have a carryover loss to absorb. The annual limitation on deduction of net losses is $3,000. Many investors have far greater losses, especially after 2008, with little hope of ever using up the entire loss. But when you have such a loss carryover, you can apply it against current-year gains. That changes the entire planning question. You may welcome profitable short-term profits as long as they are offset by the carryover. It enables you to take profits this year and free up capital without having to pay taxes on the gain.

In any case, consult with your tax professional to ensure that you know the benefits and consequences of each type of trade in advance. The basics of options can be quite straightforward—until you begin studying the tax rules.

For a detailed explanation of option tax rules, order or download a free copy of the CBOE booklet titled "Taxes and Investing" from optionseducation.org/ resources/literature/files/taxes_and_investing.pdf

The next chapter provides an overview of risk assessment in terms of return calculations and explains the many different ways to calculate returns.

3

OPTIONS IN CONTEXT

Option risks affect how you proceed; perceptions, sometimes false, can inhibit you from taking full advantage of the conservative potential of options. This chapter provides valuable details about designing conservative short positions, special margin requirements for option strategies, and calculating option returns on a comparative basis.

A ny investment strategy—from plain to exotic—contains specific attributes and can be defined in terms of risk, rates of return, and strategies for various market conditions. Options are probably the most flexible investment products available. You can use them alone, in combination with other options, or as hedge devices to protect stock positions. Options can help you to exploit market price swings, and you can utilize them in speculative or conservative ways.

Identifying the conservative applications you can use makes options a tool within your long-term portfolio and requires that you view options trading in at least two classifications. First, the primary options trader is someone who uses options as the main vehicle for producing profits. The trader is willing to take higher risks and uses long positions mainly as coverage to reduce option risks or, at the very least, may choose stocks because of their volatility and technical attributes more than for any fundamental strength. Second, the stock investor is likely to be conservative. This individual picks stocks as the primary means for putting together a portfolio and uses options to protect paper profits, provide downside protection, and augment current income. As long as options conform to the conservative standards in your portfolio, this is an appropriate series of strategies. You may want to view options not as a separate form of investing but as a method for enhancing and protecting your portfolio.

The Nature of Risk and Reward

Any assessment of an investment decision has to involve a study of risk and reward. Your conservative approach to investing is based on your sensitivity to risk as a primary means for all your decisions. You are less likely than the typical investor to react to sudden market changes out of panic or greed; your view is long term. Rather than watching index-based and volume trends every day, you track a company's fundamentals. You base your decisions on earnings reports, capital strength, and operating trends. The stocks you currently hold will be sold if and when you determine that the fundamental strength of the company has changed or if you locate another company whose stock is a better candidate for long-term growth and safety.

When options are involved, the risk equation changes. You are likely to not only alter your investing profile to take options-based risks in some circumstances, but to use options to protect paper profits without selling or to reduce your basis in stock to create downside protection. The appropriate use of options can increase the conservative nature of your portfolio because some strategies protect existing positions against loss.

Using Volatility as the Primary Risk Measurement

The usual method for defining market risk of stocks involves price volatility. This is a starting point. The more erratic the price trend, the greater the risk and the more difficulty you will have in trying to forecast future price movement. When a stock's trading range is broad, it further complicates the picture; price volatility is a problem for stock investors because owning shares in a volatile company means valuation is on an unending roller coaster ride. It is easy to say that long-term investors should not be concerned with price volatility; when living the experience, however, it can be unsettling to see a stock's value cut in half in a single trading session, double the following day, and then fall once again. It makes any form of portfolio planning difficult. Are such levels of volatility unusual? They are in some market conditions. But in the bear market of 2008, high volatility was more the rule than the exception. Many traditional buy-and-hold investors suffered such high losses that their faith in the market was shaken and, for some, changed permanently. However, rounding out a portfolio with smart options strategies can work even in the most conservative buy-and-hold strategy, by reducing risks and protecting profits.

Price volatility in a stock naturally affects option premium value as well. The greater a stock's price volatility, the greater the volatility in option premium. This reality can be a trap for the inexperienced investor who may pick stocks solely to write covered calls. While initial premium income is high, those current yields may accompany depressed prices in the stock by the time the short calls expire. Covered call writing is not a conservative strategy automatically; it relies on selecting an appropriate stock as a first step. The definition of what constitutes a conservative investment varies; it works only when stock has been selected on a conservative basis as a starting point. You may need to accept lower premium levels and lower implied volatility in exchange for safer overall portfolio positions.

The interaction between risk and opportunity is a fact of life. The higher the risk, the higher potential returns; the lower the risk, the lower those returns. However, with covered call writing, you can create an exception to the rule. Premised on the idea that you have first picked stocks that meet your conservative criteria, covered call writing is a potentially profitable method for augmenting short-term returns and overall profits, with no corresponding change in market risk. This is especially true when the stock's market value has grown since acquisition date. It is difficult to create enough of a yield when the stock's current market value is at approximately the same level today as it was at purchase, so the more price growth you see in the stock, the more profitable—and conservative—the covered call strategy. As long as the strike price of the calls would result in current income if and when exercised, you can create the certainty of profits in any of the three outcomes—exercise, expiration, and close of the position—while gaining current income. The premium income you receive may be viewed as a means for taking paper profits without selling stock. Those profits reduce your basis, providing downside protection.

> You are reviewing available options on McDonald's (MCD). The market value of stock was at $56.09 at the time, so you are reviewing 60 and 65 calls. Clearly, your selection of options will be based on your purchase price for the stock. If you pay $58 for shares, the 55 call is not as attractive as the 60. Upon exercise, you would experience a $3 capital loss on the 55 call, or a $2 gain on the 60 call. The selection of an appropriate covered call has to include a critical analysis of your basis in stock, which makes the point that if your original basis in stock is far below either option, you must make comparisons based on exercise with the certainty of profits. A study of the current

21-month options reveals that the 60 call is available at $5.20 and the 65 call is going for $3.80. Your selection of either one must consider the capital gain, because appropriate strike levels have to be selected based on your original cost of the stock.

Options Used to Mitigate Stock Investment Risk

With well-selected stocks, the option premium is likely to be "in the zone" of expectation; in other words, the low risk of the conservatively picked stock reflects the same low risk in the volatility of the option. You gain the advantage, even when dealing with safe stocks and options, in three ways:

1. **You select longer-term option writes.** The Long-term Equity AnticiPation Security (LEAPS) call creates significant profit potential in the covered call strategy. You want to use out-of-the-money calls to avoid exercise, because the purpose of covered call writing is to generate repetitive current profits; this is somewhat difficult with listed calls because time value is limited. But when you use LEAPS calls, premium levels often are high enough that the simple yield is more attractive than traditional listed options because of time. The greater the time left until expiration, the higher the time value. This does not mean you have to keep the short position open for the entire duration; you can close and replace it or roll it forward at any time, based on changing stock prices. It does mean you can acquire higher premium payments because time value premium on LEAPS calls is far higher than the premium on shorter- term calls. With the potential of closing a long-term call well before expiration, a comparative analysis of annualized yield may be tempered by the possibility of a close-and-replace strategy. Exercise is less likely on short calls with a long time until expiration, but time value falls more slowly than for calls closer to expiration.

2. **The selection of covered writes is limited to stock that has appreciated.** It would be contrary to your goals to write covered calls with strike prices close to your original basis in the stock.

Some of the best premium returns are found in calls whose current market value is close to the call's strike price. This maximizes short-call income; but the strategy makes sense only if and when your basis in the stock is well below that level. Remember, the covered call write is a means for taking profits and providing downside protection, but without necessarily selling the stock. The strategy solves the dilemma every stockholder faces: Stock has appreciated, and the temptation is to take profits, but you don't want the capital gain and you don't want to give up the long-term investment. Covered calls solve this problem, but they fit your risk profile only when exercise would yield returns you consider worthy of the exposure. For example, if you acquire stock at $28 per share and sell a 30 call for 3, exercise produces a $500 profit before trading costs ($200 on the stock plus $300 on the short call). That is an overall 17.9 percent return. Net return is less when you calculate trading costs. Now consider the return if stock has appreciated to $44 per share and you sell a 45 call for 3 ($300). Upon exercise, your pretrading cost return is 19 points (16 points on the stock and 3 points on the call), which is a 67.9 percent return. When the stock has appreciated, writing covered calls programs in those impressive profits and allows for much greater flexibility in selection of a call strike. Few investors would complain about a 67.9 percent return without increased market risk. This analysis, including both option and stock returns, is not necessarily the sole outcome for a covered write strategy. If exercise does not occur, you do not count stock profits. You consider option profits based on current stock prices only. For example, a $300 gain on stock currently valued at $28 per share is a 10.7 percent return; and when the stock is valued at $44 per share, the $300 profit represents a 6.8 percent return.

3. **Exercise is avoided with rolling techniques.** You want to repeat the cash profits from writing covered calls on appreciated stock. The best of all worlds is to keep a strong long-term growth stock while generating repetitive option profits. If the short call is exercised, you would gladly accept the high yields, but at the same time, you prefer to avoid exercise. The threat of exercise

occurs when the market price of the stock is rising, so exercise avoidance is profitable on two levels. First, you can continue writing covered calls and gaining premium income. Second, your stock gains value as the price moves upward.

Using rolling techniques achieves this. These techniques involve closing a current option and replacing it with another that expires later. For example, if you write a covered call and the stock price moves close to (or above) the strike price, you avoid exercise by (a) closing the short call and (b) opening another call that expires several months further out. The later expiring call can be at the same strike price or higher. The objective in rolling forward (to a later expiration date) and up (to a higher strike price) is to avoid exercise *and* to do so without having to pay for the roll. You often can roll forward and up while gaining additional net premium. In Chapter 5, "Options as Cash Generators," you will find discussions of the various rolling techniques to show how you can avoid exercise in the covered call strategy.

Another Kind of Volatility

As long as you employ appreciated stock, you can create consistent and low-risk profits with covered calls. Price volatility is not necessary for the strategy to work. In fact, if you accept the technical risk of high-volatility stocks, it violates your conservative standards, and covered call writing makes no sense either. Your first priority should be to buy and hold growth stocks and to replace those stocks only when the fundamentals have changed.

Price volatility is the starting point for identifying market risk, at least in the short term. However, a related test of safety in the stock is the level of fundamental volatility. This is the trend in reported revenue and earnings. If a company's operating results are somewhat predictable, showing similar growth patterns from one year to the next, it is a sign of low fundamental volatility. But if revenues and earnings change erratically from one year to the next, the high fundamental volatility translates to high risk on a fundamental level. Following are some observations concerning fundamental volatility as a measurement of risk:

- You are likely to see a corresponding level of price volatility when fundamental volatility is present. In other words, stock price *is* related directly to revenue and earnings trends.

- Fundamental volatility is as serious a measurement of safety as price volatility; in fact, because price volatility often is short term in nature, it may be less valuable as an indicator than fundamental volatility (especially if the operating trends are chronically unpredictable).

- Comparisons between price and fundamental volatility can be revealing. When they do not correspond, it may be due to nonrecurring price spikes. To make the comparison valid, study a long-term pricing chart; remove spikes if (a) they are not typical, (b) the price change is corrected immediately and prices return to previously established trading ranges, and (c) the adjusted trading range appears to correspond to fundamental volatility levels. This adjustment is statistically sensible and can confirm fundamental trends.

Market risk—the tendency for stock prices to rise and fall and the volatility those price levels demonstrate—is manageable in a number of ways involving options. The most obvious is writing covered calls to reduce net basis in stock and take paper profits. Timing covered calls for price peaks is the most advantageous. If you expect overbuying short-term trends to correct in the near future, writing a call can produce fast option profits; this is a form of profit taking that does not require you to sell shares.

Another way to manage market risk is to time options strategies for a stock's pricing trends. For example, when prices rise much more quickly than you expect, you may buy puts in anticipation of a reversal in that trend. Buying puts is normally considered speculative, but when you buy relatively cheap puts to protect stock profits, it is a form of insurance. A "cheap" put is one without a lot of time value and that is several points out of the money (OTM). For example, your stock has risen from the mid-30s to $50 per share; you expect a price retreat. The 3-month 45 put is available for 0.75 ($75). Considering the potential retreat of 10 points or more that you expect within the coming few weeks, buying insurance through the long put makes more sense than selling the stock to take profits now. Your conservative sensibilities encourage you to ignore short-term price gyrations, but you are watching the market too, and you know that this price trend could be advantageous. Whether you sell a call or buy a put, you take advantage of that price trend and protect the short-term paper profits. The higher the volatility in the market, the more likely that you can use calls and puts to take short-term profits and to hedge your stock positions through protective strategies like insurance puts.

As yet another alternative, you do not have to take action. You can listen to your conservative voice and decide to simply wait out the short-term trends, reminding yourself that the fundamentals of the company continue to indicate a hold. In fact, you may wait until the stock's volatility has settled down before even considering using options in any way. You may return to the conservative policy of employing covered call writes on appreciated stock; that strategy might not be well suited to an environment in which the stock's price is changing rapidly—even though call premium may be attractive at the moment.

Lost Opportunity Risk and Options

If you do decide to write covered calls on appreciated stock—whether in high-volatility times or otherwise—handsome yields are a realistic possibility. There is no added market risk involved when the various outcomes are considered. The only existing market risk—that the stock's price will decline—exists whether you write calls or not. In fact, writing calls reduces that risk by lowering your basis in the stock. There is another form of risk to consider, however: lost opportunity risk. If the stock's price soars far above the strike price of the covered call, you lose shares through exercise. Your stock may have to be sold at the fixed strike price when that strike price is below the current market value.

Is writing covered calls worth the lost opportunity risk? When you remember that your stocks tend to be conservative selections in the first place, how many of your issues are likely to soar in price? It certainly happens. But when you compare the certainty of short-term returns from writing covered calls to the risk of losing appreciated price in the stock, you realize that the consistency in writing covered calls produces higher overall profits. You will probably have calls exercised periodically, and you will wish you had waited so that you could have benefited from the higher stock price. But your portfolio profits will be higher from writing covered calls on appreciated stock than they will be from simply keeping your long positions without options activity. The lost opportunity is the exception rather than the rule because, by definition, a conservative selection of stocks creates consistent price trends (low volatility) and less likelihood of sudden and unexpected price changes. You can further mitigate or even eliminate the risk of exercise using rolling techniques once you have shorted options.

Perceptions about Options

Not only do options have a place in your conservative strategy but, properly employed, options can strengthen your portfolio and provide greater protection than well-selected stocks. Because prices tend to move in cycles, short-term and intermediate-term pricing may be erratic, and even the best-chosen stocks go through reversal and consolidation patterns.

One argument concerning long-term planning is that such changes in price are of no concern. As long as long-term fundamental signals continue to show strength, the conservative philosophy is to hold and accumulate stock and wait out the market. This traditional approach observes correctly that short-term pricing is unpredictable as an indicator, a belief held by followers of both the Dow theory and the random-walk hypothesis. Short-term price movement is not useful for any sort of long-term predictive use. However, it remains possible to (a) protect paper profits and even take those profits without selling shares, (b) exploit market price overreactions, and (c) generate current returns—all without taking on added market risks. The lost opportunity risk associated with committing shares of stock to a fixed strike price should be evaluated along with the rates of return, the value of downside protection, and the yield diversification you achieve with the use of options in a conservative manner.

Finding the Conservative Context for Options Trading

Options *are* high-risk, exotic, specialized, and complex products when used in certain ways. To some extent, the technician enjoys the complexity of the high-risk, high-return options strategy. This does not mean that you, as a conservative investor, have to shun options; you only have to use them in the proper context. An individual who watches a high-speed stock car race does not stop using the automobile because of the dangers of driving 200 miles per hour; instead, the observer understands that prudent speeds, obeying traffic laws, and driving defensively are conservative policies. Such policies prevent accidents and injuries.

The comparison applies to options. They are intangible and often have the character of a market "side bet." Those who believe strongly in acquiring and holding equity (a highly conservative point of view) are likely to view options as belonging solely to the short-term thinking of the speculator. This does not have to be the case. A side bet using an intangible product like an option is not always a high-risk approach to the market. It comes down to a question of *how* you use options. It would be reckless to write uncovered calls or to place large amounts of capital in long option positions. Those strategies are inappropriate for you, so they are out of the question. But there does exist an intelligent context for using options within your conservative risk profile. It is limited. You are likely to write covered calls or buy puts for insurance as the primary strategies. As you move to Chapter 6, "Alternatives to Stock Purchase," Chapter 7, "Option Strategies in Down Markets," and Chapter 8, "Combination Conservative Techniques," more advanced variations of options are introduced—but all within the conservative game plan.

It is wise, even if you limit your use of options to highly conservative strategies, to make yourself completely familiar with a full range of options strategies. The more knowledge you accumulate, the more skilled you become in selecting appropriate strategies and applying them, as well as avoiding risks you don't want to take. So the idea that "options are high risk" is not fair, because the assumption has to be qualified.

It is a mistake to make such a blanket statement. For example, "Speculating in option long positions is always high risk" is an unfair characterization. Not only are you likely to use puts to protect paper profits, but in specific market conditions, using calls simply makes sense, even with a conservative risk profile. For example, when the "market" (as measured by the Dow Jones Industrial Average, for example) falls by several hundred points (remember the lessons of 2008), several changes occur in the market, all short term. The most important is investor emotion. Everyone is fearful of further price drops. As a consequence, the idea of picking up cheap shares is appealing, but most people do not take that opportunity.

Strategic Timing and Short-Term Price Changes

Consider the possibilities in options trading when markets are exceptionally volatile. Most of your capital may be tied up in long stock positions that would produce losses if sold when market prices are low. You recognize that this is the time to buy more stock, but you are uncertain, and you do not have capital available to make a bold move even if you wanted to. This is the perfect opportunity—using a limited amount of capital, of course—to buy cheap calls. You know that sharp market drops usually rebound quickly. You also recognize the stocks whose fundamental strength supports the probability of a healthy return to the normal trading range. So, picking the bargains is not difficult; the decision to put money into the market at these moments is the difficult part.

When your portfolio is depressed, you have three choices. First, you can sell everything and just get out of the market. Second, you can wait out the cycle and hope prices rebound. Third, you can seek a rescue strategy to regain lost value as quickly as possible. This is where options can play a key role. For example, as of the end of 2008, the majority of investors had paper losses in their personal portfolio as well as in their retirement plans. This is a distressing situation; at the time, no one had any idea of how long it would take for the market to recover; some people thought it never would. Uncertainty in the economy, politics, and the market itself all worked together to increase the fear investors experienced.

In this scenario, even a conservative investor may use long calls to take advantage of the temporary depression in stock prices. The point is this: Being conservative does not mean that you have the same attitude in all market conditions. Flexibility is an essential tool in your portfolio management arsenal. When opportunities present themselves, it is prudent to take them. If you lack the capital to buy shares, or you are fearful of further price declines, options present the perfect compromise. You can limit your risk by investing only a small amount of capital; and the timing can work to your advantage given the likely price patterns in big-number changes.

This does not suggest that you should speculate in long calls. But every conservative investor has survived through big price swings and seen the results—a big drop followed by a period of uncertainty and then a rapid return to previous levels. This trend can take a few days, weeks, or even months to play out. Just as sudden price declines can be exploited with the selective purchase of calls, sudden price rallies invariably lead to corrections, a time when you can use puts to (a) protect paper profits and (b) speculate in the price correction. Even if you do not own stock, when you observe a big run-up in a stock's price and you conclude the price trend is an overreaction, buying puts can be a well-timed strategy.

In addition to unexpected stock price movements, investors are concerned about what happens to open option positions when stocks are split. Does it change the ratio between stock and option? No. When a stock splits, options are split in the same manner. For example, in a 2-for-1 split, you end up with twice as many shares at half the previous share value; you double the number of options, and the strike price is cut in half. If a stock is split and you have open options with strike prices of 45, you end up with twice as many options, each with strike prices of 22.50. A stock split keeps the values the same; only the numbers change. The same rule is applied to all open option contracts in that situation.

Short Positions: Naked or Covered

The concept of speculating on long calls or puts is contrary to the generally understood definition of conservative. As shown in the preceding discussion, there may be moments when you want to use long calls or long puts to take advantage of price changes. It may be appropriate, given the timing, and may even conform to your conservative standards. For example, if you bought stock and currently have a large paper loss, buying calls is one way to average down your basis. If you can acquire additional shares of stock at a strike price below your original basis, it could bring the average value down enough to eliminate or reduce those paper losses. This is the opposite side of the coin in which you would buy puts to protect paper profits. When appreciated stock declines in value, you could sell the puts, creating a profit to offset stock losses; or you could exercise the puts and sell shares of stock at a price higher than current market value.

Some strategies involving short calls and puts may also conform to your conservative risk profile based on prevailing market conditions and your portfolio positions. The basic covered calls strategy is the most obvious example. When you sell a call, you are taking paper profits and reducing your basis in the stock; you expose yourself to the possibility of losing future price gains in exchange for the certainty of premium income today.

The Uncovered Call: A Violation of the Conservative Theme, Usually

Is it ever justified to sell uncovered calls? In the conservative philosophy, it is not. Uncovered calls are one of the highest risk strategies possible. Chapter 6 contains an example of one situation in which writing uncovered calls can work for a conservative portfolio: the ratio write. In this strategy, more calls are written than shares owned. For example, you may write six short calls when you own 500 shares of stock. This is a combination of five covered calls and one uncovered call; but in practice, the ratio write increases cash income without exposing you to unacceptable risk. The spreading of risk among covered and uncovered positions is reasonable in some situations. With the proper structuring of ratio writes, you minimize risks and produce profits from short calls.

One exception involves topping off a ratio write with one long call. In effect, this eliminates the uncovered portion of the ratio write. For example, if you own 300 shares, full coverage involves selling three calls. If you sell four calls, you have a ratio write. This can also be viewed as the combination of three covered calls and one uncovered call. However, you can further modify this position by purchasing a single call with a higher strike price. In effect, this creates a different kind of combination: a covered call strategy on 300 shares accompanied by a spread (a strategy in which the benefits of one side of the position are offset by the risk in the other). As long as the modified ratio write can be accomplished with a net credit (money coming in rather than going out), the risk is limited. The difference in strike prices between the fourth short call and the long call is a risk if and when the stock moves about the highest short call strike price. Chapter 6 examines this modified strategy in greater detail.

Covered calls are related to ownership of stock, so exercise risk is easily controlled. Short puts are a different matter. In many instances, writing puts makes sense. Because puts cannot be covered in the same way as calls, it is easy to overlook the potential of writing uncovered puts or covering them by combining a short put with later-expiring long puts. The risks of short puts are far more limited than those of short calls, because the potential decline in value is finite. An initial analysis makes it clear that a stock can decline only to the value of zero, so it is easy to limit short puts to low-priced shares. But that standard is not always necessary. The real likely decline in value is somewhere higher than zero. It may be the tangible book value per share or, on a technical basis, the price support level for the stock.

A Stock's Likely Lowest Theoretical Price Level

Tangible book value per share is assumed to be a corporation's liquidation value, or the net value of all assets if the company simply went out of business and paid off stockholders. It is more likely that companies will cease to exist through merger or acquisition, and at a price somewhere at or above tangible book value. Does the worst-case liquidation value of the company also provide a reliable low market price level for the stock? In practice, your true support level may have little or nothing to do with the fundamental and tangible value of the corporation's assets. Some technicians prefer to identify a chart-based price-support level, but that is also unreliable; the history of trading patterns in any given stock is the history of support and resistance levels being broken through and new trading patterns established. This occurred for many companies during 2008, when nearly half of market value was lost for many stocks, and previously established support levels simply evaporated. In evaluating the likely bottom for a stock, you may want to rely partly on fundamental and partly on technical indicators.

However, your analysis should be based on the original criteria you employed when selecting the stock. Remembering the rule that *option activity should be restricted to options on stocks that you have prequalified on a conservative standard*, consider what, in your opinion, is a realistic bottom price range. With this analysis in hand, compare the difference between strike price and the probably lowest price level to the premium you receive upon selling the put. If the gap between a particular strike price and lowest likely price level is 3 points and you can sell a put for 5 points, then even given your perceived worst-case scenario for the stock, you will be ahead. This risk-free description, the worst case, allows for the possibility that the stock would be put to you upon exercise at a price above current market value. So, if the market value of shares were to fall below the put's strike price, you would be required to buy inflated-value stock.

Establishing the lowest likely price range may not be easy; it is a matter of opinion. A study of recent price trends may help, but determining the level is far from an exact science, and it is at least as difficult as identifying the likely highest price to which a stock might rise. This is why comparisons between price trends and tangible book-value-per-share are useful. If you are uncertain about the reliability of price-support level, tangible book value per share may provide a more comfortable "drop-dead price" and fundamental support level. This is especially true for the dedicated fundamental analyst. Because tangible book value per share is a fundamental indicator, it may be viewed as more reliable than the technical concept of price support level for judging risk.

Short Put Risks: Not as Drastic as Short Call Risks

The true risk to writing short puts is the difference between current market value and strike price, minus the premium you received for selling the put. This brings us to the conservative standard for selling uncovered puts: if the premium discounts the risk level to a price that you consider a *fair* price for the stock, it is conservative to sell uncovered puts—but only if you are willing to buy shares at that price. Once the short put is assigned, you can simply hold the shares and await a price rebound or recapture the paper loss through writing covered calls. The point is, in some situations, you may want to sell uncovered puts even though you are a conservative investor.

Consider the case in which prices of the stock have fallen as part of a marketwide price decline like the debacle witnessed throughout 2008. You are fairly certain that prices will rebound in the near future; but current price levels are bargains given the company's fundamentals, earnings per share, dividend history, and tangible book value per share. In this situation, you may not want to buy shares outright, so you have two choices involving options. You can speculate in calls, expecting to profit from the price rebound, but that requires an outlay of money, and it is not a conservative strategy. Or you can sell uncovered puts for which you receive a premium. It is always better to have cash coming in than going out, but in exchange for the credit, you also accept the risk of exercise. However, if you are confident that prices will rise in the near future, selling uncovered puts presents less risk than in other circumstances. For example, when prices for the stock have risen sharply, selling puts is a reckless and ill-timed decision, just as buying calls is. You expect prices to act in a particular way, and it is reliable to time option decisions when you recognize overbought and oversold conditions. Those conditions present opportunities for the timing of option trades, and uncovered puts can be structured to present great opportunity with relatively little risk.

The well-understood correlation between risk and opportunity is the *normal* situation. However, changes in a stock's market value may signal that a short-term correction is imminent. To average out your basis or to protect paper profits, you can use long or short calls at such moments. This is not the same thing as contrarian speculation, a strategy in which the speculator seeks out long shots offering great profit potential—and the likelihood of large losses. The wise timing strategy that suits your conservative standards involves careful timing of option trades with price aberrations in the stock. Such a strategy is considered conservative when you have qualified the fundamental strength of the company and when you would be happy to buy shares at the strike price of a short put position.

Margin Requirements and Trading Restrictions

There are two areas in which option investors have to live with special rules: taxes and trading restrictions. The tax rules are covered later; a more immediate concern involves the special financial requirements that apply once you move beyond the status of stockholder and begin to make actual option trades.

The first rule to be aware of involves the basic qualifications to trade. You are required to complete a questionnaire and to advise your brokerage firm that, in fact, you know enough about options and their risks to enter into trades. The brokerage firm is required to establish your qualifications. So, you probably could not begin trading tomorrow for the first time. Because options can involve considerable risks, you have to go through a special screening process by the brokerage firm. Writing covered calls is usually allowed at the lowest level of approval; writing short puts usually requires a more advanced level of experience.

The second restriction is intended to limit the volume of trading undertaken by investors with limited capital. The Securities and Exchange Commission (SEC) defines a pattern day trader as any individual who makes four or more day trades within five business days. A day trade is opening and closing a position within a single day. Once you make the fourth day trade within a five-day period, you are required to maintain at least $25,000 equity in your account (in cash and securities). For many options traders, the restriction certainly applies. So, unless you can limit activity to three or fewer, you will be treated as a pattern day trader.

Other Margin Rules

All investors must be concerned with the initial margin (the amount of value required at the time a position is opened) and with maintenance margin requirements (additional margin that is required if and when prices change in the securities involved).

Options traders must be aware of these margin requirements. The strategies involving options may look good on paper but, given margin requirements, limited capital could make combinations of positions impractical. Table 3-1 gives an overview of the basic margin requirements related to options trading.

Table 3-1   Margin Requirements, Option Trades

TYPE OF TRADE	INITIAL MARGIN	MAINTENANCE
Long call or put	100% of cost.	Same as initial.
Short uncovered call	Proceeds received plus 20% of the underlying stock market value (when out of the money) plus additional margin when stock market value exceeds the call's strike price.	Additional margin if stock's market value exceeds strike price and continues upward; potentially unlimited.
Short uncovered put	Proceeds received plus 20% of the underlying stock market value (when out of the money) plus additional margin when stock market value falls below the call's strike price.	Additional margin if stock's market value falls below strike price and continues downward; limited to the range of price down to zero.
Covered call	Standard stock margin requirement (50% of cost of the stock) plus 100% of option value when in the money.	100% of stock purchase price.

The margin rules become much more complex for advanced trading strategies and combinations. To see a complete summary of a typical broker's margin requirements, check the Interactive Brokers Web site at *www.interactivebrokers.com* and follow links for (a) individuals, to (b) trading requirements, to (c) margin, and then to (d) U.S. options.

Given the limitation on pattern day trading and the capital requirements, it would be difficult for an investor to become active in options without placing substantial capital at risk. With options, the threshold of four trades could be crossed quickly and easily within a few days, at least occasionally; it is the nature of options trading to execute a number of trades in a short period of time because market conditions present immediate opportunities.

Return Calculations: Seeking Valid Comparisons

Margin limitations certainly inhibit investor activity if only a small amount of capital is available. An equally complex problem is the calculation of returns from option activity. In attempting to measure and compare option trades—whether employing timing strategies or the safer and more reliable covered call—you face a problem. How do you measure your profits? Consider the problem of the covered call trade. You have three possible outcomes: exercise, expiration, and close of the position. In the first instance, you combine a capital gain with profits from selling a covered call; in the second two, you realize a level of profit, but you still own the stock. So you cannot compare possible returns on a like-kind basis.

You have to look at potential returns as possible scenarios and judge the covered call if any of the three outcomes occur. Comparative return analysis is a wise move, and as a conservative investor, you want to know the best-case and worst-case range of outcomes before proceeding; but remember that the time a position is open and the actual outcome make comparisons elusive. The purpose in return analysis has to be to judge the strategy in all its outcome permutations, not to arrive at comparable outcomes.

The *return if exercised* is calculated as a percentage of the stock's value at the time the strategy is entered into. For example, if you were to write a 45 call at the time the stock was at $43 per share and you received premium of 7 ($700), the return if exercised would be 16.3 percent (7 ÷ 43). Your capital gain on stock would depend on your basis in that stock and would be calculated separately. As long as you purchased the stock at a price below the short call's strike price, you can ensure a high capital gain in the event of exercise.

Limiting this discussion to the option-only return allows you to compare the various option outcomes. While return if exercised (also termed if-called rate of return) appears to be the best possible return on a short strategy, it is not always the case. To make return comparisons truly valid, you have to view them on an annualized basis. When you consider the possibility of a short call simply expiring worthless (or being closed at a profit), you can repeat the strategy. The ability to sell covered calls repeatedly turns stock into a combined long-term growth instrument and current cash cow. The combined annual income from dividends and call premiums can make nonexercised returns far more advantageous than the exercised rate of return. In fact, including dividends in the calculation of covered call return is essential; with all other factors identical, the difference in dividend yield often makes one stock more favorable than another. Dividend yield often represents a major portion of overall covered call return.

To begin analyzing various options and their potential returns, a side-by-side comparison between stocks is useful, and for each stock, potential outcome (exercise, expiration, or close) is studied. Table 3-2 summarizes the market data for the companies in the model portfolio.

Table 3-2 Market Data for Covered Call Writing: Comparisons

			21-Month Calls **		
Name of Company	Stock Symbol	Share Price *	Strike	Premium	%
Caterpillar	CAT	32.29	35	7.00	21.7%
IBM	IBM	101.27	105	13.43	13.3
Johnson & Johnson	JNJ	53.05	55	6.20	11.7
Coca-Cola	KO	45.02	45	6.20	13.8
McDonald's	MCD	56.09	60	5.20	9.3
3M	MMM	53.81	55	8.00	14.9
Altria	MO	16.99	17.50	2.06	12.1
United Parcel Service	UPS	54.65	60	6.00	11.0
Wal-Mart	WMT	50.20	55	5.90	11.8
Exxon Mobil	XOM	66.75	70	10.00	15.0

* closing prices as of April 18, 2009
** Current option premium value at the close, April 18, 2009. Source: Chicago Board Options Exchange, http:quote.cbow.com/QuoteTable.asp

In these examples, companies are shown with selected options at the money (ATM) or at the next increment above. (Coca-Cola is the exception; the current price was two cents higher than the strike used.) This includes the option premium as a percentage of the current stock price. This is a good starting point because you may want to limit your study to covered calls that will yield a minimum return of some level. Because all options in this example expire 21 months from the study date, the percentages shown are comparable. If you were using dissimilar expiration periods, you would also need to annualize these returns.

The likely return you can expect to earn on a particular option depends on the premium's relationship to the current price and should include dividend yield on the stock. Clearly, the calculation of option returns also has to consider the ramifications of exercise. Although you do not complicate your analysis by including this factor, it is clear that differences will occur. For example, the Coca-Cola option is close to the money, so exercise would include no capital gain above the value as of the analysis date. The McDonald's 60 call is about 4 points above the current share price, so in the event of exercise, you would keep the option premium *and* earn a capital gain.

Note that the potential capital gain complicates the calculation of return on the covered call. If the call is exercised, the differences in capital gain matter. For example, Coca-Cola reports a 13.8 percent return on the covered call; but the strike is approximately ATM. McDonald's offers only 9.3 percent for a covered call of the same duration; but, if exercised, the capital gain would be nearly 4 points, or an additional 7.1 percent based on current price versus strike. So the overall return on McDonald's, if exercised, is 16.4 percent versus only 13.8 if exercised for Coca-Cola.

A second factor to remember is the dividend yield. For example, Altria (which, in this example, yields 12.1 percent from option premium) pays 7.8 percent in annual dividend as of the analysis date. However, Wal-Mart reports 11.8 percent on the covered call but yields only 2.1 percent in annual dividend.

The consideration of capital gains upon exercise, and dividends, are not included in the comparison between call premiums. However, in the selection and comparison between stocks, and in the selection of a strike price, you must also consider which stocks would yield overall higher returns through covered calls. This is especially true in the case of dividends. The Chicago Board Options Exchange (CBOE) includes dividends in its calculation of overall return. Investors may actually determine which stocks to buy based on fundamental analysis *and* on the dividend yield, so dividends cannot be ignored altogether.

For example, let's assume that you had prequalified both Altria and Wal-Mart as stocks you would like to own and that the decision is based on the combination of (a) dividend yield and (b) 21-month option premium available through writing covered calls. If you annualize the 21-month returns on each company, you get the annualized option yield (divide return by 21, and then multiply by 12); then you add the current dividend yield to find the overall annualized return:

Stock	Option Premium Return Dividend 21-Month	Total Annualized	Yield	Return
Altria	12.1%	6.9%	7.8%	14.7%
Wal-Mart	11.8	6.7	2.1	8.8

This calculation demonstrates that it is not reliable to simply compare potential returns on calls. You also have to consider dividend yield, especially if you are going to select one stock over another as the stock to buy. This also assumes that all other analyses are equal and that you would be happy to own either stock. When you add in the dividend yield to the annualized return, the relative outcome changes dramatically.

All the options shown in Table 3-2 except Coca-Cola are ATM or OTM, so none of the premium is intrinsic value. This simplifies the analysis. In fact, as a conservative standard, you may set a rule for yourself concerning covered calls: Consider *only* those options that are ATM or OTM. This standard makes sense for two reasons. First, writing covered calls is a method for trading on time and extrinsic value. The speculative nature of writing ITM calls—which may also invite exercise at any time— contradicts your conservative policies. Second, writing ITM calls may jeopardize the long-term capital gains status of stock in the event of exercise and, when you have owned stock for less than one year, may toll the time counting toward achieving long-term status. Chapter 5 explains tax rules for covered call writing in more detail. The point here is that restricting your activity to time value and extrinsic value premium trades makes sense under the definition of conservative investing.

With the information in hand from Table 3-2, you can compare outcomes in the event of exercise, expiration, and close. To ensure that those comparisons are realistic, you also need to annualize returns and include dividend yield.

In the case of closing a position, the return depends on timing as well as price. For example, if you close out short calls when their value decreases by one-half, your yield before calculating trading costs is 50 percent. You then need to annualize.

You do not need to make further calculations to compare the "if-closed" calculation, because actual returns depend on the level at which you decide to close and the total number of months that positions are left open. "If-exercised" and "if-expired" comparisons, however, are necessary.

Return If Exercised

You have to assume that exercise occurs at the last day of the option's life to make valid like-kind comparisons. Although exercise could occur at any time the call is in the money (ITM), you cannot accurately compare the yield unless you make this assumption. Dividend yield varies based on the time the option is left open; assume that dividend yield is more properly treated as stock specific and not as part of the comparative option return analysis, so exclude it in your comparative analysis. If you decide which stocks to purchase based on dividend yield, it becomes quite important. However, in the following example, assume that you already own the model portfolio, and exclude dividends from the calculation. Return if exercised is shown in Table 3-3, including annualized yield.

Table 3-3 Return If Exercised: Total Return, 21-Month Options

| Name of Company Stock | Share Symbol | Price* | Strike | 21-Month Calls ** | | |
				Premium	Yield	Annualized Yield
Caterpillar	CAT	32.29	35	7.00	21.7%	12.4%
IBM	IBM	101.27	105	13.43	13.3	7.6
Johnson & Johnson	JNJ	53.05	55	6.20	11.7	6.7
Coca-Cola	KO	45.02	45	6.20	13.8	7.9
McDonald's	MCD	56.09	60	5.20	9.3	5.3
3M	MMM	53.81	55	8.00	14.9	8.5
Altria	MO	16.99	17.50	2.06	12.1	6.9
United Parcel Service	UPS	54.65	60	6.00	11.0	6.3
Wal-Mart	WMT	50.20	55	5.90	11.8	6.7
Exxon Mobil	XOM	66.75	70	10.00	15.0	8.6

* closing prices as of April 18, 2009

** To annualize returns, you must adjust the holding period to reflect the return that would have been realized if the position had been held open for exactly one year (12 ÷ 21).

Annualizing yield is important in the side-by-side analysis. You can be deceived by the numbers without looking at the percentages. For example, you may reject Altria because the potential 21-month premium is only 2.06 ($206) compared to the 5.20 ($520) you could earn on McDonald's over the same period. However, the annualized yield tells the real story. The annualized return on Altria is 6.9 percent, compared to only 5.3 percent on McDonald's.

Stock price can also be deceiving. You may compare the Altria price of $16.99 per share to the McDonald's price of $56.09 and draw conclusions about the potential for returns based on those price differences. However, ownership of 300 shares of Altria is approximately equivalent to ownership of 100 shares of McDonald's in terms of capital required. Even so, the annualized yield from writing covered calls is greater in the case of Altria.

These calculations present outcomes for the stocks being studied on a consistent basis. All comparisons involve 21-month LEAPS calls, so annualizing the returns reflects the comparative annual outcome. To continue evaluating the portfolio-wide returns in these cases, you need to also track dividend income and growth in the stock's market value. However, for option-specific returns, the results shown in Table 3-3 are accurate.

Using the alternative method of adding in dividends for the companies, we would change the outcomes on the basis shown in Table 3-4.

Table 3-4   Alternative Method of Adding Dividends

Name of Company	Dividend	Dividend (Annual) Yield	Annualized Option Yield	Total Yield
Caterpillar	CAT	5.1%	12.4%	17.5%
IBM	IBM	2.0	7.6	9.6
Johnson & Johnson	JNJ	3.6	6.7	10.3
Coca-Cola	KO	3.7	7.9	11.6
McDonald's	MCD	3.6	5.3	8.9
3M	MMM	3.8	8.5	12.3
Altria	MO	7.8	6.9	14.7

Table 3-4 Continued

Name of Company	Dividend	Dividend (Annual) Yield	Annualized Option Yield	Total Yield
United Parcel Service	UPS	3.4	6.3	9.7
Wal-Mart	WMT	2.1	6.7	8.8
Exxon Mobil	XOM	2.4	8.6	11.0

Dividend yield was calculated by dividing annual dividends paid, by the price of stock at the time the option strategy was entered. While this does *not* reflect the true dividend yield you would actually earn (that would depend on the price of stock at the time of purchase), this secondary analysis does provide valuable information. It shows how the annualized option return plus dividend yield would result in each case. Because the total yield using this method changes the total yield calculated in the previous method (making Caterpillar the most profitable stock based on option premium and dividend yield), it is more accurate to consider dividend yield as part of the return if exercised.

You cannot ignore the fact that dividend yield affects overall profitability and may also influence which stocks you would use for the covered call strategy. The most sensible approach is perhaps to calculate both with and without dividend yield and then compare outcomes.

Return If Expired

Comparing return if exercised to return if expired is useful because it shows the result of two possible outcomes. However, it is not accurate to compare the two outcomes to decide which is preferable. From the conservative point of view, the covered call strategy is sensible only if any of the possible outcomes would be justified and acceptable; but consider the problem of trying to compare exercise to expiration. Upon exercise, your stock is called away, and you then have a taxable capital gain; and that is going to vary depending on the strike you pick versus your original basis in the stock. In the case of expiration, you continue to own stock. You are free to repeat the covered call strategy after expiration. This means your yield can recur repeatedly as long as exercise never happens, so a true overall comparison is not really possible. Given the potential for repetitive returns from the covered call strategy, the rate of turnover becomes important. The more often you can replace a current covered call with another, the higher your premium income. For this reason, if the stock is far enough OTM so that the short call is worth very little, closing it and writing a replacement call with more time until expiration could be more profitable than waiting out expiration on the current call. Rather than setting a specific level for closing the position, the determining factor should rest with a combination of premium value and time remaining. Thus, you must compare outcome scenarios when the attributes are different. You want to use a basis for realistic comparison, so the purpose in these calculations is to ensure that you know all the possible outcomes.

It is valid to compare the potential return to the stock's current value. You must own the stock to enter the covered call strategy as a requirement under your conservative risk profile. Comparing yield to your original cost makes it outdated, because there is no relationship between today's covered call strike price and your original purchase price. The validity of comparing expiration returns to today's price rests with the assumption that you would select one or more covered calls based on (a) proximity between strike price of the call and today's market price, (b) related premium levels, and (c) time until expiration. The major difference between the two potential outcomes (exercise and expiration) is whether you continue to own the stock at the end of the strategy. This is where capital gains and dividend yield become important. The greater the distance between original cost and option strike price, the greater the capital gain; so in comparing return if exercised between two or more stocks, you must consider this as part of the exercise. The higher the annual dividend yield, the more value in keeping the stock; this also affects whether to select a stock for covered call writing. You may select one stock over another primarily because combined premium and dividend yield are higher than an alterative. You may also avoid using a particular stock for writing calls because of higher-than-average dividend yield (as in the case of Altria), based on your not wanting to risk high-yielding shares being called away. Referring again to overall return, you might decide to write calls on Wal-Mart, with an overall 8.8 percent return but low dividend yield. In that way, you protect your position in Altria, with its far higher dividend yield.

Dividend yield has to be an important component in the selection of stocks for covered call writing, whether you currently own the stock or are considering purchasing shares in the future. You may pursue high-yielding stocks to increase returns, or you may avoid writing covered calls to preserve dividend yield.

It may be difficult to make completely reliable comparisons between return if exercised and return if expired. First, you may decide to close a short option position well before expiration and write a replacement call, which increases the annualized return—substantially in some cases. If you do hold the position until expiration, you can repeat the experience indefinitely. In comparison, when the short call is exercised, your stock is called away; you can continue to write covered calls only by investing funds in new shares of stock and waiting out market appreciation.

Expiration may be the worst-case scenario if it yields the lower return compared to closing or having stock called away. But you have control. You do not need to keep option positions open until expiration. By comparing if-expired returns to the alternative of closing positions today and replacing them with richer premium short calls, consider the following.

- The net yield, on an annualized basis, of closing the call. That is the difference between the original sales premium and the current closing purchase premium, net of transaction expenses, calculated on an annualized basis.

- The comparative yield on a new short call, given longer time to expiration, higher time value premium, and proximity between strike price and current market value.

- The increase, if any, in the strike price level. If the stock's market value is higher today than when you sold the original call, consider selling calls with higher strike prices. This increases your capital gain in the event of exercise, yet it keeps your position OTM and maintains your conservative standard for covered call writing.

With these variables in mind, the worst case is difficult to quantify. Because the comparison is not entirely valid between stocks, it is not accurate to assign a preference of one outcome over another. All the factors—including exercise, dividend yield, and capital gains—have to be considered as part of your analysis. The original cost of stock, proximity between cost and strike price, and proximity between current value and strike price affect your decision, and those factors may vary considerably between stocks.

Long-Term Goals as a Guiding Force

Return comparisons, of course, are not the only forms of analysis needed to select an appropriate options strategy. Your long-term goals are the guiding force that ultimately determines whether a strategy makes sense. So, if you want to keep shares of stock and are willing to give up current returns from writing covered calls, that is a clear goal. In that situation, covered calls are inappropriate. However, if you see covered call writing as a means for (a) taking paper profits without selling stock, (b) providing downside protection through reducing your basis in stock, and (c) enhancing current income beyond dividends, a covered-call-writing program can help you manage your portfolio, exploit temporary market price changes, and overcome the worry about paper profits and losses.

Working within a conservative framework is not always an absolute or easily defined criterion for how to invest or what products to select. Your level of conservatism changes with market circumstances. The various options strategies enable you to take advantage of market high points without disposing of stock you prefer to keep. Degrees of conservatism are possible and may not be fixed. It might be considered conservative to use options at market extremes as long as large amounts of capital are not risked or exercise of short positions produces an undesirable outcome. That is an individual decision, and no universal standard can identify whether it is appropriate.

Current circumstances affect how you invest, and they should. As explained in Chapter 7, it is not conservative to invest in the same manner in every situation. You need strategies for managing your portfolios in down markets as well as in up markets; and options in their various configurations are powerful tools for protecting your long-term positions and for identifying and taking profit opportunities without compromising your goals.

There is a tendency to classify specific options strategies universally, so taking long positions is *always* thought to be high-risk, and writing covered positions is *always viewed as* safe. Neither of these is true, of course. For example, writing covered calls is ill-advised when the stock price is depressed, especially if the current price of an underlying stock is lower than your basis. If you think prices are going to climb in the future to reverse the downtrend, timing of the covered call write would be poor. The best time is during high volatility and when the stock's price has run up and, in your opinion, is temporarily higher than its normal trading range. Not only will higher strike prices be available, but the implied volatility in the option could make it a profitable covered call opportunity.

A more subtle variation of risk involves how you utilize cash. For example, when you receive option premium, where can you invest it? If you hope to continue earning a rate of return you think of as a minimum in your portfolio, you want to invest cash receipts in some way. Dividends can be reinvested automatically if companies whose stock you own offer dividend reinvestment plans (DRIPs), in which partial shares of stock can be acquired automatically in place of dividend cash payments. This makes sense because it creates a compound rate of return on dividend income. However, it is not as easy to create the same automatic compound returns when you sell options. Some choices include the following.

- Place funds received for selling options in well-selected mutual funds. Select reinvestment of all income so that your money continues earning compound rates. For example, you can invest option premium received from covered call writing in odd-lot shares of the same company; this creates a compound return on the current dividend yield.

- Group covered call sales to create enough funds to acquire shares in another company that you want to buy; or buy shares and write calls at the same time, paying the net debit required for both transactions. Make sure the company is on your list of stocks that meet your fundamental requirements, remembering to ensure that conservative risk rules apply. This action, combined with dividend reinvestment and the potential for additional option writing, puts premium income back to work as quickly as possible.

- Invest premium income in other investments, satisfy margin requirements, or add funds to your personal cash reserve. Premium income can augment a cash reserve as circumstances change, so you do not have to dispose of other assets; premium income can also serve as a source for your cash safety net.

Exercise as a Desirable Outcome

One aspect of options that is often ignored is the desirability of exercise in some circumstances. Exercise is usually avoided as part of an overall strategic approach based on your wanting to enhance current income while doing all you can to keep well-selected, long-term growth stocks. In the covered call strategy, exercise is most likely when the stock's price is rising, so escaping exercise provides more capital gains in the stock, to be realized later. Avoiding exercise by rolling out of positions is a practical method for managing covered call positions; even if exercise does occur in the future, it is always preferable at a higher strike price. In the following circumstances, you will welcome exercise.

- **Writing deep ITM calls, even with tax consequences in mind.** If you have a substantial carryover loss to bring forward, you are limited to a maximum of $3,000 per year in capital losses you can claim. When your carryover is far above that level, you will not be concerned about the loss of long-term status you suffer when writing deep ITM covered calls. In fact, in that situation, your covered-call-writing strategy could be designed to invite exercise. Because deep ITM, soon-to-expire calls consist mostly of intrinsic value, changes in the stock's market value are matched dollar for dollar by changes in the call's premium. Covered calls provide complete downside protection to the extent of intrinsic value in this case; for example, if your covered call contains 20 points of intrinsic value, you receive the entire premium when you write the call; and the price drops for each point loss in the stock or rises with each point gained in the stock. The call can be closed for a purchase price below the original sale level if stock prices drop, so your lost points in the stock can be recovered in the changed option premium. This strategy works only when two conditions are present: (1) you have substantial carry-over loss and don't care about losing long-term treatment for covered call transactions, and (2) your basis in the stock is lower than the strike price or lower than the strike price minus the call premium. (For example, if you bought stock at $35 per share and it is now worth $60, you may decide to sell a 30 call. That will bring you 30 points of intrinsic value plus whatever time value premium is available. It is entirely possible when stock has appreciated to this extent to receive a total call premium that exceeds your basis in the stock. That makes any outcome risk free; if you can take out not only your basis, but extra profits as well, you have no net capital investment, but you still own long shares against a short call. So, following such a transaction, a decline in the stock price could produce a profit in the call due to changes in intrinsic value.

- **Selling puts as a form of contingent purchase when the strike price makes sense.** If you are willing to buy stock at the short put strike price, minus the premium, exercise is a desirable outcome. For example, stock is currently valued at $33 per share, and you can get 4 points for the 30 put. Upon exercise, you would acquire shares at the fixed strike price of $30 per share; your basis would be $26 per share due to the $400 put premium you were paid. The ideal condition is to experience exercise above $26, meaning your net basis would be lower than market value (not counting trading fees).

- **Accepting exercise when fundamental indicators have changed.** You may find yourself in the interesting position of owning stock with a short covered call, to also discover that you no longer want to own the stock. If the call is ITM, you can simply accept exercise in this situation and take your profit. If tax consequences are not important to you (for example, if you have a large carryover loss), you could also roll down to a lower strike price, gain 5 points in additional profits, and accept the certainty of exercise. If you don't want to wait for the outcome but prefer to exercise more quickly, you can roll down with the same strike price; you can even execute an unusual rollback, replacing the original exercise price with one on an earlier date. Combined with a roll-down, this creates net premium income while accepting exercise as an exit strategy on shares of stock. The acceptance of exercise in this case may be more practical than closing a covered option position and perhaps taking a loss on the transaction just so that you are free to sell shares of stock. As with the case of a deep ITM call written originally, this decision can affect the tax status of your stock; it is most practical when you want to absorb a large carryover loss or when you are allowed to execute options within a tax-deferred plan.

Inviting exercise is one method of dealing with ever-changing market conditions. As a conservative investor, you continually struggle with the problem of market volatility. Even when you believe stock is worth holding for the long term, how can you ensure that today's paper profits are not lost in future market price movements? You can use several conservative strategies to accomplish these defensive goals. In Chapter 4, "Managing Profits and Losses," you find ideas for the interesting use of calls to protect paper outfits.

4

MANAGING PROFITS AND LOSSES

Everyone contends with short-term price fluctuations, and even the most conservative investor may be susceptible to profit-taking. Options can be employed to protect profits and even to take those profits without selling stock. On the other side of the short-term price question, options can be used effectively to eliminate loss positions through rescue strategies.

T he conservative risk profile discourages short-term decisions, and speculation is contrary to your sensible investing philosophy. Your general buy-hold-sell rule is buy well-selected, high-quality stocks, hold for the long term, and sell only when the fundamentals change. This smart investing approach does not preclude protecting profits when price levels become volatile. You do not want to begin as a conservative and end up as a speculator. However, there are ways to take profits without selling stock and without increasing market risks. In some instances, taking market risks makes sense, even though it is not generally a wise move to make.

Begin by making distinctions between various investor profiles. As a general rule, a conservative investor is interested in preserving capital and, as a result, wants to avoid risks. In stock market terms, risk usually refers to volatility (technical risk) or weak financial position (fundamental risk). A moderate investor is willing to assume somewhat greater risks as long as the potential for higher profits is present as well. A speculator or aggressive investor seeks the highest possible returns—often short-term—and is willing to accept the highest levels of risk.

These terms are by no means black and white, nor are they permanent. A particular profile is likely to change as financial and individual circumstances change. With investing experience, any profile is going to evolve based on the positive or negative outcomes of past decisions. Current market conditions also affect a particular risk profile. Self-defining labels rarely apply to anyone in every respect. In the following discussions, the assumption is that your profile is generally conservative, even though that will not always apply. These discussions also assume that, even while you may view yourself as conservative or moderate, you accept the premise that—under some circumstances—your risk profile is going to be more flexible than the label may imply.

The label you use to define yourself is likely to be challenged when you come to the question of when and how to take profits. Recalling that profit-taking normally involves selling stock, it is contrary to your conservative profile to dispose of stock you would rather keep. But when you involve options, your choices expand significantly. Option strategies provide methods for protecting paper profits as they exist today, making smart moves when market conditions change, and taking profits without needing to sell stock.

Your Conservative Dilemma

A conservative policy is intended to protect your investments from loss. By selecting long-term quality companies, you eliminate the volatility that threatens your portfolio's value, and you set the goal of building equity over many years. Even so, you have to contend with ever-changing market conditions and the prospect of needing to modify your mix of stocks. The most readily available information is short-term by nature, so you have to continually ensure that your portfolio-based buy-hold-sell decisions are made using *valid* information.

Short-term indicators can be distracting. Momentary volatility in issues you own, especially when price spikes are part of marketwide volatility, can be distracting. Without gaining independent confirmation of apparent changes in trends, it is easy to make mistakes. For example, you may decide to sell stock to avoid further price declines when selling is not necessary, or you may buy additional shares when prices surge, only to realize later that a correction was virtually certain. Reacting to short-term indicators and trends is human nature, but it can adversely affect the timing of decisions in your conservative portfolio.

The ongoing conflict between short-term market trends and your long-term mindset is efficiently managed with options. Used in the proper context—for managing price volatility and not as a primary and speculative change in policy—options help smooth out the price volatility that characterizes the market while protecting profits. Ask yourself these questions.

- How often are paper profits one-time opportunities?
- With high-quality stocks, do you still consider long-term growth potential likely?
- Have you sold stocks prematurely, fearing the loss of profits?

Deciding How to Establish Your Policies

You can probably relate to all these questions because they have a familiar ring. If you have observed trends over time, you know that the price gyrations occurring this week and this month have a short-term aspect and a long-term aspect. You are keenly aware of what occurs from one day to the next, and you see daily reactions to political and business news, to earnings reports, to rumors of economic trends, and to an unending number of other reasons for prices to rise or fall. But in the long-term context, short-term price changes and the daily reasons for price volatility really have nothing to do with long-term value. Conservative investing emphasizes fundamental corporate strength—competitive position, excellence of management, diversification, healthy capitalization, consistent dividend record, and so on—and is based on faith in long-term fundamental indicators. With this in mind, it is most logical to invest in high-quality stocks, monitor the fundamentals, and ignore short-term trends altogether.

Even the most ardent fundamental investor may not want to take this approach exclusively. Profit taking is tempting. There is a way to take profits without selling stock. Some forms of trading can be made with little or no market risk. In Chapter 5, "Options as Cash Generators," you see how covered call writing using appreciated stock achieves this end. The well-timed purchase of puts protects profits with limited risk and provides the choice of selling stock at a fixed price (in the event of a rapid price decline) or closing the long put and taking your profits.

Selling stock when its price demonstrates short-term change is usually contrary to your conservative strategy. However, rapid price movement may also signal a change in the company attributes. If the fundamentals have changed and that manifests itself in the price movement you experience in the short term, the long-put strategy gives you a way out should you decide to exercise. So, using this strategy does not contradict your conservative rule. In fact, the insurance aspect is conservative, and the contingency of providing a profitable exit strategy is both conservative and prudent.

Managing Profits with Options

Investors often ignore the real problem of "managing" profits. (It may seem odd to refer to the "management" of profits because the usual thinking is, you either sell to take profits or leave them intact; but, in fact, management is precisely what you want to do, even when your primary emphasis is on long-term growth.)

The traditional suggestion to buy long-term stocks and ignore short-term volatility is generally good advice. But ironically, it may also be irresponsible to simply leave it at that. Your ongoing portfolio management involves many chores, mostly centered on monitoring fundamental indicators. If and when corporate strength, competitive position, dividend payments, earnings trends, capitalization, and other fundamentals change, you may decide to sell shares and redirect a portion of your capital elsewhere. This is basic and sensible.

Basing Decisions on the Fundamentals

Conservative portfolio management is based on the fundamentals. Short-term price volatility—a technical indicator—can also be an early warning of emerging changes in the fundamentals. If volatility is a symptom of other problems—notably, of changes in fundamental strength—watching prices carefully is a smart suggestion. It is not reliable, however; most market theories agree that short-term movement cannot be used as a predictive tool. When price volatility does appear, it is worth checking. It may serve as a signal of some kind, so seeking confirmation in the fundamentals just makes sense.

If price volatility is related to a serious decline in fundamental strength, it helps identify a change far earlier than do traditional methods. Price volatility does not consistently provide early signals; much of the short-term volatility represents marketwide short-term trends, overreaction to news and events, or buying and selling trends among institutional investors that have little or nothing to do with the stock's long-term growth potential. So, to the extent that you pay attention to daily or weekly price trends, it remains important to keep that indicator in context.

The traditional advice given to conservative investors wanting to ensure safety is to diversify their portfolios. Although diversification is a basic and sensible idea, it does nothing to contend with short-term price volatility. Even with the best diversification, you still experience price surges and declines; you still want to take profits or buy more stock at depressed prices; and you must resist the temptation to react to short-term trends for all the wrong reasons. Diversification protects you against specific risks, but it does nothing to ensure that you will not have to live through price volatility.

Yet another expansion of the diversified portfolio is to adopt a model for asset allocation. Under this variation, you "allocate" portions of your capital in different markets: stocks, mutual funds, real estate, cash reserves, precious metals, and so on. Asset allocation makes sense for the same reasons that diversification does, but it does not protect your portfolio from short-term volatility.

Allocation may not be adequate to protect capital. Simply moving money around among different markets provides a degree of safety to your capital, but it does not protect you from all forms of market risk. The portion of your net worth that is invested in the stock market is subject to short-term market risk, no matter how strong the long-term growth of your stocks. By the same argument, the short-term values in real estate, precious metals, the money market, bonds, and other allocated investments are vulnerable to short-term market risk as well. The most conservative investor contends with market risk continually. Even those who stay out of the market cannot avoid loss altogether; the gradual loss of buying power resulting from inflation, and the lost opportunity risk of being out of all markets, combine to form a more serious problem than short-term volatility.

The Reality of Risk

You cannot avoid all forms of risk. You can simply ignore short-term trends and adopt the traditional conservative plan: Monitor well-selected stocks and sell only if and when the fundamentals change. Otherwise, ignore all short-term price volatility and wait out the market. Or you can recognize the potential of short-term price volatility as a possible signal worth confirming through an examination of the fundamentals, and even take advantage of price movement, using options to limit exposure to additional risk, smooth out price volatility, and take profits without having to sell stock.

The two methods of protecting profits with options are buying puts and selling covered calls. Each of the attributes of these strategies is worth comparing. Table 4-1 summarizes the features of the long put and the short call.

Table 4-1 Long Put and Short Call Features

Buying Puts	Selling Calls
A form of insurance on long stock holdings.	Contingent sale in the event of exercise.
Stock price decline is offset by increased put premium value.	Stock price decline is offset by reduced call premium value.
Price offset is unlimited as long as the put exists.	Price offset is limited to premium received in sale of call.
You pay to acquire the put.	You are paid for selling the call.
Time value declines may offset your in-the-money gains.	Time value decline is profitable in the short position.

The decision to use long puts or short calls rests with your long-term opinions about long or short positions. If you view long puts as strictly working to provide insurance, it is conservative to protect profits without risking stock positions. In comparison, covered call writing presents the possibility of exercise in exchange for money flowing in rather than out and for providing a reduction in your basis, thus programmed higher profits in the event of exercise. This downside protection makes short calls more attractive in most respects. But picking one or the other is a matter of preference and, to some extent, it depends on what you originally paid for stock. If your basis is vastly appreciated, you may be happy in the event of exercise, so the short call makes sense. However, if you view covered calls as inappropriate because you do not want to have shares called away, the long put may be the best method for protecting your profits.

Overcoming the Profit-Taking Problem

The debate about whether or not it is conservative to use options depends on the timing and motives behind your decision. Of course, buying options purely to speculate would be inconsistent with your conservative goals.

As a starting point in this discussion, you need to identify the lowest likely price level for the stock. Support is a technical term, of course, and most conservative investors do not use support and resistance as decision-making tools. However, an understanding of the support level within your conservative risk profile helps you coordinate option strategies that enable profit-taking without needing to sell stock.

At any given time, you probably have a fair idea of the support level for stock, based on recent historical price trends. This support level, a technical tool, is by no means reliable or appropriate in your conservative, fundamentally based methodology. However, when you use options to identify short-term risk (as an avenue to identifying how and when to use options for taking profits, for example), it is also important to identify support level. The technical definition of support—the lowest price at which stock is likely to trade within the current price range—is the most reliable definition in the context of making profits without selling stock.

Realizing Profits without Selling Stock

The premise is that, as a conservative investor, you do not want to make profits just because the current price of stock is higher than your basis; at the same time, it would certainly be desirable to make those profits without selling stock. Given this premise, a few guidelines are valuable within your portfolio strategy.

1. It is appropriate to use long puts to protect existing portfolio positions. The long put, as insurance, represents a limited risk and ensures that current profitable price levels are protected.

2. It is appropriate to use long calls only as a form of contingent purchase, when long-term options (LEAPS) are available and when the purpose is to reserve the possibility of exercising those

calls to purchase shares of stock. (See Chapter 6, "Alternatives to Stock Purchase," for more in-depth discussions of this strategy.)

3. Long calls are further useful if and when prices of stocks you currently own have fallen rapidly due to marketwide price declines; this presents a buying opportunity, but you may be unwilling to purchase additional shares as a means of exploiting the temporary condition. Calls can be exercised to acquire additional shares to reduce your overall basis in the stock. This is a conservative strategy only if and when you want to acquire additional shares of the stock.

4. Short puts are useful as a form of contingent purchase (in which you would have shares put to you at the strike price if and when exercised) only when you would be pleased to purchase shares at the net price (strike price reduced by put premium you receive). In this situation, risk level should be thought of as the difference between strike price and price-support level, minus the net premium you receive for selling puts. Remember, support level is by no means an absolute value. You may employ certain fundamental tests such as profit and dividend history, tangible book value per share, and other indicators to find what you consider the stock's support level. To find the net risk associated with short-put strategies, calculate the price level of exercise-adjusted price (strike price less support level), and reduce this price by the benefit of the net premium you receive. The net risk is defined as follows:

$$[S - L] - [P - T] = R$$

S = strike price of short put

L = support level

P = premium received

T = transaction costs

R = net risk level

5. You can use short puts in place of long calls when prices of stock you own have declined and you expect near-term prices to rise. This assumes you are willing to acquire shares at the strike price if the put is ultimately exercised, based on the criterion in point 4.

When is the decision to employ options speculative, and when is it a valid conservative strategy? One consideration is whether you already have a position in the stock. As long as your purpose in using options is to protect profits, exploit price spikes, or average down your cost of stock, your conservative standards are compatible with using options in a variety of ways. If you use options to time market price movement in stocks you do not own, it is only appropriate for contingent purchase strategies, qualified by the preceding conditions. Otherwise, using options just as a means for profiting in stocks you do not own is speculative.

Further Defining Your Personal Investing Standards

Is it even necessary to protect profits, average down your basis, or exploit obvious market price spikes? The answer depends on your position, timing, and degree of advantage or disadvantage to a particular strategy. For example, if you own stock you want to hold for the long term, but a large correction recently occurred, how long will it take to get back to your original basis? It could take many months, or it could take years. Meanwhile, capital is tied up in a paper loss position.

In this situation, options can be useful for managing and even reversing the loss, erasing it and restoring a basis nearer to current market value. You can use short puts based on several assumptions. The first assumption is that the stock has reached its low and is going to begin rising; if your timing is correct, selling puts produces income, but the puts will expire worthless. That premium income reduces your basis in stock. Look at a hypothetical market example: In January, you purchased 100 shares of stock and paid $85 per share. Twenty-one months later, in October, share value closed at $67.65 per share. You sold a 65 put and received a premium of 6.80 ($680). This reduced your basis in stock to $78.20.

Because the short put could be exercised if the stock's price continued to decline below the put's strike price, that strike price (net of put premium) has to be considered in the context of the continued long-term strength of the company. It has to qualify as a long-term hold. Now modify the example: You originally bought 100 shares at $85, and 21 months later, the market value was $67.65. You sold two 40 puts at $6.80 and received $13.60. This reduced your basis in the stock to $71.40 per share (without calculating trading costs: $85.00 minus $13.60). The strategy works as long as you would be happy to increase your basis by an additional 200 shares of this company. In the event of exercise, your average basis in the stock would be $67.13 per share, as shown in Table 4-2. This compares favorably to the current market price of stock as of the sample close: $67.65. The average basis in stock is calculated by totaling the net cost of all 300 shares, including the reduction in basis from put premium:

Table 4-2   Average Basis

Original cost, 100 shares	$85.00
Minus premium for selling 2 puts	−13.60
Net basis, original 100 shares	$71.40
Plus basis, 200 shares @ $65 per share	130.00
Net basis, all 300 shares	$201.40
Average ($201.40 ÷ 3)	$67.13

This series of transactions is summarized in Figure 4-1.

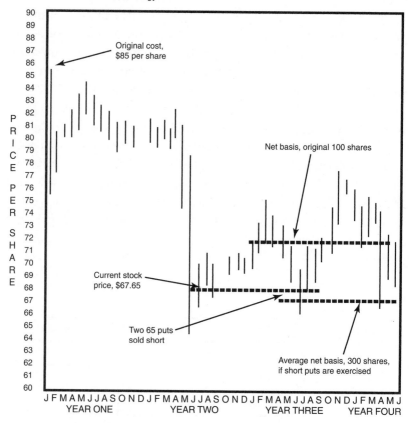

Figure 4-1 Short put rescue strategy

When a Rescue Strategy Is Appropriate

This rescue strategy is appropriate only when (a) fundamental strength continues to qualify the stock as a long-term growth investment, (b) you have capital available to purchase 200 more shares, and (c) you are willing to have that amount invested in a single stock. The historical drop in price levels in the example is a problem; however, if the fundamental value of this stock has not changed and you want to continue to hold shares, this rescue strategy helps reduce basis *and* acquire more shares.

If the current market value were to rebound above $70 per share, you could sell the 200 shares acquired via short puts. Your average basis is

$67.13, so a sale of 200 shares at $70 would result in a capital gain of $574 before transaction costs. But, in reality, your original basis of the 200 shares would be $85 per share on 100 shares and $65 per share on the second 100 shares, plus a 4.40-point short-term gain on the put premium:

Capital loss, original 100 shares ($85 – $65)	$–2,000
Capital gain, second 100 shares ($70 – $65)	+500
Profit from selling two puts @ 6.80	+1,360
Net profit or loss	$–140

The precise timing of gain recognition and the question of short term versus long term varies on these three profit/loss components. The point to be remembered, however, is that with a current market value in the stock of $67.65 per share, this series of transactions reduces the basis in the 100-share position from $85 to $67.13, with a net $140 loss for tax purposes. You continue to own 100 shares with a basis of $67.13, and your $420 loss can be claimed this year on your tax return. Considering the dramatic two-year drop in market value of the stock in this example, the rescue strategy worked well. Such declines in value have not been unusual in recent years, so the rescue strategy is worth considering. You ended up with 100 shares with dramatically reduced market value and a small net loss reported, offset by a paper profit. This is what makes the strategy both practical and profitable when market value has declined in the stock.

Reverting to a Secondary Strategy

A second possible strategy following the acquisition of stock through exercised short puts is to revert to a covered call strategy. Given the same circumstances as in the preceding example, you started out with 100 shares purchased at $85 per share. The average basis has been reduced to $67.13 per share on 300 shares, and the stock's current market value is at $67.65 per share. Because your original position was limited to 100 shares, you may be willing to have 200 shares called away at a profit. So, among various covered call strategies, you could write two calls, each with strike prices of 70. In the event of exercise, 200 shares would be sold at 5 points higher than your current basis, so your capital gain would be $1,000. In addition, you would keep the premium income from selling the calls. Assume that 21-month 70 calls were valued at 8.30 each; in this case, the strategy would produce additional profits through covered calls of $1,660 for two covered calls.

The outcome of this strategy is positive from all angles:

- You end up with 100 shares, but your basis is reduced from $85 to $67.13.

- You earn a premium from writing two short puts and two short calls, all of which is yours to keep.

- You have a capital gain on the 200 shares acquired and then called away.

- You come out of the series of transactions with 100 shares of stock, which is unencumbered and can be held for long-term growth (but at 17.87 points lower basis than originally), or to provide coverage for additional short call positions.

This series of transactions resulted in an important net change. You began and ended the position with 100 shares of stock, but your basis was reduced by 17.87 points. Your realized net capital gains create a small loss, along with a reduced basis in stock. In this example, you did not need to sell your original 100 shares but were able to employ a combination of short puts and short calls to recover from the market decline. The risk in this situation was managed through the use of options trades. The positions are justified as long as you have prequalified the company, as always, and this is critical given the steep declines in many stocks during 2008, for example; the point is that options can effectively adjust basis, manage volatility, and protect profits. In either outcome in the preceding example, the put premium you receive reduced the basis in stock so it was a sound fit for your conservative portfolio.

If the puts in the preceding example were not exercised, you could have waited out expiration, or you could have closed them prior to expiration at a profit. Once they were expired or closed, you would be free to write subsequent short puts. However, if the price of stock rebounded during the life of the puts, you would not have needed or wanted to repeat the short put strategy. If the puts' value declined, you could have entered a closing purchase transaction. The net difference between your original sale and later purchase would have been profitable and, once the puts were closed, you could replace the positions with new short puts, if desired.

The greatest problem with strategies like this is the complexity of the transaction. To execute a series of trades involving short puts and short calls, changes in basis, and the number of shares owned, some conservative investors are understandably discouraged. It requires confidence and skill to deal with the details. For example, if you want to write short puts, your broker requires that you have funds on deposit to pay for stock in the event of exercise: the cost of stock plus transaction fees, minus premium earned from the short sale. Considering that the purpose of this transaction is to manage a decline in market value and to turn it into a profitable position, it is worth overcoming the initial learning curve. However, you also should ensure that before you enter the short positions, you fully understand the potential consequences, as well as the benefits, of every possible outcome.

Managing the Inertia Problem

For some conservative investors, the problem is not mastering the complexities of options trading; in fact, some may be quite comfortable with options and the various strategic possibilities they offer. A greater problem may be inertia.

When market prices move quickly, the natural tendency is to close out positions to cut further losses, or to become overcautious and fail to act when the timing is right. The fear reaction is untypical of conservative investors. You know the stock is a viable long-term hold, so you are unlikely to panic if prices drop out. You know that this temporary situation will turn around at some point in the future. Inertia, on the other hand, is more difficult to deal with. When prices fall unexpectedly, taking decisive action is a struggle between two forces: the desire to make smart, well-timed moves, and the fear that the entire market and its conditions have changed and a more defensive posture is justified. In hindsight, everyone knows that inertia is just another word for lost opportunity; but it is difficult to act when that opportunity arises.

Inertia Management

Following are some suggestions for dealing with the inertia problem.

- **Set goals in advance.** With specific goals set in advance, you improve the clarity of your decisions. Sudden, even unexpected changes in the market as a whole or in the profile of a particular stock prompt a specific and timely decision. Conservative investors are not concerned with daily price timing but do want to pay attention to fundamental changes. Price volatility often signals a change in the fundamentals, so your goals have to allow for the unexpected. For example, if your criteria for holding a stock require continued improvement in quarterly revenues, return on sales, capitalization ratios, increased dividend payments, and other useful indicators, what happens when one of those trends stops or turns around? If you decide in advance that you must sell shares at that point, take action. The goals should involve far more than questions of current price and profit and loss. As important as it is to your goals to make a profit, you know that, from a conservative viewpoint, holding shares when risks have increased can be dangerous as well.

  In setting action goals, know that selling shares does not have to be the only possible decision. In reaction to changing news, you may decide, for example, to take other action. Increased price volatility may prompt you to sell if you can break even or make a profit, or to buy one put per 100 shares to provide downside price protection. A high market price condition along with changed fundamentals may prompt you to sell a covered call for limited downside protection or to sell and take profits and then move capital to another issue. Selling shares is not the only possible way to cut losses; options can help you to adopt a defensive position while preserving your long-term holdings.

- **Follow your own rules without exception.** Prearranged goals give you comfort and clarity, and programmed reactions offset emotions. The emotional block to taking decisive action is a common flaw in the market; you can overcome this flaw by operating from the base of your own rules. Once your rules are set and analyzed critically, follow them without fail, even if your instinct tells you to wait and see or to take a different action. When prices become volatile, don't lower your guard and speculate. The real test of conservatism is how you act when prices are volatile and there is more to lose.

- **Develop two-part strategies.** What if prices rise? What if prices continue to fall? Plan your actions based on both best-case and worst-case scenarios. You have a particular course of action if and when prices rise in volatile times and a different course of action when stock prices fall. Remember, volatility itself is what changes your risk level, and you must identify an action plan. If the volatility is temporary, you can use options to smooth out the rough ride while expanding possible secondary actions if you later decide the fundamentals have also changed. If that changed volatility is permanent, seek an exit strategy. If you can sell at a profit and the fundamentals have changed, take action immediately. If not, you may have to accept a loss, or you may be able to use options to protect yourself against further losses and to provide opportunities for developing a profitable situation in the near future.

- **Consider closing positions when risk attributes have changed.** Volatility is often more than cyclical market change; it may also be a symptom of a change in the stock's fundamental profile, indicating the need for further investigation. When your stock has been trading in a narrow price range and suddenly breaks out and behaves erratically, you must determine why. Is the volatility occurring throughout the market? Is current news causing the change, and if so, do you expect the price range to return to normal levels? Does the volatility follow recent earnings reports, and is there anything in the operating results that you should act upon? If fundamental conditions have changed, you may want to revisit your assumptions concerning the company; perhaps you'll conclude that attributes have changed and you need to sell that stock.

It may be worth redefining your investment policies on a conservative theme. It is not realistic to expect to always make profitable decisions; but you do expect that by selecting stocks wisely, your portfolio will perform better than market averages. Although options can certainly help in this goal, it may be more prudent to sell shares that have become less safe. Your capital may serve you better elsewhere. The conservative theme of your portfolio should not dictate profit levels, but your actions. By following those themes, you avoid the common problem that investors face: ending up with a portfolio of stocks acquired above current market value. Inexperienced investors tend to take profits whenever they are available, so by selection, they end up with a portfolio full of underperforming stocks. This is contrary to any investor's goals. Because you are a conservative investor, it is important to know not only when to take profits, but also when to take losses.

Taxes and Profits

The various strategies you employ to either protect paper profits or minimize paper losses may be profitable or not, depending on your tax status. If a profitable or breakeven situation is calculated on a pretax basis, it may end up at a net loss after tax liabilities are calculated.

To assess strategic decisions with tax liabilities in mind, include the following points in your analysis.

- **Carryover loss status.** As a planning tool, carryover losses are easily forgotten or ignored. Many investors have fairly large losses from past years that can be used to offset current-year gains. If your carryover loss is substantial, you may absorb that loss by taking gains this year that you might not have taken otherwise. As inconvenient as carryover losses are, they provide a planning opportunity. For example, as long as you avoid the 30-day wash sale rule, large realized profits can be absorbed by carryover losses, and the current position can be replaced with a lower basis. However, if you use options to protect current value in stock, you could jeopardize the tax advantage. For example, if you own appreciated stock, you can sell shares this year to offset a carryover loss. If you wait 31 days or more, you can repurchase shares and establish the current price as your new basis. If you also sell puts or buy calls to protect your current basis in the event of a price decline, they may be treated as related transactions. You also may not be able to claim the loss on stock if you have opened option transactions. These so-called "offsetting positions" are complicated. If you sell in-the-money (ITM) puts within the 30-day period—meaning the put is likely to be exercised—you may risk losing the right to claim a loss on the stock. The sale of stock and exercise of the put (meaning a reacquisition of the same stock) could negate the sale under the wash sale rule.

To be on the safe side, a true sale of stock should occur without use of options. Wait the 31 days and repurchase stock, or sell ITM puts at the strike price close to your sale price. When the put is exercised, reacquire the stock, discounted by the premium you received when you sold the put. Or, you can simply wait the 31 days and buy the stock without using options in the transaction.

- **Your true effective tax rate.** When you calculate the tax effect of capital gains on stock or options, be sure to include both federal and state taxes. Your "true" effective rate is the combined rate of both. The effective rate is defined as taxes on any earnings you report within your effective tax bracket. For example, if your annual income places you in the 33 percent federal tax bracket, any *additional* reported income is taxed at that level. However, you may also be taxed by your state. For example, if your tax rate for state earnings is 8 percent, your combined effective tax rate is 41 percent. You may need to make additional calculations. For example, although federal long-term capital gains rates are fixed at a lower rate, your state may not provide a long-term gains provision for reduced tax rates.

  The adjustment could be complex. In calculating a long-term gain, for example, you may need to reduce the federal rate from 33 percent to 15 percent but calculate the state tax based on the full rate assessed. At the same time, you may have a federal carryover loss, but no corresponding loss (or a different one) on the state level. To compare tax rules for each state, check the Web site taxadmin.org/fta/rate/ind_inc.html.

- **The timing of your profits and losses.** Traditional tax planning involves preplanned timing of taxable gains and, equally important, of tax losses. You can time your profits and losses based on your tax status this year. However, your priority in timing of transactions should be set first on your conservative goals. Only when it makes no difference should the tax questions come into play. For example, if a sale this year would create a net loss, but you already have a large loss carryover, there is no tax advantage to selling shares before the end of the year. In this case, you could buy puts to protect your current value and wait until next year, when you may need the loss. If the tax advantage next year would be greater than the cost of buying the put, it makes sense to employ this strategy.

To the extent that you can plan profits and losses to offset one another, you can minimize your tax liability. Tax avoidance is legal, but it requires planning and consultation with your tax adviser. Profits and losses can be offset based on the timing of profitable sales with disposal of loss-status assets. Profits can also be offset against carryover losses. In the past, stock profits and losses could be offset against nondeferred gains from selling a primary residence. Today, though, profits from selling your primary residence are tax free up to $500,000 for married couples ($250,000 if you are single) and cannot be deferred. This is a great advantage, but timing and coordination between residence sales and your investment portfolio provides no year-to-year planning advantage.

■ **Offsetting profits and losses in the same year.** One of the most effective planning devices is to simply match profits against current-year losses. The outcome is to have little or no net change on your effective tax rate. If your rate is close to the point where additional income would push your taxes into the next bracket, preplanning makes sense. If you intend to take profits, it may be smart to also dispose of underperforming stock. You gain two advantages by coordinating the timing of these transactions. First, you shelter gains by offsetting them with investment losses. Second, you dispose of stocks that have not performed as you hoped. This is far more conservative than making decisions in isolation. You may experience subsequent year swings in your tax bracket and liability if you do not plan. For example, this year, you may sell several stocks and realize capital gains, which are taxed; and next year, you may sell several stocks that have lost value, creating a carryover loss of limited year-to-year value. By not planning ahead, you may create a problem for yourself over future tax years. Not only do you face the possible jump in your tax bracket in the profitable year, but you create problems by placing your investment losses into a single year without offsetting gains. Although all your gains are taxed in the year reported, your maximum annual capital loss is $3,000. It makes no sense to create a carry-over loss when, with some preplanning, you can time those losses so to use as offsets to reduce current-year tax liabilities.

■ **Unintended tax consequences.** The tax rules for options-related transactions are complex. For many individuals, the tax rules are too complicated even without options, so many people who simply buy and sell stocks, mutual funds, and real estate hire tax experts to help them comply with the law. When you add options to the mix, the complexity makes professional help more important than ever. Be sure your tax professional is completely knowledgeable in the area of tax rules for options. You must pay for the professional advice not only at tax season but throughout the year. The complexity of rules, notably for in-the-money covered calls, can have consequences, including the loss of long-term capital gain status on your stock portfolio. Consult with your expert before making trades so that you understand the rules and know beforehand which types of trades can cause significant loss of tax advantage.

Options Used for Riding Out Volatility

Everyone has to contend with short-term price volatility. As a conservative investor, you focus on fundamental attributes of the company and use short-term indicators only to test your ongoing assumptions. If those assumptions change, your hold strategy may become a sell. However, as long as you intend to continue holding stock, options can be valuable in riding out short-term volatility as an alternative to profit taking in the traditional manner. With options, you can minimize short-term losses and even take profits while continuing to own shares of stock.

In the next chapter, the intriguing possibilities of the covered call strategy, including the special tax rules that apply to short options strategies, are explored in depth.

5

OPTIONS AS CASH GENERATORS

Covered call writing is a conservative strategy. The key is in exploiting time value premium. For the strategy to make sense, your basis in stock must justify the short position, the option premium must be adequate to justify the risk of exercise, and you must know the tax ramifications before you open short positions. Tax rules for short options are odd and complex, but you cannot ignore them.

The covered call is among the most attractive of *conservative* option strategies. It provides an impressive rate of return when properly structured, and it does not increase the most common forms of risk. In fact, market risk—your exposure to lost value in your stock—is *reduced* with the covered call strategy.

In this chapter, the conservative possibilities of covered calls are explained, starting with the underlying premise necessary to succeed with this strategy. Various outcome scenarios are provided to help you form realistic judgments about when and if the covered call strategy makes sense. Your analysis is best made with tax consequences in mind; for example, capital gains rules for covered call strategies affect your decision and the timing of these short positions.

One of the more intriguing strategies involving covered calls is the forward-and-up roll, a technique used to avoid exercise while increasing potential profits in the event of future exercise. This idea works best after a run-up in stock prices that occurs after entry into the covered call strategy. Covered calls also work as a means for intentionally generating a sale of stock while creating more profit than would be possible through a straight stock sale.

The Covered Call Concept

No strategy is completely risk free, not even owning stock in well-managed, strongly capitalized companies. But in the case of a covered call, you seek to enhance your profits without incurring added *market risk*, and this advantage is both practical and inevitable. For many investors, the lost opportunity risk is worth the additional income that covered call strategies generate. (Lost opportunity risk is discussed later in this chapter.)

A covered call strategy has two elements. First is the ownership of 100 shares of stock for each option to be covered; second is the short position in the call option. If you own 100 shares, you sell one call to achieve the one-to-one "covered" status. The call grants the right to the buyer on the other side of the transaction to buy your 100 shares (to call them away) at the set strike price at any time from the date of sale until expiration. As long as the current price of stock is below the strike price, the call will not be exercised.

> You own 100 shares of 3M. The current price is $53.81. If you consider covered calls with strike prices of 55, 60, and 65, these positions are not exercised unless the market value of the stock rises above those strike price levels before the call expires.

Who Makes the Decision?

When you enter a covered call position, you are *selling* the call against stock you own. This means you give the right to exercise to the buyer, and that decision is entirely in the buyer's hands. You are allowed to keep the cash you receive upon selling the short call, whether the call is exercised, closed, or simply expires. You also continue to receive dividends during the period you are short on the call. The big question comes down to this: Is it worthwhile to risk having 100 shares of stock called away if and when the stock's price moves above the call's strike price?

To answer that all-important question, you need to analyze the transaction, review the yield outcomes based on all possible stock price movements, and calculate the after-tax yield from the covered call as well as potential capital gains and dividends on the called-away stock.

The *advantage* to selling covered calls is that it produces instant cash. You are paid for selling the call. For example, if you can achieve an immediate 10 percent return on your stock by selling a call, is it worthwhile? The answer, of course, depends on your original purchase prices versus today's stock value as well as the potential call-away price. These elements determine your overall yield on the investment in the event of exercise.

The disadvantage to selling covered calls is that you tie up 100 shares for each call sold, and you cannot escape from the covered position without closing out that short call. For example, if you sell a call and receive payment (the premium), and you later decide you do not want to continue holding that stock position, you have to buy the call to close. (Remember, the initial transaction was a sale; to close that out, you need to buy the call with a closing purchase transaction.)

You should close the position under one of two circumstances. First, if the value of the short call has declined since the position was opened, you can pay the current price and close out the position. The net difference (the original sales price minus the closing purchase price, net of trading expense) will be a capital gain, which is taxable in the year the position is closed. Second, you may want to close the position if the value of stock has moved upward beyond the strike price. In this situation, you face the possibility of exercise, which can happen at any time when the call is in the money (ITM, or when the current market price of stock is higher than the strike price of the call). When the stock's price moves above the strike price, the net premium value of the short call may be *lower* than it was when you sold it. This is true because the call's time value declines as the exercise date draws near. In this situation, it is prudent to buy and avoid exercise while still realizing a net gain on the call transaction. Incidentally, once you close out the covered call position, you are free to repeat the trade, using calls with higher strike prices and later expiration dates.

If the stock's price moves above strike price so that your short call is in the money, the call's value may also have increased. You can still avoid exercise without taking a net loss using a technique called rolling (replacement of one call with another). This strategy is explained in detail later in this chapter.

Examples: Ten Stocks and Covered Calls

To illustrate how the basic covered call strategy works, examine the ten companies in the model portfolio, sharing three common attributes:

1. Both listed options and Long-term Equity AnticiPation Security (LEAPS) are available on the stocks.

2. All these stocks are assumed to have current market value *above* the original basis. (There is no justification for engaging in covered calls for stocks whose market value is lower than the basis; the conservative strategy works only when the stocks have appreciated in value since the time of purchase. This does not mean writing ITM calls is always a bad idea. If your basis in stock is far lower than the current value, ITM short calls may be viable.)

3. All stocks show current moderate price volatility levels. (If volatility in a stock is high, so is market risk; if it is too low, option premiums also are low, and the strategy may not be justified.)

These stocks' attributes are summarized in Table 5-1.

Table 5-1 Sample Stocks for Covered Calls

Name of Company	Symbol	Current Price*	Dividend Yield
Caterpillar	CAT	32.29	5.1
IBM	IBM	101.2	72.0
Johnson & Johnson	JNJ	53.05	3.6
Coca-Cola	KO	45.02	3.7
McDonald's	MCD	56.09	3.6
3M	MMM	53.8	13.8
Altria	MO	16.9	97.8
United Parcel Service	UPS	54.65	3.4
Wal-Mart	WMT	50.20	2.1
Exxon Mobil	XOM	66.75	2.4

* closing prices as of April 18, 2009

Working within Pre-Established Standards

The covered call strategy works at specific strike price levels, so you will want to proceed on the premise that stocks you own contain all these attributes. If they do not, the covered call strategy will not conform to your conservative standards. The first step is to select strike prices that are (a) at or out of the money (OTM) and (b) higher than your original basis in the stock.

In Table 5-1, note that Altria reports the highest dividend yield of 7.8 percent. Because your conservative covered call strategy is based on stock attributes, the high current yield is attractive; while you may not consider dividend yield for stocks currently owned as part of the selection process, the yield can affect your decision to purchase particular company stock given that fundamental indicators are otherwise equal. If you owned all ten of these stocks in your portfolio, you would expect to also experience a varying range of potential profits from covered call strategies. By the same logic, you might also own other stocks whose option premiums would not meet your expectations. Referring again to Table 5-1, you may decide to *avoid* writing covered calls of Altria specifically because of the high dividend yield. It may be preferable to ensure that you retain these high-yielding shares and reserve covered call writing for the lowest yielding stocks on the list, notably IBM (yielding only 2.0 percent), Wal-Mart (2.1 percent), and Exxon Mobil (2.4 percent).

You next analyze a series of options in comparative form. If you compare options with different expiration terms, you should annualize those returns. For example, you might decide to use LEAPS calls, all of which expire in 21 months. A summary of call option values expiring in 21 months is shown in Table 5-2.

Table 5-2   Covered Call Premiums, 21 Months Until Expiration

Name of Company	Symbol	Current Price *	21-Month Strikes	Call Premium
Caterpillar	CAT	32.29	35	7.00
			40	5.15
IBM	IBM	101.27	110	13.43

Table 5-2 Continued

Name of Company	Symbol	Current Price *	21-Month Strikes	Call Premium
Johnson & Johnson	JNJ	53.05	55	6.20
Coca-Cola	KO	45.02	47.50	5.10
			50	4.00
McDonald's	MCD	56.09	60	5.20
			65	3.80
3M	MMM	53.81	55	8.00
			60	6.30
Altria	MO	16.99	17.50	2.06
			20	1.32
United Parcel Service	UPS	54.65	60	6.00
Wal-Mart	WMT	50.20	55	5.90
			60	4.15
Exxon Mobil	XOM	66.75	70	10.00
			75	8.23

* closing prices as of April 18, 2009

Calculating the Gain Comparatively

Let's review how these values must be read. In the case of the Exxon Mobil options, the 21-month option with a strike price of 70 is currently worth 10.00 ($1,000). So, if you sold this option today, you would receive $1,000 (minus trading fees) as premium for the sale.

If you sold the 75 option, you would be paid 8.23 ($823) per option. You can perform a fast return calculation based on the difference between today's value and strike price to see what you would gain if each call were exercised. Upon exercise, your 100 shares of stock would be called away at the strike price: in the first instance, $70 per share, and in the second, $75 per share. The following calculations are based on *today's* price, however, and not on what you actually paid for the stock. Based on the current price, if the short call were exercised in the month of expiration, you would gain (excluding dividend income and not allowing for taxes) the following:

21-Month Call
Strike Price 70

Sale of stock	$7,000
Less: Current value	- 6,675
Stock profit	$325
Return ($325 ÷ $6,675)	4.9%
Call premium	$1,000
Option yield ($1,000 ÷ 6,675)	15.0%

21-Month Call
Strike Price 75

Sale of stock	$7,500
Less: Current value	- 6,675
Stock profit	$825
Return ($825 ÷ $6,675)	12.4%
Call premium	$823
Option yield ($823 ÷ 6,675)	12.3%

By showing both the stock *and* option profits, an important point comes out: While you do not include the stock's capital gain as a means for picking one covered call over another, the return if exercised varies based on strike price. In this example, the lower strike price of 70 produces a higher option gain but a lower stock capital gain, and the higher strike price of 75 produces an option and capital gain that are nearly equal. The 70 strike price example produces a 19.9 percent overall gain, and the 75 strike price produces a 24.7 percent overall gain. So, although you should not mix the outcomes in stock and option profit, the selection of one strike price over another is essential if you expect to make expected profits based on various scenarios. In the example, the higher strike price produces a more desirable outcome, even though the option premium return is lower.

If you annualize these rates of return—again, based only on stock sale and option premium—you must adjust the reported gain to show the yield based on a 12-month holding period:

21-Month Call
Strike Price 70
Stock gain $(4.9\% \div 21) \times 12 = 2.8\%$
Option gain $(15.0\% \div 21) \times 12 = 8.6\%$

21-Month Call
Strike Price 75
Stock gain $(12.4\% \div 21) \times 12 = 7.1\%$
Option gain $(12.3\% \div 21) \times 12 = 7.0\%$

This example demonstrates that in comparing two options, you arrive at a rate of return based on stock gains and another separate return based on option premium. You do not want to combine these because it remains important to compare option outcomes if exercised and if expired, excluding any capital gains on stock. The point relates only to the selection of strike price based on various exercise outcomes and demonstrates that overall returns are substantially different when stock profits are also considered.

Actual comparisons should be based on your purchase price of stock, include a calculation of dividend income, and consider your tax liability as part of the calculation.[1] More on taxation of covered calls is found later in this chapter.

Smart Conservative Ground Rules

All strategies have positive and negative aspects. The covered call strategy is conservative, assuming that you understand the transaction's specific attributes and that you are sure the numbers work in your favor. You need to observe a few basic ground rules as you proceed through the analysis to ensure a truly *conservative* application of the covered call strategy:

---

1.   Annualizing option returns is important because holding periods are likely to vary from a few weeks or months to several years. The basic annualization formula involves dividing the yield by the holding period (in months) and then multiplying the result by 12 (months); this produces the average annual yield.

- **Your original purchase price has to justify the strategy.** The most conservative use of covered calls exists when you own stock that has appreciated in value. The lower your basis in comparison to today's market value of stock, the more flexibility you have in devising a conservative options strategy. In fact, the use of covered calls is a sensible way to protect a portion of your paper profits without needing to take those profits. For example, if you have a 30-point paper profit, selling a covered call and receiving a premium of 10 ($1,000) gives you 10 points of downside protection, or one-third of your total unrealized profit. If you sell a series of covered calls over time, it is even possible to take all your profits out of the position without selling stock. For example, if you received a premium of 10 on three subsequent calls over a period of many months, with each one expiring and being replaced in turn, the entire 30 points of paper profits can be taken as capital gains.

- **The premium value you will receive has to provide enough yield to justify the covered call exposure.** If you plan to use your stock as cover for a short option position, you must be able to justify it in terms of profit levels. Check returns from option premium on an annualized basis. So, if you own shares of many different stocks, you will naturally seek out those option positions that yield the best returns. In comparing one option position to another, be aware of the rate of return and the time until expiration. A 5 percent return you earn in 6 months is far more profitable than a 10 percent return that takes 24 months. Also remember that you will not always keep the short position open all the way until expiration. You can close out short positions at any time. For example, one profitable strategy is to sell a covered call, wait for the time value to decline, and then enter a buy-to-close order, realizing the net difference as a profit. After the position is closed, you can open another covered call using the same stock, but with more time value and profit potential.

- **You are willing to accept exercise as one of the possible outcomes.** In every covered call position, you have to accept the possibility that your 100 shares of stock will be called away. In fact, some investors are drawn to options with the original idea of accepting exercise and selling shares, only to realize that repetitive covered call selling may be more profitable. If you do not want exercise under any circumstances, you should not write covered calls. For example, if you have a large amount of profit but you don't want to sell until you reach the long-term holding period, writing covered calls and risking exercise is ill-advised. However, for many investors, covered call writing is a smart alternative to simply selling shares. Keeping shares of stock and the associated dividend income and selling calls to realize short-term profits is one effective way to achieve current returns.

The idea that you must be willing to accept exercise is not a problem if, in fact, exercise produces capital gains in addition to option returns. The risk in such a transaction is that the covered call could be exercised and you would be required to sell your 100 shares of stock. But a risk that comes with a return is one that most investors gladly accept—assuming that it is structured to produce profits if and when the short call is exercised.

■ **You are aware of the tax consequences in the event of exercise.** If you trade in options without considering the effect on your stock positions, taxation is easy to understand. If you sell a call and it expires worthless, your gain is treated as short term regardless of how long it was held. So, tax treatment of LEAPS options is different than for most other investments. (Incidentally, less conservative investors who go long on options may have either short- or long-term gains or losses, depending on the usual rule concerning the holding period.) You must understand how capital gains rules apply to a particular strategy and consider the tax consequences as part of your overall return calculation.

■ **The primary risk to the covered call strategy is possible loss of future market gains if and when stock prices exceed the call's strike price.** This lost opportunity risk should be understood before you enter into any covered call strategy.

You purchased stock at $35 per share. Today, it is valued at $40. You sell a covered call expiring in one year and receive a premium of $300. The strike price is $45 per share. If the stock rises above $45, your stock will be called away. At the time you enter the transaction, you justify the decision based on your purchase price, which is $10 per share below the strike price. Furthermore, strike price is 5 points higher than today's stock value, so the entire premium represents nonintrinsic value. Finally, the $300 premium is extra income equal to 8.6 percent of your original purchase price. This analysis makes sense; however, let's say the stock's market value soars to $60 per share and your stock is called away at the strike price of $45 per share. Your lost opportunity cost for this transaction is $1,200, the difference between market value of stock and strike price of the call, minus the premium received for selling the option ($6,000 - $4,500 - $300 = $1,200).

In this example, the lost opportunity arises from the stock's market value climbing 15 points above the call's strike price. In the analysis of a covered call strategy, you have two risk factors to consider. You know (given the example) that you can create consistent high returns with no increase in market risk. You also know that for stocks you own that have appreciated in value since you purchased shares, this scenario can be repeated many times unless a particular call is exercised. In exchange for consistent high returns, you must look at the other side: In some cases, a stock's market value rises above strike price, and you may lose the potential profits had you not entered into the covered call strategy. That is the lost opportunity.

Here is the essential question: Are you willing to give up the consistent higher-than-average returns on all stocks on which you can write covered calls in exchange for the lost opportunity that might occur on occasion? You need to assess lost opportunity risk in the context of your conservative portfolio, considering your willingness to accept possible exercise, dividend yield comparisons between stocks, proximity of strike prices to current market value, and the amount of profit in the current position based on original purchase price. The stocks you own today should have a good chance of growing in market value gradually over time. Lost opportunity risk cannot be ignored, but that risk may be less significant in your conservative portfolio when compared to the certainty of profits from writing covered calls.

You can mitigate lost opportunity risk using a secondary covered call strategy, rolling forward and up, discussed later in this chapter. Even though stock prices may rise more quickly than you expect in some cases, the lost opportunity risk is not absolute. You can (a) close option positions to avoid lost opportunity risk; (b) avoid risk by employing covered calls on only a portion of your holdings (for example, covering 100 shares when you own 500 shares, so only 20 percent of your holdings in a particular stock are even exposed to the lost opportunity risk); and (c) employ rolling techniques to escape the lost opportunity risk or to mitigate the future lost opportunity you experience when stock prices rise even further.

Lost opportunity is a "delightful problem" for conservative investors. It is an opportunity to accept exercise at ensured high-yield levels; it allows you to roll out of one position and replace it with another to increase profits even more; and if you have employed covered calls on only a portion of your holdings, it means the balance of shares on that company continue to appreciate in value. Many investors would be quite pleased to face a lost opportunity under these circumstances.

- **The covered call strategy commits the capital invested in stock for as long as the short call remains open.** Because a conservative strategy requires that your long stock position is maintained as an offset to the short call, your shares are committed until the short position is closed. You escape this commitment when you buy to close the call, when the call is exercised, or when the call expires. If you plan to keep the covered call position open until expiration many months in the future, for example, this means that you cannot sell shares until the call is closed or canceled. (You can sell shares, of course, but that would transform the highly conservative covered call strategy into a high-risk uncovered call strategy.)

Is it worthwhile to keep shares committed? As a conservative investor, a basic assumption made here is that you own shares of a particular company as a long-term investment and would not want to sell. The alternative to the covered calls strategy is to take no action but simply to continue your hold strategy in the stock. Covered call writing does not change this basic strategy; it only employs the stock to enhance profits via option premium. So, yes, assuming your portfolio strategy does not change, it *is* worthwhile to keep shares committed.

A second point to remember is that even though your shares are committed or tied up relative to the short call, you will continue receiving dividends as long as you own your shares. So, if part of your conservative strategy is to invest in high-yielding stocks, the covered call does not change this strategy. If you are also using a dividend reinvestment program to achieve compound returns on your dividend income, this will continue to occur. So, remaining committed to keeping the stock is consistent with your existing conservative strategy.

■ Most important of all, your primary portfolio strategy has to remain the same, seeking long-term investment in the stock of properly selected companies, not in selecting stocks based only on potential covered call returns. One danger in using options to enhance profits is that it could change your entire investment strategy. As a conservative investor, your first rule should be that, no matter what, the proper selection of companies based on fundamental strength and growth prospects must remain the primary means of stock selection and the primary deciding factor for any decision to buy, hold, or sell shares.

You have built a strong portfolio of stocks with growing dividend payment history and a consistent long-term growth record. However, in looking through the options listings, you discover that some other stocks have options yielding much higher premium levels than your stocks. You sell your holdings and replace them with stocks on which higher yields can be achieved with covered call writing.

This is a big mistake. One essential rule in the options market is that higher-risk stocks (defined by the primary market risk factor—volatility) exhibit a correspondingly higher volatility in option time value premium. As a consequence, if you concentrate on stock selection with option premium as your primary criterion, you will be replacing a conservative portfolio with a high-risk one.

A Conservative Approach

Proceeding from the ground rules for covered call writing, the next step is to determine exactly what makes elements of the strategy advantageous. As a conservative investor, what are the primary attributes you need to enter a profitable conservative strategy? There are three: appreciated value in the stock, time and extrinsic value premium, and downside protection.

Element 1: Appreciated Value in the Stock

As long as the current value is higher than your basis, you have great profit flexibility in entering a covered call strategy. In other words, with those paper profits, you can build in a greater certainty of profits. For example, consider how different the return scenario looks in the two following examples.

EXAMPLE 1: COVERED CALLS WITHOUT SUBSTANTIAL APPRECIATED VALUE IN THE STOCK

You purchased Exxon Mobil stock at $65 per share; today, shares are worth $66.75. You sell a 9-month 70 strike call and receive a premium of $6.01. If exercised, total return on stock and on option transactions (without adjusting for trading costs, annualization, or taxes) would be

Capital gain = $7,000 less $6,500 basis = $500
Capital gain = 7.1% (before annualizing)
Option premium = $601
Option return = *9.0%* ($601 ÷ $6,675)

EXAMPLE 2: COVERED CALLS WITH SUBSTANTIAL APPRECIATED VALUE IN THE STOCK

You purchased Exxon Mobil stock at $54 per share; today, shares are worth $66.75. You sell a 9-month call with a strike price of 70 and receive a premium of $6.01. If exercised, total return on stock and on option transactions (without adjusting for trading costs, annualization, or taxes) would be

Capital gain = $7,000 strike price less $5,400 basis = $1,600
Capital gain = 29.6% (before annualizing)
Option premium = $601
Option return = *9.0%* ($601 ÷ $6,675)

Clearly, the greater appreciation from higher capital gains enhances the overall return from combined capital gains and the option premium. The conservative covered call strategy requires that the scenario produce such returns if the call were exercised. However, it is also important to remember that in comparing option-specific outcomes, you do not consider the capital gain as a part of the total return. The previous example illustrates that exercise produces higher profits for appreciated stock than for stock that has not appreciated. It simply makes the point that you should prefer to use appreciated stock in covered call strategies.

Exercise is one of the possible outcomes, and you cannot just ignore the potential capital gain. That may even be desirable. However, the majority of covered call writers would prefer to gain option profits without going through exercise so that they can repeat the strategy many times. You can avoid exercise in a number of ways; however, if you look at exercise as a worst-case outcome, you will want to ensure before entering the position that it is justified by the level of profitability upon exercise.

Element 2: Time and Extrinsic Value Premium

The key to successful covered call writing is in the time-value premium. To review, every option's premium contains three parts. *Intrinsic value* is the value of ITM points. For example, if the strike price of the call is $40 and the current market value of stock is $43, the call contains 3 points of intrinsic value. *Time value is the value assigned to time remaining until expiration.* *Extrinsic value* is any premium above intrinsic and time value; it represents the volatility of the option. If the call is at the money (ATM) or OTM, there is no intrinsic value. For example, if the stock is valued today at $43 and the 40 call premium value is 5 ($500), it contains 3 points of intrinsic value and 2 points of time and extrinsic value. If the stock value is at or below $40 per share, a call with a 40 strike price consists entirely of time and extrinsic value premium.

Time works *for* the seller and *against* the buyer. Buying options can be highly speculative because the buyer has to hope not only that the stock rises enough to create intrinsic value prior to expiration but that the growth in price also rises far enough to offset lost time value. Because time value evaporates as expiration approaches, this is difficult to achieve. For example, a buyer may purchase a 40 call and pay $500 (5 points) when the stock is valued at $39 per share. In this situation, the premium is all time and extrinsic value. That stock must rise to at least $45 per share *just to break even* by expiration. (The buyer paid 5 points for time and extrinsic value.) Even before considering the cost of trading on both sides of the transaction, the buyer must experience considerable growth in the stock's market value to create a profit.

In comparison, time and extrinsic value from the seller's point of view are the advantage. Knowing that time value declines no matter how the stock's price moves by expiration, the time value premium is a cushion, made even more generous when extrinsic value is high. In the circumstances described earlier, imagine the advantage the seller enjoys even when the stock's market value rises. For example, let's say the seller *sells* the $40 call at 5 when the stock is at $39 per share. By expiration, the stock is at $43. This is not enough for the buyer to profit; the 3 points of intrinsic value are still 2 points lower than the premium the buyer paid. However, the seller has a different point of view. As expiration approaches, the concern is that the call will be exercised for the 3 points ITM. The seller can close the position by buying the call to close. Before considering trading costs, the profit is $200. The call was sold for $500 and then purchased for $300. The seller makes a profit, whereas the buyer cannot in the same circumstances. (Sellers can also roll out of this position.)

With traditional listed options, the life span is generally as short as 8 months. Although time value is an important part of the seller's equation, greater time and extrinsic value profit potential is found in the LEAPS calls. The LEAPS option has a life span up to 30 months, so option time value is substantially higher. For example, a comparison of various options on IBM calls with stock at $101.27 and strike price at 110 demonstrates the point:

Time to Expiration	Option Value	Return	Annualized Return
21 months	13.43	13.3	7.6%
9 months	7.90	7.8	10.4
6 months	6.30	6.2	12.4
3 months	3.41	3.4	13.6

This example shows that the longer period produces a higher dollar yield but a lower annualized yield. You are dealing strictly with time and extrinsic value. The stock's price is below the $110-per-share strike price level, so *all* premium is time and extrinsic value for the 110 call. The longer you are willing to keep your long stock positions exposed with a short call cover, the greater the time value and extrinsic value premium; but as the example also shows, the yield on an annualized basis tends to be higher for shorter-term options.

Element 3: Downside Protection

Every investor whose stock has appreciated in value worries about losing paper profits, so profit taking is more likely as these paper profits increase. Well-disciplined conservative strategy tells you that you should not give in to the temptation to speculate on short-term price movements—that is, by taking profits. However, as the old adage tells you, "Wall Street climbs a wall of worry."

Selling covered calls against appreciated stocks is one way to offset your personal wall of worry. The premium you receive from selling covered calls is, in a sense, a way of taking profits without giving up ownership of shares. Those profits are yours to keep in the event of expiration or exercise; and if you close the position by buying the short call, the difference between sell and buy price represents profit or loss. In any of these events, you continue owning stock and receiving dividends.

The net premium you earn from selling calls can be viewed in another way: as downside protection. For example, if your original basis in stock is $40.00 per share and you sell a call for a premium of 4 ($400), that is a 10 percent reduction in your basis. Your adjusted basis in stock is $36 per share, not $40, because you have gained $400 by selling the covered call. Viewing covered calls in this way, you achieve a broader range of profit margin, meaning more downside protection. The more premium you receive from selling calls over time, the greater your downside protection.

Tax Ramifications of Covered Calls

Calculating returns without also figuring out the after-tax outcome is not realistic. Not only must you consider a tax liability, you need to be aware that the tax rules can drastically affect your tax rate on capital gains. The current rules for federal taxes on option trades are more complex than for most forms of investing. For conservative investors, a crucial point to remember is that selling OTM calls is the least complicated strategy, for two reasons. First, the entire premium consists of time value and extrinsic value. Second, the tax rules are simple as long as you restrict your trades to OTM positions so there is no effect on the calculation of short-term or long-term capital gains holding periods. However, once you sell an ITM call, the whole question becomes much more complicated. Here is a rundown of the tax rules governing options.

- **Rules for option buyers.** If you buy options, the profit or loss can either be long term or short term depending on how long you own the long option. The net amount is reported on federal tax Schedule D (Capital Gains and Losses) in the year of sale. If the transaction is completed within one year or less, it is taxed as a short-term capital gain or loss. If the total holding period was longer than one year, it is treated as a long-term gain or loss.

- **Rules for option sellers.** The rules for option sellers are quite different than for other types of investments. The payment you receive at the time of sale is not taxed at that point. The tax "event" occurs when the position is closed, expired, or exercised. If you sell an option in one year and it is closed in the next, the tax is not calculated until the latter year.

One important exception to the general rule governing short-term and long-term tax rates is that if you keep a short call until expiration, it is treated as a short-term gain or loss, no matter how long the position was open. For example, you may sell a covered LEAPS call that does not expire for 30 months. Upon expiration, the gain is considered short term. If you close out the position with a buy order prior to expiration, it is treated as short-term if it was open for one year or less, or as long-term if the holding period went more than a year.

If the call is exercised and your stock is called away, the gain is figured including the premium you received from the sale of the call and the gain on stock. For example, if your capital gain was $2,400 and you received $830 for the option, *all* the gain—$3,230—is treated in the same manner. That treatment depends on the holding period of the stock and whether the call is defined under IRS rules as a "qualified" covered call. Nonqualified covered calls affect the calculation of the long-term gain holding period. As long as the option you sell is ATM or OTM, the holding period for your stock is not affected or stopped. If the call is ITM and it meets the definition of qualified, the holding period is not changed. If the call is nonqualified, however, the holding period counting toward long-term gain treatment is done away with and, for the purposes of calculating gain, the time limit begins anew once the call position has been closed.

> You own stock currently valued at $75 per share. You sell covered call options with an $80 strike price. There is no effect on the calculation of the stock's holding period, because the position is OTM; the holding period for the stock's eventual capital gain calculation continues to run. If you purchased the stock more than one year ago, you already qualify for long-term capital gains treatment if and when the call is exercised. If your holding period is less than a year, the time continues to run without interruption.

> You own stock currently valued at $75 per share. You sell a covered call ITM (below the current value of the stock). In this case, the status of long-term or short-term gain is determined by the rules for qualification for the call. If the call is defined as unqualified, the holding period of stock is suspended as long as the call position is open. Your stock's holding period is eliminated entirely and starts over once the call is closed. So, if you have owned stock for less than a full year, selling an ITM call, even if qualified, is unwise; the time limit stops running as long as the call is open, and if the call is nonqualified, you lose any time already accumulated toward the one-year long-term holding period. However, if you have already met the requirements for long-term gain treatment, this is not changed by opening an unqualified covered call.

A qualified covered call must have more than 30 days until expiration. ITM calls with fewer than 30 days to expiration are not qualified. For calls with expiration occurring in more than 30 days, qualification depends on the stock's closing price and on option strike price level. This is where the calculation becomes complicated. Based on the previous day's closing price of stock at the time the call is sold, it is necessary to calculate the lowest qualified strike price. (Remember, as long as the call is OTM, there is no need to qualify its status. There is no effect on calculation of holding periods.)

Six Levels of Separation (of Your Money) for Taxes

The following applies only to in-the-money covered calls. There are six separate levels of calculation.

1. **The previous day's closing stock price is $25 or less, and the option has more than 30 days to go until expiration.** A qualified covered call must be no lower than one strike price *below* the closing stock price, but no qualified call is counted if the strike price is less than 85 percent of the stock price. This is somewhat mind-boggling, and the average investor has to wonder how such limitations were arrived at, what they are meant to achieve or prevent, and why the calculation has to be so complex. The purpose in limiting qualification is to apply special rules for "offsetting positions" in which risks are reduced so that tax benefits and deferrals are minimized. The qualification price ranges of calls in this classification are summarized in Table 5-3.

2. **The previous day's closing stock price is between $25.01 and $60.00, and the option has more than 30 days until expiration.** A qualified covered call must be no lower than one strike price below the previous day's closing stock price.

3. **The previous day's closing stock price is between $60.01 and $150, and the option expires in 31 to 90 days.** A qualified covered call must be no lower than one strike price below the previous day's closing stock price, but not more than $10 ITM.

4. **The previous day's closing stock price is between $60.01 and $150, and the option expires beyond 90 days.** A qualified covered call must be no lower than one strike price below the previous day's closing stock price, but not more than $10 ITM.

5. **The previous day's closing stock price is greater than $150 per share, and the option will expire between 31 and 90 days.** A qualified covered call must be no lower than one strike price below the previous day's closing stock price.

6. **The previous day's closing stock price is greater than $150 per share, and the option expires beyond 90 days.** A qualified covered call must be no lower than two strike prices below the previous day's closing stock price.

The tax rules for writing ITM covered calls are complex and potentially costly in terms of tax consequences. Because the long-term gain period can be suspended (for qualified calls) or even eliminated and started over (for nonqualified calls), most conservative investors find no justification in writing ITM calls. However, even beyond tax considerations, the question of a call's status dictates that OTM covered calls make sense. Your advantage as a seller is found in time and extrinsic value premium.

In conclusion, the conservative investor should seek OTM covered calls exclusively. This simplifies the tax calculations and conforms to the commonsense standards defining a conservative strategy. One exception to this general rule is if you have large carryover losses, you may not be concerned with taxation of current-year capital gains. Because annual capital losses are limited to $3,000 maximum, a large carryover loss may be used to absorb current-year gains. So, even if you lose long-term capital gains status for exercised stock, that large carryover loss presents a planning advantage; you can engage in ITM covered call writing without worrying about long-term or short-term restrictions.

Table 5-3 Qualified Covered Calls

Stock Closing Price	85%	Qualified Calls Price Range*
$25	21.25	21.25–24.75
24	20.40	20.50–23.75
23	19.55	19.75–22.75
22	18.70	18.75–21.75
21	17.85	18.00–20.75
$20	17.00	17.00–19.75
19	16.15	16.25–18.75
18	15.30	15.50–17.75
17	14.45	14.50–16.76
16	13.60	13.75–15.75
$15	12.75	12.75–14.75
14	11.90	12.00–13.75
13	11.05	11.25–12.75
12	10.20	10.25–11.75
11	9.35	9.50–10.75
10	8.50	8.50–9.75
$9	7.65	7.75–8.75
8	6.80	7.00–7.75
7	5.95	6.00–6.75
6	5.10	5.25–5.75
5	4.25	4.25–4.75
$4	3.40	3.50–3.75
3	2.55	2.75 only
2	1.70	1.75 only
1	0.85	1.00 only

* This range assumes that calls are traded in increments of $0.25.

Rolling Forward and Up: Exercise Avoidance

You can easily avoid the complexities of the tax rules by utilizing only OTM covered calls. For conservative investors, this makes good sense even without considering how federal taxes affect the strategy. It can and does affect planning if you intend to create a forced sale using deep ITM calls ("deep" means more than 5 points below strike price). Under the definitions in the tax rules, that would convert all stock sales to short term because the options would be nonqualified.

Rather than *seeking* forced exercise, most conservative investors prefer to keep ownership of the stock and use options to maximize short-term income, hopefully in a repetitive fashion. So, exercise avoidance is a far more attractive strategy for most people. In some instances, a stock's trading range remains narrow enough that option profits can be achieved with little effort or lost opportunity risk; relatively low price volatility means there is little chance of exercise. However, a stock's price can exceed the strike price, which makes it a viable conservative strategy to avoid exercise.

Because covered call writers have to accept the possibility of exercise, why avoid it? Although exercise is a real possibility, it is often preferable to keep well-selected stocks in the portfolio and to take steps to (a) avoid having it called away, (b) be able to continue writing subsequent calls, and (c) in the event of exercise, maximize income from the transaction. All this requires employing a rolling technique.

The Types of Rolls

In a roll, you close out a current open position while you open a subsequent position that has one of three possible attributes.

1. **A roll forward.** The new covered call expires later than the old covered call but at the same strike price. Caution: If the stock price moves *above* this strike price, you risk converting your OTM covered call into an ITM call, so the entire tax picture of stock profits changes.

2. **A roll up.** The new covered call expires at the same time but at a higher strike price. With this strategy, expiration remains the

same, but you "buy" another 5 points of profit in the event of exercise. The difference of 5 points may be only 2 or 3 points of cost, so if you expect the stock's price to continue rising, losing a few points in the exchange of one option for another is not a negative in every instance. For example, the net difference in buying out of the current position and opening the new one is 2 points, but you gain 5 points in the higher strike price, while converting your ITM short call to a new, OTM short call.

3. **A roll forward and up.** The new covered call expires later than the old covered call *and* at a higher strike price. This is the most desirable rolling method. It is possible to execute a forward-and-up roll while still producing a net credit. This means more premium income as well as a higher potential exercise price. By avoiding exercise, you gain more net income, *and* you also gain 5 points (assuming the calls are trading within 5-point increments, as most medium-range stock priced calls do). You give up more time in exchange.

You originally sold a call with a strike price of 55 and expiring in January, five months away. At that time, the stock was trading at $57 per share. You received $600 when you sold the covered call. Today, the stock has moved up to $57 per share, and you want to avoid exercise.

If you exchange the January 55 call for an April 60 call, you will receive a net premium because the latter call has more time value. You gain the 5 points in the event of exercise, which yields an additional $500 profit on the stock.

The Exercise Acceptance Strategy

A final strategy worth mentioning is the exercise acceptance strategy. Most conservative investors are content to keep their long-term stocks and to use well-selected OTM calls to create additional profits along with downside protection. However, what if you would be happy to see your call exercised?

Selling covered calls is a profitable alternative to simply owning stock. You can also force exercise by intentionally writing ITM calls. However, because this ensures the loss of long-term status of capital gains when exercise occurs, the strategy has to be studied on an after-tax basis. When you have a large carryover loss from previous years, it could be an effective way to create large option premium gains and absorb unused carryover. Your annual net-loss deduction is limited to $3,000, so if you have a $30,000 carryover, it would take 10 years to use it up without future offsetting capital gains. It is desirable to absorb that loss as soon as possible; so in this case, creating a large gain in stock and options by writing deep ITM covered calls (virtually ensuring exercise) would be beneficial because the loss of long-term status is sheltered by the carryover loss.

Remembering to Limit Yourself to Conservative Strategies

You probably consider covered calls a conservative strategy because no increased market risk is involved. The alternative, simply owning shares of stock, has an inherent market risk, and discounting the basis by generating call premium reduces the basis in stock, which also lowers the net market risk. Covered call writing involves lost opportunity risk; in reviewing likely scenarios for a number of stocks, you know that such lost opportunities occur in a minority of cases, while consistent high returns from covered calls are certain.

In the next chapter, you will find interesting ways to use options as an alternative to the outright purchase of shares of stock. Contingent purchase strategies make options powerful tools, especially during volatile markets.

6

ALTERNATIVES TO STOCK PURCHASE

Most investors start by looking for stocks they want to buy. But with options, there are many other ways—safer ways—to enter the market. Contingent purchase using either long calls or short puts is a powerful weapon in your strategic arsenal. You can also roll options forward to avoid exercise or apply them to recover paper loss positions. This chapter explores these ideas and demonstrates how the ratio write can be converted into a risk-free conservative strategy.

Options open up a range of contingent strategies. Covered calls are interesting because they are the ultimate low-risk form of contingent sale. If and when exercised, the covered call is designed to produce current income consisting of both dividend income and call premium.

Contingent sale—represented by the covered call strategy—is the most conservative use of options. However, you can also use options to leverage capital in several forms of contingent purchase. As an alternative to buying shares of stock, you can either buy calls or sell puts with the intention of acquiring stock before expiration. This strategy is appropriate when the market is volatile or when marketwide prices have fallen significantly. You recognize the buying opportunity, yet you do not want to risk capital on stock that might continue to fall even more.

Because time is invariably an issue, Long-term Equity AnticiPation Security (LEAPS) options are more likely to work in contingent strategies. The ability to leave positions open for as long as 30 months makes LEAPS well suited for this range of strategies, whereas traditional listed options do not survive long enough for contingency to mature in every case. The risks are simply too great that the option's life will end before stock prices move adequately. This is especially true when you employ contingent strategies with long calls.

Leverage and Options

The contingent-purchase strategy is based on the assumption that a number of conditions exist at the moment:

- **The market is volatile; prices are down.** The most likely market condition for contingent purchase is when prices have moved downward or are highly volatile. You want to be in the market, but you hesitate to take equity positions, fearing ongoing volatility. The dilemma is a combination of (a) volatile conditions and (b) concern that you will lose opportunities if you don't act now.

- **You have capital available to open option positions.** You must have capital available either to purchase calls or to leave on margin in the event that short puts are exercised. Looking to the future, if you do decide to exercise long-call positions, you need capital to complete your purchase as well. So, on the long side, you need to be able to buy calls—preferably in several stocks— and later, to exercise. On the short side, you are required to deposit funds to buy stock (equal to the purchase price minus put premium you earn or, on margin, a portion of the purchase price, usually one-half). These requirements naturally limit the extent of contingent purchase in which you can afford to engage at any given time.

- **You want to open contingent purchase positions in several stocks.** The importance of diversification as a conservative model cannot be overemphasized. The basic theory behind contingent purchase is that you do not know whether a particular stock will rise or fall in the future, so you select stocks that meet your fundamental criteria, and you open contingent purchase positions in that range of stocks. If you can afford to engage in contingent purchase on four or five stocks at the same time, you increase your chances that they will end up being profitable. The essential starting point is that stocks you pick must be stocks you would want to purchase if you were simply buying shares. In any contingent-purchase strategy, you limit your activity to stocks that meet your conservative standards based on your fundamental criteria.

- **You believe that contingent purchase—given current circumstances—is an appropriate conservative strategy.** This strategy, like all market strategies, must be assessed in context and as part of a larger portfolio strategy. It is inadvisable to place all your capital in options as part of a contingent-purchase strategy; your conservative portfolio should contain a foundation of strong growth stocks. Contingent purchase can be used to fix the price of additional shares of stock you already own or to ensure your right to buy shares in new stocks if and when price movement goes in the right direction. But given market conditions and your personal rules for picking stocks, the underlying issues have to be appropriate. If you select stocks for contingent purchase based only on option pricing, you violate the basic rules for portfolio management. Conservative investing is always based on equity value of the stock, and options are considered only as a secondary possible strategic means for acquiring shares.

Applications of Contingent-Purchase Strategies

Contingent purchase is a way to fix the price of stock if and when you decide to buy shares in the future (in the case of long calls) or if stock is put to you (in the case of short puts). In either case, the basic rules remain:

- You would be pleased to acquire stock at the indicated strike price.
- You can afford to buy the stock.
- You have performed a fundamental analysis and found the company suitable.
- The contingent-purchase strategy is appropriate, and you are comfortable with it as an alternative to simply buying shares at the current price.

Just as any options strategy is wrong when based solely on option premium levels, using contingent purchase without intending to buy stock is wrong. Contingent purchase is appropriate only if you intend to buy shares, and your purpose in employing the strategy should be to limit current risk and not to incur more. If you are following four stocks that meet your criteria, but you are not sure that all will increase in value, contingent purchase allows you to leverage capital among all four while limiting your risk exposure. Even if only some of those stocks increase in value, you can profit from the overall contingent-purchase strategy. By fixing premium prices, you keep purchase as one possible outcome without undertaking excessive market risk. You may exercise long calls (or have short puts exercised), the options can expire worthless, or the positions can be closed before expiration.

Contingent-purchase strategies require watching so that you know when to act and when to wait. This does not mean you have to track prices on a daily basis, but frequent monitoring can help you to time subsequent decisions to maximize profits or to reduce undesired losses. Depending on the contingent strategy you employ, time may work for or against you. The use of LEAPS is appropriate given the length of time until expiration, which makes the range of contingent-purchase strategies realistic, and working with options lasting as long as 30 months gives you a lot of flexibility. In the market, 30 months is a long time, and a lot can occur in that period. If you look back over the past three years and review the changes in market conditions and prices of individual stocks, you will appreciate the potential of long-term contingent purchase investing.

Later in this chapter, you see how even a long position's cost can be mitigated with offsetting long-term short positions, as a form of cover. Given the right circumstances, you may recapture the entire cost of the long position without incurring additional risk.

It is risk, when all else is considered, that ultimately determines whether you employ contingent-purchase strategies. No matter how profitable and safe a strategy seems to be, it has to work as a good fit for your conservative profile. This limits the kinds of strategies you will be willing to use. Option strategies come in all shares and sizes, and many are highly speculative.

If you pick options incorrectly or ignore the underlying risks, using option strategies simply won't work for you. But contingent-purchase strategies are sensible and conservative, assuming the following:

- The fundamentals of the underlying stock meet your standards.
- You consider the strike price a good price for the stock.
- The funds are available to open positions and, later, to exercise.

The Long-Call Contingent-Purchase Strategy

The first contingent strategy involves buying calls instead of stock. This would be a speculative move if the only purpose was to create profits in call premium. However, as long as your intention is to buy shares, this strategy fixes your future purchase price at the strike price. If you buy calls in several stocks and only some increase in value, you would exercise those calls only on profitable positions. Contingent purchase limits your capital risk. For example, if you spend $500 on call premium and the stock later falls 15 points, you can never lose more than your $500 investment. However, if you had bought 100 shares of stock in the same circumstances, you would suffer a loss of $1,500. So, the primary advantage of the long-call contingent-purchase strategy is limitation of risk. Its primary risk is loss of value—notably time value.

If you buy LEAPS calls with a long time until expiration—which is essential for this to qualify as a conservative strategy—you pay for the time value. The question of whether the contingent purchase is worthwhile is determined by (a) call premium, (b) strike price of the underlying stock, (c) time until expiration, and (d) your desire to fix the price for possible future purchase. One of the more difficult situations occurs when you know that the current price of stock is attractive, but you either cannot afford to buy or you are concerned about short-term volatility. Buying LEAPS calls as a contingent-purchase strategy overcomes this dilemma.

Diversifying Exposure with Several Stocks in Play

The strategy should involve several stocks. This diversifies your exposure in a long-option position, and the very reason you are considering contingent purchase is that you do not know what future price levels will be for any particular stock. So using several well-selected stocks make sense as part of a coordinated strategy.

Here is how a contingent-purchase program might work using long calls: a review of the ten model portfolio stocks is shown in Table 6-1, which summarizes available LEAPS calls.

Table 6-1   Stocks for Contingent Purchase Using Long Calls

Name of Company	Current Symbol	Price	9-Month Calls			21-Month Calls		
			1	2	3	1	2	3
Caterpillar	CAT	32.29						
Strikes xx 35 40			xx	4.70	3.00	xx	7.00	5.15
IBM	IBM	101.27						
Strikes 100 105 110			12.28	9.90	7.90	17.70	xx	13.43

Table 6-1 Continued

Name of Company	Current Symbol	Price	9-Month Calls			21-Month Calls		
			1	2	3	1	2	3
Johnson & Johnson	JNJ	53.05						
Strikes xx xx 55			xx	xx	3.60	xx	xx	6.20
Coca-Cola	KO	45.02						
Strikes 45 50 55			4.10	2.11	0.95	6.20	4.00	2.45
McDonald's	MCD	56.09						
Strikes xx 60 65			xx	3.50	1.90	xx	5.20	3.80
3M	MMM	53.81						
Strikes xx 55 60			xx	5.44	3.30	xx	8.00	6.30
Altria	MO	16.99						
Strikes 17.50 20 22.50			1.34	0.60	0.20	2.06	1.32	0.73
United Parcel Service	UPS	54.65						
Strikes xx 55 60			xx	5.70	3.60	xx	xx	6.00
Wal-Mart	WMT	50.20						
Strikes 55 60 65			3.20	1.73	0.88	5.90	4.15	2.85
Exxon Mobil	XOM	66.75						
Strikes xx 70 75			xx	6.01	4.30	xx	10.00	8.23

If you bought one call for each stock, the overall price would depend on the proximity between current market value and strike price. If you compare the strike prices selected for each stock to current market price, you can see how these values change.

For the basic contingent-purchase strategy to be profitable, you need a net increase in market value equal to or greater than the investment level. For example, if you purchased a 9-month call at 105 for IBM (costing 9.90), the stock would need to rise to nearly $115 per share before your breakeven point (not counting transaction fees). You would need the stock's value to rise *above* that level to justify the long-call contingent-purchase strategy. Although this is a disadvantage, you have a lot of time for the outcome to materialize—9 months for the first set of calls or 21 months for the second set of calls.

Reducing Contingent Purchase Risks

Contingent purchase risk can be reduced in a variety of ways. Here are three ideas:

1. **Use a higher strike price.** Table 6-1 shows three strike price levels. If you preferred the third increment over the first or second strike prices, your investment basis would be lower because there would be more points to go to expiration.

2. **Invest in longer-term calls.** For example, you gain a full year buying the 21-month calls instead of the 9-month calls.

3. **Reduce the cost of long calls by using short-call offsets.** The most effective way to cut risks and make contingent purchase a profitable strategy is to write short calls against your long-call positions.

The Covered Long Call

The major risk involved with long-call contingent purchase is the same as for all long-call strategies: If expiration occurs before an adequate price increase occurs in the underlying stock, it is extremely difficult to make a profit. So, *risk* involves the same problem as every other long-option strategy: Time works against you. Even if the stock's market value rises, you still need to overcome the time-value problem.

There is a way to achieve this. Assuming that some or all of the stocks in this example increase in value before expiration, you can employ a secondary strategy designed to recapture the premium cost of the long call. The basic strategy is to sell a call with a higher strike price and earlier expiration than the long positions. Does this work out?

Let's assume that you bought one of each of the closing strike price 21-month calls for the 10 model portfolio stocks at the strike immediately above current market value of the stock. You hope that during the next 21 months, the price will appreciate enough in these 10 stocks to make the contingent purchase a profitable strategy. At the same time, you want to get back some or all of the money you invested in long LEAPS calls. To make this illustration comparable, let's assume that all 10 stocks were to increase between 5 and 10 points in the near future—not enough to ensure profitability on the long-call purchases, but enough to put the secondary strategy into effect. To estimate the future value of calls given the increased market value of the underlying stock, review current premium values for calls 5 points above current value. For example, in the case of Caterpillar, where the 21-month 35-strike price was 7.00, you would review calls with current strike prices of 40. In the case of each stock, compare the long-call cost to the current value of one price increment above those positions.

Future premium values are estimated based on two assumptions. First, the market value of each stock will rise by 5 to 10 points. Second, the current premium values for calls with strike prices 10 points lower represent fair estimates of future premium value. For example, in the case of Caterpillar, estimate the value of the 40 short call by using the current 30 call's value. The 30 call for Caterpillar was valued at 9.10.

Extrapolating Future Strike Prices

In making this comparison, assume that the relative value of calls will remain about the same in the future as they are today. Because future strike prices of the short positions are higher than the corresponding original long positions, exercise is a no-risk outcome. If the short calls are exercised, they are offset by 5 points lower value in each of the long calls; those long calls could be surrendered to satisfy the call in each instance. For example, if you bought a Caterpillar 30 for $910 and later sold a Caterpillar 35, exercise would create a 5-point profit for you. You would use your long call to offset the exercised short call. The risk is eliminated because of the following:

- Each long position provides cover for the short positions.
- Exercise of short positions creates a profit of 5 points of intrinsic value between the short and long positions.
- Expiration of short positions occurs 12 months prior to long positions; if the short calls expire, you end up with continuing long positions, but all the premium income you received for the short is profit.

This illustration is based on the belief that the market value of these shares will grow within the next 21 months. Hopefully, if your stock selection skills are good, your contingent purchase experience can take the course shown in the example. When you enter into a contingent-purchase strategy when marketwide prices are low, chances are better than average that this course of price change will occur.

The long-call contingent plan with short-call offset is an example of how your disadvantage can be turned to an advantage. When you are long in calls, you have a time disadvantage. Using higher strike price, shorter expiring calls flip the time value in your favor. You buy time value on the long side, but you sell it on the short side. Given the example in which market value of underlying shares has grown, this is a good method for making the strategy work well. You preserve the original locked-in strike price, but you recapture your long-premium investment.

The strategy assumes that the higher strike priced short calls will expire worthless. You risk exercise in this strategy, but that would produce a 5-point profit as long as you use the next increment of strike prices for the short positions. You can also roll forward to avoid or defer exercise. However, remember that this strategy remains conservative only as long as the short position does not expire later than the long position.

Using the Forward Roll Effectively

Rolling forward is attractive when the underlying stock's price is rising. The purpose in rolling is to avoid exercise; it is most desirable to execute a forward roll that creates a net credit whenever possible, defers or avoids exercise and, ideally, moves exercise further away from in-the-money (ITM) status (up for calls or down for puts). When you have bought a long-term call and cover it with a short, the short call should expire before the long.

For example, let's say you originally purchase a Caterpillar 25 call expiring in 21 months and later sell a 30 call scheduled to expire in seven months. Today, the stock's market price is 2.29 points above the short call's strike price (stock is 32.29 versus short call strike of 30). You could roll the short position forward two months to defer exercise; you could also roll forward and up to the next strike increment; that puts the call out of the money by 3 points. In this case, you could buy to close the seven-month short call for 6 and sell a nine-month call at 30 for 6.76; or sell a 35 call for 4.70. In the latter case, you move the strike up 5 points, which is a clear advantage, but it costs you 1.30 (6.00 less 4.70). Is the cost of $130 worth increasing potential exercise price by $500? That becomes the issue in rolling forward and up.

An alternative is to roll both long and short positions. Roll the short call forward and up to escape the ITM status; also roll the long position forward. By closing the current position and opening one with a later expiration, you have to pay additional premium. However, as long as premium levels for the long and short positions offset one another within a close range, this adjustment is worthwhile. You replace the short-call strike price with a new short call 5 points higher. This avoids exercise or, in the event of exercise, creates a 5-point increase in future profit.

Another choice is to replace the current long position with a later expiring call and increase to the next higher strike increment. Because this position is already ITM, you can buy the higher call for an intrinsic value of 5 points. So, although you increase your future purchase price at exercise by 5 points, you save 5 points today by replacing the existing long call with a higher strike price. The four choices in this situation, illustrated in Figure 6-1, are as follows.

1. Roll the short call forward to a later expiring position.
2. Roll the short call forward and up to the next strike increment.
3. Roll the short position forward and up, and roll the long position forward.
4. Roll both positions forward and up.

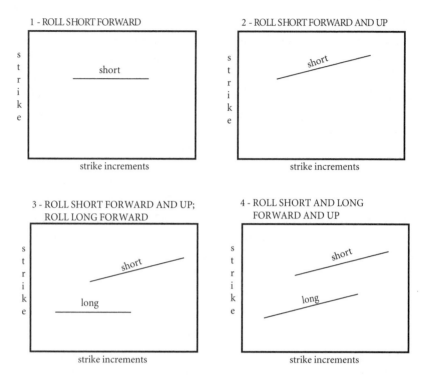

Figure 6-1 Rolling strategies, contingent purchase cover

The viability of these rolling techniques depends on current option premium values. As a general rule, rolling forward produces higher income because you are "buying" more time. Rolling up is likely to offset that time advantage, especially when you move from ITM to out-of-the-money (OTM) status. In picking a rolling strategy, consider the net balance between credit and debit, compared to the advantages gained by avoiding exercise or changing strike price.

Short Puts and Contingent Purchase

You are not limited to long LEAPS calls to enter a contingent-purchase strategy. You can also use short puts. When you sell puts, you are required by your brokerage firm to have adequate funds on deposit to satisfy exercise of the put, if and when that occurs. The benefit of the put strategy is that money flows to you rather than away from you. Time value is also an advantage. You receive a premium for selling the put, and that premium value declines over time, even when the stock's value falls to ITM price levels. Extrinsic value may offset intrinsic value to a degree for long-term contracts.

Begin with a review of the strike price. If you would be happy to acquire shares at that price, based on the fundamentals, the short put is an excellent strategy. It can go in one of two possible directions. First, the stock does not move ITM, in which case you can later buy the puts to close at a profit or allow them to expire. Second, the stock's market value declines below strike price; in this event, you can either wait for exercise or roll forward and down to avoid or defer exercise. When you roll forward and down, you expose yourself to more time, but you reduce the basis in the event of later exercise by one strike price increment.

The Value of Selling Puts

In the section concerning long calls, diversification was shown to be sensible because the long position was employed. In a strategy with short positions, the same rationale applies in the sense that you do not know which stock will rise and which will fall in market value. At the same time, you probably would not want to acquire shares of all ten stocks in the model portfolio if current market value declined below the indicated strike price levels. You can use the short-put contingent-purchase strategy on any single stock or on a combination of stocks, depending on your willingness to leave funds on deposit and based on the attractiveness of this strategy.

If you decided to short puts on all these stocks, you could also vary the strike prices and expiration dates. Table 6-2 presents 9-month and 21-month expirations to demonstrate how the time value in short puts can work to your advantage. Although you would not have to select puts with the same expirations, you can judge this strategy by making comparisons.

Table 6-2 Stocks for Contingent Purchase Using Short Puts

Name of Company	Symbol	Current Price	9-Month Puts			21-Month Puts		
			1	2	3	1	2	3
Caterpillar	CAT	32.29						
Strikes 30 25 22.50			5.15	3.20	2.28	8.25	5.82	4.70
IBM	IBM	101.27						
Strikes 100 95 90			12.15	10.00	7.80	18.30	16.10	15.90
Johnson & Johnson	JNJ	53.05						
Strikes 50 45 40			4.10	2.35	1.40	7.20	5.40	3.74
Coca-Cola	KO	45.02						
Strikes 45 42.50 40			4.95	4.30	3.00	8.00	7.00	5.70
McDonald's	MCD	56.09						
Strikes 55 50 45			6.07	3.90	2.50	9.80	7.70	5.90
3M	MMM	53.81						
Strikes 50 45 40			5.39	3.40	2.00	8.60	6.29	4.90
Altria	MO	16.99						
Strikes 15 12.50 10			1.37	0.65	0.25	2.88	1.69	0.99
United Parcel Service	UPS	54.65						
Strikes 50 45 xx			5.40	3.50	xx	8.28	5.80	xx
Wal-Mart	WMT	50.20						
Strikes 50 45 40			5.45	3.56	2.12	8.21	6.35	4.45
Exxon Mobil	XOM	66.75						
Strikes 65 60 55			7.50	5.45	3.70	11.75	9.45	7.40

In determining whether it makes more sense to employ 9-month or 21-month puts, you need to remember that the difference in time is one full year. Annualizing returns for each alternative is the only way to fairly compare the two choices.

The Value of Shorter Exposure Terms

Given the shorter time span of the nine-month mix of puts, it is preferable to employ these for several reasons.

- Less time is required for leaving funds on deposit. The money you have to leave on deposit in the event of exercise—whether involving one stock or all—will be committed a full year less if you use the shorter expiring options.

- Turnover profits are higher. By using puts with closer expiration, you are free to repeat this strategy if and when the short puts expire. As a result, you can create more short-term profits or contingent purchase opportunities.

- Time value premium declines more rapidly in shorter-term positions. Time value premium tends to evaporate with greater speed in the months prior to expiration than in preceding months. Thus, the 9-month puts lose time value much more rapidly than the 21-month puts within the coming nine months. If you determine that it would be better to close and replace these short positions prior to expiration, it would be more profitable with the 9-month puts.

The same question has to be asked for all strategies. Is it conservative? Does this strategy suit your risk profile, and would you be happy to acquire stock on the basis of exercised short puts? Although stock values would be lower than the strike in the event of exercise, your basis would be discounted by the premium received. You would probably not want to enter short contingent-purchase positions on a portfolio of ten stocks at the same time; this example simply illustrates the overall effect of doing so for each stock in the model portfolio. The strategy is more applicable to most situations by looking at a single stock and calculating the likely outcomes based on its price movement.

For example, if you sold the 9-month IBM 95 put, your premium income would be 10 points, so your basis in the stock upon exercise would be $1,000 (before calculating net trading costs). As long as the exercise occurred when the stock's market value was between $85 and $95 per share, this contingent purchase would not create a paper loss. However, even when exercise does create a loss, you can employ rescue strategies to offset it. In comparison, selling the 21-month 95 put, premium income would be $1,610; the extended safety price range would go down to $79; but the position would remain open an additional 12 months.

Rescue Strategy Using Calls

Let's say you sell a put as part of your contingent-purchase strategy and the put is exercised. It creates a paper loss. What can you do to recover in this situation?

The solution depends on the point value of the net loss. In the case of selling a nine-month IBM put at 95, the $1,000 premium protects the net stock position down to $85 per share (compared to current value of $101.27). However, what if market value declined below that level?

The first strategy to employ is the roll forward and down to avoid or defer exercise. For example, once the IBM stock price fell below the strike price of 95, you could replace the 95 put with a later expiring 90 put. Even so, if the stock were to continue to decline, it could eventually be exercised. Market prices can fall suddenly, so you do not always have the opportunity to employ a rolling strategy. Exercise could occur without warning.

Rescue Strategy Based on Smart Stock Choices

When you end up with stock put to you above current market value and your basis still produces a net loss, you have three choices. First, you can simply wait out the market.

Second, you can sell a covered call to offset the paper loss. The danger in the covered call position is that it may be exercised. You do not want to set up a situation in which exercise would create an overall net loss, so premium level of the call has to be adequate to offset the paper loss, trading costs, and income tax on your gain. If that is not possible, it makes no sense to write a call.

The third choice is to employ a combination of average-down strategies and short calls. This strategy assumes that you are willing to buy more shares of the stock. Remember, the underlying assumption for all of these conservative strategies is that (a) you have prequalified the stock, (b) your hold decision continues to apply, and (c) you would be happy to acquire more shares. For example, let's assume that your net basis in IBM is $91 per share ($101 purchase, reduced by $1,000 for selling the 95 put) and that market value has fallen to about $87 per share. The put is exercised and you are required to buy 100 shares at $95 per share. Your net loss on the transaction is $400 ($101.27 less $1,000 put premium = approximately $91 per share; buy 100 shares at $95 = $400 net loss.

If you were to buy 200 more shares, your average basis would be $89.67 per share (net 95 + 87 + 87 = 269; and 269 ÷ 3 = 89.67). With this adjusted basis, you could sell OTM calls with strikes of 90 or 95. This further reduces your basis by the premium value of the calls, while reverting to the covered call strategy. In this example, with average cost of $89.67 per share, you may also assume that you can find a 90 call available for about 5 points in premium and three months until expiration. (This estimate is based on the current value of the 105 call for 105, valued at 5.20 three months out, with strike at 101.27.) So, if you bought an additional 200 shares at 87 on top of the current net value of 95, the average basis would change to $89.67 per share, and you could sell three calls with a strike price of 90, receiving about 5 points for each. This further reduces the net basis to $84.67.

In the event of exercise, the 300 shares would be called away at $90 per share compared to your adjusted basis of $84.67 per share. Total profit before trading costs and taxes is $5.33 per share, or $1,599. This rescue strategy is illustrated in Figure 6-2.

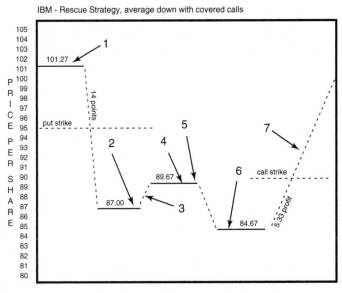

Figure 6-2   Rescue strategy, average down with covered calls

The strategy has seven segments, as reflected in the figure.

1. The original purchase price of shares was $101.27; a 95 put was sold and later exercised with a strike price of $95 per share, after stock price fell to $87 per share.

2. The stock price fell 14 points to $87, and the put was exercised with a 95 strike.

3. An additional 200 shares are purchased at $87 per share.

4. The new net basis is $89.67 per share.

5. Three 90 calls are sold at 5.

6. The new basis is $84.67 per share.

7. The calls are exercised at $90, creating a profit of $5.33 per share, for a total of $1,599.

Programming a Profitable Result

Even though the sequence of events depicted in Figure 6-2 included a significant point decline in the stock, when the stock's price recovered and the last calls were exercised, the outcome was profitable. But what if the stock's price did not recover? The new basis (step 6) was $84.67 per share, but what if the current market value remained at $87? In this situation, if the calls expired worthless—which would happen as long as market value remained below $70 per share—you would be free to sell the shares, simply hold for long-term appreciation, or use more option strategies.

There is a tendency to think about stocks in terms of current market value in relation to past market value. If a stock is at $101 per share and over time it falls to $89, the general opinion is that its value has fallen. So value—as defined in terms of market price—tends to be a relative idea. However, as the rescue strategy reveals, you can forget about relative value and use options to reduce your basis. This adjusts the perception that the stock has fallen from the original cost of $101 to $89; if you reduce your basis to $84.67 through various options strategies, the realistic gap is only 5.67 points, not 12 points. When combined with price averaging, the use of covered calls can turn a loss situation into a smaller paper gap or even into an overall profitable situation.

The Ratio Write: Adjusting to Make It Conservative

A somewhat less conservative strategy is the ratio write. However, risks can be eliminated so that the ratio write fits within the definition of conservative risk. First, an explanation of the unadjusted strategy: The ratio write is a method in which you partially cover your calls. For example, if you own 300 shares and you sell 4 calls, it is a 4-to-3 ratio write. You could view this as having 3 covered calls and 1 uncovered call, or as a 75 percent coverage ratio. The higher the number of shares, the lower the risk. For example, 400 shares with 5 uncovered calls is an approach with less risk than 300 shares with 4 uncovered calls.

The advantage of the ratio write is that it increases premium income with only moderate increase in risk. A variation on the ratio write is to spread strike prices over a range. For example, if your basis in 400 shares of stock is $22 per share, and the stock is now worth $21, you may decide to write 5 calls; you could employ a combination of 2 calls with striking prices of $25 and 3 with later expiring strike prices of $30. The risk is relatively low for two reasons. First, all calls are OTM, and the two upper-level strike prices are 9 points higher than the current market value. Second, two of the calls will expire sooner, and that eliminates all the market risk for the remaining calls, while eliminating the uncovered portion of the ratio write. If the stock's price exceeded the strike price of 25, you could roll forward and up on any or all of these positions to avoid exercise.

In this example of the ratio write, the strategy could be rolled forward and up indefinitely to avoid exercise and to keep risks at a manageable level. Even if the 25 calls were exercised, the 30 calls could either be closed or rolled; so unless the stock's price soared quickly past the higher strike price, risk of exercise would not be immediate.

Converting the Ratio Write into a Conservative Strategy

Even with this logic, the ratio write continues to present risks that, on the surface at least, contradict your risk profile. The solution involves using a method for reducing worst-case risk by offsetting the exposed top-side uncovered call. That is achieved by going long on a higher strike price call to offset the uncovered position.

For example, consider a range of options on UPS. If you own 300 shares with an original basis of $50.00 per share and the current price is $54.65 per share, you could enter a ratio write with 55 strikes. For example, you could enter a ratio covered call position involving 4 calls, but you could also buy an additional call, which essentially eliminates *all* the ratio risk. The following represents one possible variation of this strategy:

Sell two three-month 55 calls @ 3.50	$700
Sell two six-month 60 calls @ 2.80	560
Buy one six-month 65 call @ 1.25	- 125
Net credit	$1,135

In this situation, you have created a combination yielding 6.9 percent return in 6 months, which annualizes out at 13.8 percent. Half of the exposure lasts three months, and the other half goes out six months. The exposed additional 100 shares are protected by the six-month 65 long call. In the worst-case scenario—all short positions exercised—you could use the long call to satisfy assignment of the fourth short call, costing you $500 (the difference between the 65 strike of the long call and the 60 strike of the unprotected short call). However, your overall cash credit is $1,135 on these positions, so you would still have $635 remaining as net profit. Remember, this is worst case; it assumes no rolling forward, and it assumes that the stock's price rises above $65 per share prior to expiration. In addition, exercise would represent capital gains—assuming your basis of $50 per share—or a profit of $2,000 ($1,000 on each of two exercised 55 calls and $1,000 on one exercised call at 60). The overall outcome for exercise of all these positions, without counting dividend income, transaction costs, or taxes, would be as follows:

Capital gain, 200 shares with basis of $50, exercised at $55	$1,000
Capital gain, 100 shares with basis of $50, exercised at $60	1,000
Loss, uncovered short 60 call versus long 65 call	-500
Net credit earned on option positions	1,135
Total gain before dividends, costs, and taxes	$1,635

This worst-case analysis assumes a rapid increase in the stock's price, necessitating the purchase of an "insurance call" at the top of the transaction. However, splitting the ratio between different expiration dates and strike prices provides a degree of protection in most situations. It may not be necessary to assume worst-case outcome and still remain within your risk profile range. You may consider this worst case because stock was called away, so the ratio write is appropriate based on the same rules for any form of covered calls: You have to be willing to accept exercise as one of the possible outcomes. In the example, using the single long call at the top of the transaction eliminates the ratio-write risk entirely, while leaving you exposed to the net covered call exposure.

Ratio Writes for Rescue Strategies and Higher Current Returns

The ratio write is not only a useful rescue strategy for depressed stock; it may also serve as a powerful tool for creating higher returns from options with minimal risk, even when the price of the stock is below your original basis. However, to ensure the safety of your position, the split of expiration dates and strike prices is recommended.

Rescue Strategy Using Puts

You can create a rescue strategy with short puts in place of the purchase of additional shares. Short puts can be used as a form of contingent purchase, and an alternate rescue strategy can be employed to reduce average price while creating additional downside protection through put premium income.

The Risk of Continued Price Declines

The difference in this variety of the rescue strategy is that there is a further chance for price decline. This is why you should employ such a strategy only when acquisition of more shares is desirable based on your fundamental analysis of the stock. If additional short puts are exercised, you could revert to the original rescue strategy and write covered calls. However, using short puts allows you to create a lower net basis in stock without necessarily having to acquire more shares. If the short puts expire, you create a reduced basis in the original 100 shares by virtue of put premium.

In the worst case outcome, you increase the number of shares owned. The advantage of having more shares is clear: Profits would be three times those of the 100-share rescue. However, using short puts may be more conservative because you would not be required to buy shares unless prices decline below strike price. Given that average share prices have a continually reduced basis, the question becomes, are you willing to buy more shares as market prices decline? As long as you believe that the stock's long-term value remains strong, this may be desirable; or you may conclude that, as strong an investment as it is, there is simply too much volatility. You would prefer, then, to create a situation in which the net basis is lower than the current market value so you can sell shares at a profit. The stark outcome used to seem unlikely; but the large declines in stock values in 2008, even of companies once considered quite safe, make the point that you have to live with risk if you are in the market. The advantage with options strategies over simple ownership of stock is found in the hedging or mitigation of market risk. You have stock-based market risk simply by owning stock. Options actually reduce or eliminate the risk.

Both varieties of the rescue strategy achieve your goal of reducing exposure and recapturing paper losses. If you can reduce your basis to create a profitable outcome, the rescue strategies are valuable ways to manage your portfolio. The decision to use calls or puts depends on your attitude toward the company, available resources, and your willingness to wait out the stock's market trends.

Covered Calls for Contingent Sale

Looking beyond contingent purchase, you also may want to consider contingent-sale strategies. The most conservative form of contingent sale is the covered call write. When you own 100 shares and you sell a call, you invite the possibility of exercise. One strategy—writing deep ITM calls to create exercise intentionally—makes sense, but *only* if you first consider the tax implications.

For example, using the example of McDonald's, with the stock at 56.09, one-month calls are available for 11.00 (45 strike) or 8.80 (47.50 strike). These are almost all intrinsic value, so if you want to create exercise, it makes little difference which one you pick. Strike prices are 2.5 points apart, and option premium levels are 2.20 points apart. Every point of movement in stock price will be matched point-for-point in changes in option premium, so short-term changes in the stock could create immediate profit opportunities as an alternative to exercise.

However, writing deep ITM calls has a potential tax consequence. You could lose long-term capital gains treatment by writing what are called unqualified covered calls—those more than one strike increment below the current value of the stock. Before entering a strategy like this, you need to analyze the tax consequences.

Picking the Right Conditions for Forced Exercise

The strategy of creating a forced exercise as a form of contingent sale makes sense under two conditions. First, your original basis in the stock should be low enough that the exercise price would create a profit. For example, if you purchased the stock at $50 per share, selling the 45 call would combine a 5-point capital loss with an 11-point profit on the call, with net return before trading costs and taxes of $600. It would be preferable, of course, if your original basis in stock was low enough so that exercise of the deep ITM call would produce a profit in both stock and option trades.

The second condition is an awareness of the tax rules. When you sell ITM covered calls, you may lose long-term status for taxing of capital gains. In the event of exercise, the entire transaction could be taxed at the short-term rate. The difference in long-term and short-term rates could be substantial, perhaps even offsetting the option premium with increased tax liability. However, if you have a significant capital loss carryover, current-year short-term gains will be absorbed by the carryover loss. In fact, creating current-year gains may be a smart tax move, because annual loss limitations are only $3,000, and it could take many years to completely use up a capital loss carryover. For some unfortunate ex-stockholders of Enron, WorldCom, or any number of dot-coms that lost half of their value in 2008, the carryover loss may never be entirely absorbed unless future gains are realized to offset those losses from year to year.

One of the great advantages to covered call writing is the ability to use well-selected stock as cover for a string of covered call profits. This strategy—based on the fundamental value of the stocks in your portfolio—enables you to keep stock in most circumstances, while enhancing current income. This can work over many years if you write OTM calls, use high-dividend stocks, reinvest your short-term income, and avoid exercise. If stock is worth holding on to for the long term, it is worth avoiding exercise through a series of rolls forward and up. The forward roll increases the time value, while roll-up increases the strike price so that if exercise does occur later, you will increase your stock profit by that point spread as well.

The possible alternatives to outright stock purchase demonstrate how you can use options to leverage your capital, employ conservative techniques to offset time value risks, and put rescue strategies into effect when a stock's price moves downward. The covered long-LEAPS-call strategy even employs shorter expiring short calls to balance out long-position time value. All these strategies make it possible to deal with volatile market conditions, improve your portfolio diversification, and lock in prices on a range of stocks that you might want to buy in the near future.

The next chapter expands on these concepts to show how options can offset paper losses and maximize conditions in down markets.

7

OPTION STRATEGIES IN DOWN MARKETS

Some options moves qualify as conservative strategies—as long as the purpose is to manage the portfolio rather than to simply speculate. You can use long puts or calls to manage price change, and short puts—with their limited risk—present great opportunities as long as they are used solely when you would be happy to acquire more shares of the underlying stock. This chapter provides a conservative context to these ideas, explains how to evaluate your stock positions when prices have fallen, and examines options strategies to reduce market risk.

The chronic problem every investor faces is the inevitability of cycles. The stock market experiences these cycles in numerous ways. The severity and duration of a cycle determines the success of your program, if only because timing is so crucial. Even though you invest with the long term in mind, you prefer to adhere to the advice to buy low and sell high—instead of the other way around. Chapter 6, "Alternatives to Stock Purchase," showed how to devise a rescue strategy when stocks move in an unexpected direction as part of a contingent-purchase plan. In this chapter, you find a variety of additional option strategies worth considering.

Thinking Outside the Market Box

What characterizes the "crowd mentality" of the market? Fear and greed often have more to do with decision making than does prudent or analytical, strategic thinking. Although an academic approach—usually taken by someone with no money at risk—may dictate against fear and greed, it is far more difficult to ignore those emotional responses to market trends when you have capital at risk.

Knowing this, how can you proceed? How can you manage and resist fear and greed to avoid making the common mistakes? Investors often describe themselves as conservative, but they act irrationally when sudden and unexpected trends emerge. They may also say they base decisions on the fundamentals, but they watch index movements, short-term price trends, and other newsy but not especially useful forms of information. Valid fundamental data is less exciting than current-day price movement and far more difficult to convey in a 10-second television or radio news bite. As a consequence, the majority of news that investors receive through television and radio is useless. The print media are more useful to the extent that stories go into greater depth and may be more analytical. Coverage by the leading financial newspapers and magazines is superior to television and radio media, primarily because the venue is more suited to the kind of fundamental and analytical information you need.

Remembering the Fundamentals

The success of your conservative approach to investing is based partially on the quality of research and information you have available. You may use one or more of the dozens of free Internet Web sites and subscription services; print services, including newspapers and magazines; and stock market services. The amount of time and money you are willing to spend determines how information based your decisions are; ultimately, going directly to a company's Web site and reviewing quarterly and annual financial statements is a fine starting point. This assumes that you can glean information from the financial information provided by corporations and their auditing firms. To a large extent, as long as you understand how to interpret the important indicators, you can make sound decisions.

A sensible way to narrow your field of investigation is to identify a few high-quality fundamental indicators and then investigate companies meeting your criteria. This is preferable to listening to analysts and Wall Street personalities and then buying stocks they recommend, often without fundamental reasons for doing so.

If you want to act as a contrarian in the way you pick stocks, you have to first ask yourself, is the market efficient? If so, does the *majority* tend to make sensible market decisions? In fact, the majority often does not make good decisions, so a contrarian approach to stock selection makes sense. It may be the ultimate contrarian approach to define yourself as a conservative investor and at the same time use options to manage market price swings.

The long-term conservative point of view is that taking a long stock position in well-chosen companies is the primary, and perhaps the only, method for investing success. Most refer to this approach as value investing. However, this approach may not be conservative at all. If you entrust your portfolio to short-term price gyrations, you are at the mercy of a chaotic and ever-changing market. It makes more sense to view your portfolio in two segments. First, the foundation of your conservative portfolio will always be defined with well-selected companies whose long-term value ultimately dictates where their stock prices will head. Attributes of such companies include consistent growth in dividend payments, strong and consistent capitalization, and competitive growth in revenues accompanied by consistent earnings. Second, you can manage market gyrations with the selective use of options, which is prudent and conservative as long as the purpose in using options is not speculative and as long as option richness does not dictate which stocks you hold or buy. Options are a secondary tool to help you manage market volatility, increase short-term profits, protect paper profits through hedging strategies, and devise rescue strategies when your portfolio experiences paper losses. All of these goals are conservative.

Conservative versus Speculative: Remembering the Difference

Timing is crucial in the use of options. A speculator is likely to devise strategies and select options based primarily on implied volatility and a perception of how stocks will react in the short term. However, because speculators leverage their capital in high-risk scenarios, they do not appreciate the long-term goals that you develop as your first priority. The uses of options in the two instances—speculative and conservative—are vastly different. You use options successfully if you time strategies to take advantage of short-term price changes in stocks you own, to protect paper profits, or to average prices when your stock values have declined but you continue to believe those companies are quality investments.

Options can help you to overcome the short-term timing problem, enabling you to acquire more shares when prices are low. When prices are high, options are effective at protecting paper profits without having to sell shares. Using long puts, you can offset price decline by selling puts at a profit or by exercising them to sell shares at the market top. If you use covered calls, you can cash out your paper profits without selling stock.

Such examples of options used to time price changes in your stock make the point that many conservative strategies can help you to build wealth in your portfolio while resisting the temptation to think conservatively but act speculatively.

The Long Put: The Overlooked Option

The tendency to favor long calls over long puts—a common phenomenon among speculators—arises from the tendency for investors to be optimistic. Realistically, you know that market values rise *and* fall, but those who speculate in long options invariably believe that a stock's price will begin rising immediately after they buy a call. It is not as common for speculators to consider buying puts in the belief that the stock will fall in value.

This generalization applies to most, but not all, speculators. However, because so much emphasis is placed on calls, long puts often are overlooked and at times undervalued as a result. Your conservative risk profile may present situations in which buying long puts not only makes sense, but conforms to your standards.

When the Stock's Price Rises

Two scenarios are worth considering. First, and most likely, is one in which a stock's price rises quickly. The temptation is to sell shares at the market top and take profits. This is a dilemma. You want to keep shares for the long term, but you also want to protect paper profits. If you don't want to sell shares, buying long puts is a sensible alternative. You do not need to spend a lot of money on long puts either. If you expect a correction within two to three months, you can probably find an out-of-the-money (OTM) put for a relatively small premium with a two- to three-month expiration. Buying longer-expiring puts provides longer terms of insurance and profit protection.

For example, assume that you purchased shares of various stocks and they have appreciated. Use the ten stocks in the model portfolio to summarize available puts expiring in nine months, as shown in Table 7-1.

Table 7-1 Long Puts to Protect Paper Profits

Name of Company	Current Symbol	Price	9-Month Put Premium		
			1	2	3
Caterpillar	CAT	32.29			
Strikes 30 25 22.50			5.15	3.20	2.28
IBM	IBM	101.27			
Strikes 100 95 90			12.15	10.00	7.80
Johnson & Johnson	JNJ	53.05			
Strikes 50 45 40			4.10	2.35	1.40
Coca-Cola	KO	45.02			
Strikes 45 42.50 40			4.95	4.30	3.00
McDonald's	MCD	56.09			
Strikes 55 50 45			6.07	3.90	2.50
3M	MMM	53.81			
Strikes 50 45 40			5.39	3.40	2.00
Altria	MO	16.99			
Strikes 15 12.50 10			1.37	0.65	0.25
United Parcel Service	UPS	54.65			
Strikes 55 50 45			7.68	5.40	3.50
Wal-Mart	WMT	50.20			
Strikes 50 45 40			5.45	3.56	2.12
Exxon Mobil	XOM	66.75			
Strikes 65 60 55			7.50	5.45	3.70

In each case, the examples cover a range of current price strike prices from the closest increment to the stock's price, and two strike prices below that price. For example, UPS was worth $54.65 per share, so the table looks at puts with strike prices of 55, 50, and 45. If the UPS market value declines below those strike price levels between the current date and expiration (nine months later), you can either sell the puts at a profit or exercise them. If you sell at a profit, you offset lost paper profits with a current option profit. If you exercise, you sell UPS shares at the strike price. For example, if you purchase one 50 put per 100 shares, paying $540, and the stock falls to $39 per share, you can exercise before the expiration deadline and sell shares at $50 per share, the put strike price. That would produce a pretransaction cost profit of $5.60 per share (11 points between market and strike values minus the cost of $5.40 per share).

Low-cost puts can be used to protect profits. By "low cost," in this example, you gain nine months of protection for $540. Given past market gyrations, that could be a bargain. You can employ long puts to protect paper profits and to provide yourself the choice between exercising and selling those puts if and when prices retreat. You can protect against price decline in the case of UPS stock below $50 per share for a premium cost of $560 (or below $45 per share, at a cost of $350 per put).

If you have bought shares of stocks that tend to rise and fall on average with marketwide direction, a rapid price increase could create an over-bought position in many, if not all, of your portfolio issues. So, the use of puts to protect paper profits is a prudent method for dealing with short-term price trends. Because the assumed market trend is short term, a nine-month protection period is a long time in terms of market price trends. Rapid price spikes tend to correct within a short timeframe, so if you have read the market correctly, this strategy—even given its limited life span—is both realistic and conservative. Shorter-term options provide protection for shorter time periods, often with advantageous pricing. For example, compare the prices for UPS 50 puts at various expirations:[1]

---

1.   Based on closing bid prices, April 18, 2009; source: CBOE delayed quotes, *www.cboe.com*.

Months to Expiration	Premium Cost
21	8.28
9	5.40
6	3.90
3	2.45
1	1.12

You can see from this comparison that, depending on the amount of time you want to have the protection, the premium cost varies considerably. You can buy 21 months of downside protection for $828 or one month of protection for only $112 (before transaction costs).

Balancing time and cost enables you to identify a practical means for managing short-term price fluctuation in your long stock positions. The alternative is to ignore short-term price gyrations and simply hold stocks for long-term appreciation. This is also a conservative approach. Because short-term price movement is often irrational and not caused by any fundamental changes in the companies themselves, you can either avoid management of short-term price changes or use options to exploit price spikes and to create the opportunity for additional profits without substantial capital risk.

The strategy of buying puts to insure paper profits (or even to provide a safe floor for your purchase price of shares) is a system for managing short-term volatility while continuing to execute the long-term conservative policies you have established in your portfolio. This is not mere speculation; it is a method for protecting current value at a relatively small cost, just as is purchasing fire and casualty insurance on your home even though the chances of a loss are slim. In the case of your portfolio, it is doubtful that properly selected stocks will experience large price declines, but when market prices rise too quickly, a short-term correction presents an opportunity to protect profits for a relatively small cost.

When the Stock's Price Falls

In the second scenario, long puts are used when market prices fall rapidly. In this situation, you may recognize a buying opportunity on an intellectual level, but you also fear further declines. So, you use long puts to provide an immediate floor for stocks in your portfolio. In cases of extreme short-term volatility, you can combine long puts with long calls. Long puts protect your capital value in case of a further decline; at the same time, a price rebound would make the long calls profitable.

The two scenarios for using long puts—when your stock prices either rise or fall rapidly—are based on the premise that you want to protect the value of shares you own and want to keep. This qualifies both strategic uses of long puts as conservative in nature. Speculators have no interest in protecting long stock value; in fact, the true speculator does not even own stock unless it serves as a vehicle for executing some related strategy, such as covered call writing. Were you to play market price swings, you would be defined as a speculator. However, the strategies described here are designed to serve as insurance for your paper profits, reduction of further losses, or an opportunity to take paper profits if and when they materialize. The thoughtful selection of long puts makes sense in these extreme market environments. It can also make sense to buy puts for insurance. For example, if you buy shares and you want to guarantee that the market value will not fall below your net basis, using puts as insurance is wise even when market prices are not especially volatile. It is conservative to insure long positions. A basic assumption is that your stocks will rise in value. Realistically, you also know that you could be wrong, at least in the short or intermediate term.

Short Puts: A Variety of Strategies

In a down market, you face the dilemma well known to all investors. You want to take advantage of buying opportunities, but you're not sure where the market is going. The conservative point of view should be to recognize down markets as the chance to pick up more shares of your favorite stocks. This not only represents a bargain; it is also a way to create new short-term profits. When you buy cheap shares, you lower your overall basis in a stock, and that improves long-term as well as current income potential.

Given the fear factor in down markets, you may hesitate to put a lot of capital into shares. What if the market continues to fall? What if it takes months instead of days to recover? What if 2008 is repeated? Anyone can look back over past pricing patterns and identify the obvious timing of purchases, but it is far more difficult to do in advance. This is where short puts are especially valuable. There is always the possibility that stock prices will fall and not recover. This danger exists whether you use options or not; it is a well-known investment risk. The value of using options is that strategies may exploit *temporary* price declines. When prices fall and remain down, options reduce the losses (if you use short options) or provide the opportunity for recovery with limited additional cost (if you use long options). For many conservative investors facing possible losses, using options in short strategies is more appealing than going long, because at the very least, it involves receiving payment instead of spending more capital.

When you sell puts, you receive the premium payment. If the stock's market value falls below strike price, the put is exercised. You can avoid exercise by rolling forward and down; or you can accept exercise and have 100 shares put to you. However, in down markets, selling puts can be a valuable method for acquiring additional shares of stocks at a reduced price, thus reducing your basis in stock through the profits you earn from shorting puts.

Conservative Ground Rules for Short Puts

Following are seven conservative ground rules for selling puts in down markets.

1. **Sell puts on stocks you already own.** Conservative standards state that you will buy and hold stock that meets your fundamental criteria. If those criteria continue to hold even when the stock's market value falls, you may view selling puts as a sensible and conservative strategy. This gives you the potential to pick up more shares, lower your average basis, and increase current income.

2. **Select strike prices based on support level.** The stocks you select for writing puts, like all stocks, are likely to trade in a predictable price range. Conservative stocks normally have a fairly narrow trading range and strong support. But when marketwide price declines occur, your conservative stocks may spike downward temporarily.

3. **Sell puts that provide a minimal rate of return.** What rate of return will you earn on short puts if exercised? As a general rule (and not a universal one), you may want to look for puts that represent a 10 percent return on strike price. Identifying a percentage helps you to avoid a common problem: choosing a higher dollar amount without comparing rates of return. For example, perhaps you have two stocks on which you want to write puts, but you've decided to go with only one. The current market value of one stock is $40 and the other is $65. The $65 stock has puts available at 5, and the $40 stock has puts at 4. The $500 premium on the first stock is higher than the $400 premium on the second. However, on a percentage basis, you would be wiser to pick the second stock and take the 10 percent return. This is a better return than the 7.7 percent on the $65 stock. (This comparison assumes the same time to go until expiration, because annualized returns can also change the comparative picture.)

4. **Coordinate the strike price and current market value.** In picking short puts, you want to gain the best possible premium, but you also want to avoid exercise. The farther OTM, the better you avoid exercise, but the lower the premium will be. So, you may look for puts with strike prices between 3 and 7 points lower than current market value. Why this range? It is the most likely range for creating desirable levels of premium profits. If the strike price is any closer to the current market value, a relatively small decline in the stock will put you in the money (ITM) and could lead to exercise. If strike price is further out, you are less likely to generate adequate premium to justify the short position exposure.

5. **Pick the expiration time based on your market perceptions.** How long should you leave yourself exposed in the short position? The longer until expiration, the greater the time value; the shorter that time, the lower the risk. The key is to compare those puts offering the desired 10 percent return with proximity between strike price and current market value. How long an exposure period is required? Is it worthwhile? How long do you

estimate it will take for the market to rebound? The decision has to be based on your willingness to remain at risk.

6. **Pick exit levels or roll levels when you initiate the transaction.** You may set a rule for yourself. For example, you may decide that once the stock's market value declines to within one point of the strike price, you will roll forward and down to avoid exercise. You may also decide that if and when the put's premium value declines to one-half its original value, you will close the position and take a profit, perhaps then replacing the short put with another. For example, if the stock's price rose while the short position was open, you may be able to sell a put with a higher strike price, generating additional premium profits.

7. **Plan out secondary strategies in the event of exercise.** What if the price of the stock falls below the strike price, and before you have the opportunity to roll out of the position, the put is exercised? In that case, you need a rescue strategy. One conservative choice would be to do nothing. If the put exercise reduces your overall basis, you will have more shares at a lower overall cost. Remember, as long as the fundamental value of the company is strong, this is a short-term situation and not a problem. In fact, it is a long-term advantage because your average price of shares has been reduced. Another secondary strategy may involve either selling additional puts or reverting to a covered call strategy. With more shares, you can write more covered calls. The basic rule is that if exercised, the covered call position must produce an overall net profit in the stock (after calculating the net basis due to average costs and further reduced by short-put and short-call premium). In that case, writing OTM calls (which are 100 percent time and extrinsic value) further reduces your net basis. Exercise can be subsequently avoided in a rising market by rolling forward and up.

An example shows how this strategy may work. Table 7-2 summarizes the annualized returns you would earn by writing several different puts on IBM. The annualized yield is calculated by first finding the simple rate of return between option premium and strike price, and then reflecting that return as if the position were open for 12 months.

Table 7-2   Short Put Annualized Rates of Return

IBM Expiration and Strike Prices	(A) Premium	(B) Simple Return	(C) Months to ÷ Expiration	× 12 =	Annualized Return
One Month:					
100	4.00	4.0%	1		48.0%
95	2.20	2.3	1		27.6
90	1.15	1.3	1		15.6
Three Months:					
100	6.90	6.9%	3		27.6%
95	4.84	5.1	3		20.4
90	3.30	3.7	3		14.8
Six Months:					
100	11.00	11.0%	6		22.0%
95	8.00	8.4	6		16.8
90	6.20	6.9	6		13.8
Nine Months:					
100	12.15	12.2%	9		16.3%
95	10.00	10.5	9		14.0
90	7.80	8.7	9		11.6
21 Months:					
100	18.30	18.3%	21		10.5%
95	16.10	16.9	21		9.7
90	15.90	17.7	21		10.1

The table reveals that shorter-term options earn a higher annualized yield than longer-term options. It also demonstrates that puts that are further OTM are less vulnerable to exercise but tend to yield lower annualized rates. This lower yield is reduced for longer-term puts. For example, the annualized returns for 21-month puts are within less than

1 percent of one another even though the exercise range covers 10 points. This makes the point that the further out until exercise, the more sense it makes to pick an OTM put.

Comparing Rates of Return for Dissimilar Strike Prices

The comparison between different strike prices and expiration dates is complex, even when the returns are annualized. When you consider the ramifications of different strike prices with the potential for exercise in mind, it changes the comparison completely; for example, if the stock continued to decline, you would prefer to take exercise at the lowest possible strike price, given the desired rate of return. The comparison between returns at various strike prices provides a valuable analytical tool for making an informed, conservative decision.

The selection of the better-positioned put represents a lower risk for another reason: If the market value of the stock were to change in either direction in the next three months, for example, you could select different options in future short strategies based on the desirability of maintaining a gap between the current market price and strike price that meets your standards. For example, in selecting options with the short put strategy in mind, you could limit your exposure to puts with strike prices between 5 and 10 points below the current market value and with three to six months until expiration.

When you consider the alternative—buying shares at today's price to average down your basis—it is apparent that selling the put is more profitable but requires less capital (limited to margin requirement minus premium received).

When selecting short puts, plan an exit or roll strategy and identify a rescue strategy in the event the stock declines in value. You will likely be able to roll forward and down at a credit (or perhaps at a small cost when trading expenses are considered). The value of rolling is not based on the exchange of premium cost or benefit, but more on the reduction of potential exercise price by 5 points.

Three Types of Rescue Strategies

A sensible and conservative strategy is to develop a contingency plan to rescue the stock if and when your put is exercised. (This is comparable to an exit strategy or other contingency plan you employ in managing your portfolio even if you don't use options.) If the short put is exercised, it will mean current market value will be below the strike price, so you would end up with more shares at a reduced basis from your original cost but at a basis *above* current market value. Your rescue strategy in this case may take three forms:

1. **Take no further action.** You can wait out the market in the belief that although the downward price movement is lasting longer than you thought, the stock's value will rebound. Because you continue to believe the stock is a quality investment, there is no long-term problem with waiting out the market. Having sold the put, you have reduced the overall basis in stock, and its value will eventually rise. Because you averaged down your basis, it will take less time to return your investment to breakeven or profitable status.

2. **Sell short puts again.** You can repeat the strategy in the belief that the price level is lower than the stock's long-term support. In severe marketwide price declines, this situation can occur, but it does not necessarily signal a disaster. It can be viewed as yet another opportunity to average down your basis. However, you also need to decide when to stop shorting puts. A conservative standard may dictate that you not continue to buy stock as prices fall, regardless of where you believe the stock's lowest likely level resides.

3. **Sell covered calls.** You have acquired additional shares, and this provides the potential to revert to a covered call strategy. Your true basis in stock is the average share price of all shares you own, minus the put premium you received. Can you sell covered calls on those shares and—in the event of exercise—produce a net profit overall? That is an important first question because if it is not possible, it makes no sense to invite a net loss upon exercise. Second, you must select calls on the same basis as your selection

of puts: for example, limiting your positions to a predetermined minimum annualized yield and number of points OTM.

Using Calls in Down Markets

Using puts to average down your basis and acquire more shares—or to increase income when those short puts are not exercised—is one way to manage your portfolio in a down market. You can also use calls based on the same arguments.

Long calls can maximize your position as long as you remember these guidelines.

- **Buy calls on stocks already qualified or owned.** The conservative use of long calls has to be based on the fundamental value of the underlying stock, so limit your call-buying activity to stocks you already own and intend to hold for the long term or to stocks you have already qualified based on your risk profile and conservative investing standards. If you intend to exercise the calls when the stock's price rises, do so to increase your holdings while averaging down your basis.

- **Buy calls only when the stock's price is low.** Timing is everything with options. Speculators often pay little if any attention to the underlying stock; they are concerned solely with option values and potential for short-term gain. However, because all your decisions are related to your long stock portfolio (and perhaps to its potential expansion), you should buy calls only when the underlying stock's price has declined dramatically. The "normal" trading range for the stock should be well above current market price, increasing the probability that the decline is a spike, a reaction to a marketwide decline or to a temporary decline in the sector. In those cases, a reversal should occur in the short term, so timing your call purchase to such moments is essential.

- **Identify and define an exit strategy.** When will you close the long-call position? In some cases, your purpose will be strictly to exploit a short-term price decline in a stock you have qualified, so you will want to know exactly when to sell the position and take your profit. For example, you may decide to sell if and when premium values will double in value; or you may identify a specific premium price level. If you intend to exercise the call (again, assuming the stock's price rises above the call's strike price), at what level will you exercise? Although you might decide you want more shares today, you could change your mind in the future based on emerging fundamentals.

- **Select strike prices with your intent in mind.** You should select a strike price you consider an attractive price for the stock based on the trading range prior to the price decline. This is premised on your belief that the stock's market value will return to that level before the long call's expiration, so strike price has to be selected with exercise in mind. If you decide later to just sell the call instead of exercising it, that is a subsequent decision. At the onset of the position, you want to pick a strike price that will average down your basis when you exercise. For example, if you bought 200 shares at $84, and today's price is $72, which strike price is most appealing? If you buy one 75 call and later exercise it, your average basis is $81. If you buy two 75 calls, your average is $79.50. Another way to average down involves dramatically increasing your holdings using long calls. For example, if you originally bought 100 shares at $84 and today sold two 75 calls, your exercised average basis would be $78. So, if the stock's market value at the time of exercise was $78 or above, you would have recaptured all the paper losses associated with the price decline.

The combination of long puts and short calls can be quite interesting. Consider the possible outcomes. The cost of the long call may be covered by the premium you receive for the put. If the market price rises, the call grows in value and the put becomes worthless, so you benefit for no cost or low cost. If the market price declines further, the put may be exercised (or rolled forward and down) and the call may expire worthless. However, even though the call becomes worthless, the zero cost (or close to zero cost) of the position provides increased upside potential with no more downside risk than you would experience by simply selling puts.

- **Coordinate cost and expiration so that the strategy is logical.** In picking long calls in down markets, limit the premium cost, because all the premium is in time value. Also, allow enough time until expiration that the stock can rebound to its previously established trading range. This suggestion assumes that you limit your long-call positions to OTM calls and that you have a sense of how long it may take for prices to return to normal levels. If you have survived through previous market-price changes, you know that short-term movement is usually an overreaction to current economic news and that the situation tends to correct itself in a short period. However, you also know that investors are cautious during volatile periods, and a reversal of a price decline can take more time. So, picking the right call is a matter of judgment.

Calls Used for Leverage, but Not for Speculation

The selection of calls in your conservative portfolio is a matter of leverage rather than speculation. The difference is based on ownership of the stock or on restricting the activity to the short list of stocks you have analyzed and qualified. It makes sense to have a list of stocks you would purchase if given the chance, and a price decline is the perfect opportunity to buy shares—assuming you are right about the timing and extent of the decline itself. Given this uncertainty, using long calls is more conservative than putting a large sum of capital into the purchase of shares. With calls, your potential loss is limited to call premium, and the potential profit is theoretically unlimited. When you buy stock, the same profit potential exists, but you risk further price decline if you time market volatility incorrectly.

The question of using long calls is a problem when you consider how time value affects price movement. If you have only a few months to go before expiration, you need the stock to appreciate enough to both create intrinsic value and offset declining time value. Consider the case of buying a call 4 points OTM and paying a premium of 3. By expiration, the stock must increase 4 points plus another 3 points to break even. In addition, you pay trading costs when you buy and again when you sell. If you use the average of a half point for the complete two-part trade, you need the stock to rise 7.5 points to break even. If you want to double your premium investment, the stock must rise 10.5 points by expiration. With listed options, this is a problem; but with Long-term Equity AnticiPation Security (LEAPS), the potential use of long calls gives you much greater flexibility.

Rather than limiting your selection of calls to the next eight months or so, you can consider using LEAPS calls of up to 30 months. The longer the time until expiration, the more you pay, but if the stock's price is depressed and you're not sure how long it will take for prices to return to normal levels, LEAPS calls can provide flexibility by allowing more time for strategies to season. An analysis of a range of prices, as demonstrated in Chapter 6, reveals this flexibility. In Chapter 6, Table 6-1 lists a series of long calls with contingent purchase in mind. The same list demonstrates the potential for long calls as part of a rescue strategy during down markets. It shows that for relatively small risk, you can lock in the share price in anticipation of a change in market price. LEAPS calls extend your period significantly.

You can also employ ratio-writing techniques in down markets to speed up your recovery and to close the gap between net basis and current market value. For example, if you own 400 shares and you write five calls, your ratio will produce more income than strict one-to-one coverage provides. (You eliminate the uncovered call risk by purchasing a higher long call.) Although ratio writing is one method to rescue paper loss positions, with well-chosen stocks your premise for holding them is a belief that prices will recover in the near future. Other rescue techniques are more prudent and contain less market risk; a ratio write may turn out to be a poor strategy if the stock's market value rises more rapidly than you expected and you end up exiting the position through exercise of stock you would rather keep.

Evaluating Your Stock Positions

Whenever a stock's price falls, you have to ask whether the decline is part of a short-term technical correction that will reverse in the future. If so, the buying opportunities should not be ignored. However, there is also the chance that the stock's volatility and technical safety have changed. Why?

Changes in stock volatility can be caused by a number of company-specific reasons. Marketwide volatility is better understood because investors tend, as a whole, to think of the market singularly. This can be a deceptive point of view, because a long-term quality investment may demonstrate short-term volatility, so it may appear higher risk than you thought it was. A temporary problem can be ignored or exploited with the well-timed use of options.

Rescue Strategies and Opportunity

A conservative options strategy makes sense as part of a rescue strategy or as a way to take advantage of down-market buying opportunities. Such opportunities are often best dealt with using options because that is a safer and more conservative approach than buying more stock. Timing, in all investment strategies, is both the key to profits and the potential gateway to losses. However, conservative investors, referring faithfully to in-depth analysis of the fundamentals, are less likely to fall victim to short-term price changes. Your decisions, if based on conservative investing standards and well-understood fundamental indicators, will likely be more successful than the average technical investor's, because you do not buy into short-term trends; you prefer to exploit those trends to find real bargains in market pricing.

Another question has to be asked, however: Have the fundamentals changed? Among the many causes of stock-specific volatility, a plateau of a growth trend is one of many signals that a growth period is slowing down or even stopping. All trends eventually flatten out; nothing continues in the same direction forever. If you look back over stock market history, you realize that companies like Polaroid—with heavy dependence on now-obsolete photo technology—lost its market leadership position because its products did not evolve with the times. Some experts believe the same problem may be happening to Kodak in the digital camera industry. Similar changes have happened to many industries due to either exhaustion of markets or technological change. Railroads, steel, public utilities, dot-com companies, and retail sectors have changed drastically over the past 50 years. New technology and the Internet, new modes of travel, energy efficiency, and changing methods of consumer shopping are examples of how the past growth companies have been replaced or forced to evolve. Today's leaders must change with ever-emerging technology, or they too will become obsolete.

Examining the Causes of Price Volatility

Fundamentals do change, often for reasons beyond anyone's control, so when stock volatility changes, the related volatility in conservative investments cannot be automatically blamed on the marketwide trend. The fundamentals deserve another look. Among the possible causes for individual stock volatility are the following:

- **Cyclical movement.** Many sectors have predictable cycles, and at various points in those cycles, price volatility is predictably higher than at others. As one of the many factors worth reviewing, even if you are the most dedicated fundamental investor, you will benefit by studying cyclical price trends. Coordinated review of fundamental cyclical change with those price and volume trends may reveal a correlation that explains the change in volatility and perhaps even signals immediate buying (or selling) opportunities in that stock.

- **Economic and political developments.** Some sectors are more sensitive than others to outside changes. Beyond marketwide cycles, also consider the cause and effect of economic and political situations on specific sectors.

- **Basic revenue and earnings changes.** A strong growth curve usually combines a consistent rate of growth in revenues, well-controlled ratios to cost and expense levels, and growing dollar amounts of earnings with a consistent net return. These fundamental indicators are perhaps the most popular for spotting long-term trends and, of equal importance, a slowdown or reversal in those trends. Assuming that you have faith in the accuracy of reported operating results, you probably rely heavily on these trends.

- **High core earnings adjustments.** Core earnings—the revenue and expenses related specifically to a company's primary product or service—are not always the only items reported on operating statements. Noncore items may include proceeds from the sale of an operating subsidiary or fixed assets; one-time adjustments due to accounting changes and other extraordinary items; and pro forma profits from invested assets such as pension plan assets. Some expenses are properly a part of core earnings but may be excluded, such as the exercise value of employee stock options granted during the year.

You may notice a direct relationship between core-earnings adjustments (a fundamental indicator) and price volatility (a technical indicator). This important relationship has been documented.[2] As a general observation, the greater year-to-year core-earnings adjustments, the greater the tendency for market price to fluctuate, and vice versa.

Investigating the possibility that a company's fundamentals have changed is crucial, even when short-term market volatility is the obvious cause. It is often the case that stock volatility reflects economic or sectorwide changes, so volatility itself may be a symptom of fundamental change. It is, at the very least, a possibility worth looking into. Your conservative risk profile requires that once the conservative investing standards in your portfolio change, you must also move from hold to sell. It is unrealistic to expect that stocks you own today will continue indefinitely to offer all the features you require in your portfolio. It is more realistic to select stocks that have those attributes today but to continually monitor each stock you own and, if and when changes occur, replace those stocks with other issues that better suit your requirements.

Deciding When to Sell and Replace Stock

When you decide it is time to dispose of stock, it is fairly simple to sell and replace if you are holding stock at a profitable position. As a matter of policy, you may want to employ options in various ways to turn paper losses into paper profits on all stocks you intend to keep and on all stocks in which you would like to increase your holdings. If you can achieve this goal, your portfolio will be likely to remain in good shape. But there is also a strong likelihood that once it is time to sell a particular stock, its price

---

2. My book *Stock Profits: Getting to The Core*, Financial Times Prentice Hall, 2005, pp. 245–246, demonstrates the direct relationship between technical and fundamental volatility (the latter being attributed largely to core-earnings adjustments).

will be depressed. There is a tendency to want to keep stocks as long as their price is *higher* than the original basis and to take a second look only when the price falls. In that situation, do you accept the loss or use options to recapture your basis before you sell? The dilemma is that you decide you want to sell the stock, but doing so will create an immediate loss.

If the stock's attributes have changed significantly, you are probably better off to wisely accept the loss and put your money elsewhere, preferably in shares of stock you can use for covered call writing. That is a far more profitable strategy than hoping for a price recovery, especially if you have already noted a decline in fundamental value. It is less likely than ever that you will recapture your full basis under these circumstances. As difficult as it is to accept losses, that may be the most conservative decision.

Another alternative is to use options in a combination strategy to provide potential recapture of value, along with protection against further price decline. When you combine a long put with a strike price immediately below current market value with a covered call above current value, you may be able to recapture your paper loss without additional risk—assuming some conditions are present.

- **The net cost of the position should be as close to zero as possible.** This is a rescue strategy combined with a desired exit from the long stock position. The cost of opening the long put should be offset by the premium you earn from selling the short call. This is not the time to spend more money on options; it is the time to provide downside protection against further price decline (long put) while being able and willing to sell shares through exercise (short call).

- **The call's strike price should be adequate to produce a net profit upon exercise or to yield a desirable exit price.** The call's strike price may be high enough to produce an overall net profit on the total position. That is the most desirable outcome, of course, but it will create a net loss. Your alternative—simply selling shares at today's market price—would not be as profitable as long as your short call's strike price is higher. So, selling the call may be the preferred position, even though it still produces a loss.

- **The exposure time should be limited; you want to exit this position.** Given that you want to exit this position, you do not want to be committed to a long-term covered call position. The premium levels have to be high enough to justify the exposure, but with expiration occurring soon enough that you are willing to wait.

- **The long put should expire at or after the short call, but not before.** As part of your exit strategy, you cannot risk further price decline. If the net cost of the long put and short call are close to zero, you are protected against any downside movement. If the stock moves below the put's strike price, each point is protected (because your combined option cost is at or near zero). However, be sure that the long put will expire at the same time as the short call or later. Otherwise, your stock position is vulnerable to further price decline, and thus additional losses. If the put were to expire first, you would own long stock and be short a call. If the stock's value declined at that point, you would have a bigger loss than you face today.

Stock Positions and Risk Evaluation

If you want to coordinate your various portfolio management requirements by using options, you must first classify risks and keep them in perspective. Inexperienced options traders commonly forget to pay attention to stock fundamentals, picking options in isolation. Even if a speculator uses only long-option positions and never buys or sells stock, fundamental analysis invariably affects (a) the success of an option trade; (b) pricing trends based on support, resistance, and overbought or oversold conditions; and (c) timing of purchase and sell decisions for options.

Risk evaluation of stock based on both price volatility and fundamental volatility (levels of period-to-period changes in revenue and earnings trends) are at the heart of risk analysis. The two types of analysis—technical and fundamental—are directly related and have a cause and effect on one another. The tendency to look at only one set of indicators is a mistake because to truly understand the causes of market trends, you need both.

The Relationship between Stock Safety and Options

The better the fundamentals for a company, the safer your selection of options. A stock whose price volatility makes it high risk is invariably also a high fundamental risk. Companies are unlikely to have safe fundamentals but high-risk technical indicators, or vice versa. The two go hand in hand. The same point applies to option strategies. If your stocks are selected based on corporate strength, excellence of management, strong revenue and earnings trends, dividend history, and competitive stance within a sector, the option choices will match the stock's fundamental strength.

Some observers counter that safe stocks do not offer great potential in option trades. In other words, extrinsic value, reflecting volatility, is not as strong in safe stocks as it is in highly volatile stocks, and the real short-term option opportunities are found in highly volatile situations. That is all true. However, the program in your conservative portfolio is not to maximize option income at the risk of your long-term portfolio; the purpose is to manage portfolio positions in a variety of strategies using options: puts to insure paper profits, basic covered call writing, contingent purchase using long puts or short calls, and rescue strategies in down markets. You do not want to expose yourself to high-risk situations because option income is likely to be better; in fact, income levels of short-term option positions are indicative of higher risk levels if and when those strategies require that you take long positions in high-volatility stocks. No matter which strategies you employ, the essential safety of your long stock positions is the highest priority.

That is why some down-market conditions indicate your best course of action is simply to sell. Cut your losses and invest capital in other companies whose value is greater and whose long-term growth prospects are more promising. Accepting losses is part of investing in the market, and few people will suggest that any line of strategies can make your portfolio foolproof. You will continue to have losses in the future, just as you have in the past. However, well-selected option strategies can protect you against losses, help you solidify paper profits, improve short-term income, and reduce your basis in stock positions—all without having to assume higher levels of risk and, in many cases, without added market risk.

Examining Your Risk Profile

Even when you have defined yourself as conservative, it can be instructive to review your attitude toward long positions in stocks. There are three likely points of view, and you may even hold these views in different ways for different issues in your portfolio.

1. **Long-term hold for conservative stock growth.** The traditional conservative view is that you should select stocks based on long-term value, growth potential, dividend record, and capital strength; keep them for the long term; and use them to build wealth over many years. This ideal continues to provide an intelligent investing method for many individuals.

2. **A vehicle for current income via covered calls.** Many investors select stocks using sound conservative principles, but with the primary idea of earning consistent current income from writing covered calls. This is also a sound investment program. It is entirely possible to earn option-generated current income with no added market risk, as demonstrated in Chapter 5, "Options as Cash Generators." This strategy works best when stocks have been picked using sound fundamental analysis associated with conservative investing.

3. **A combination, the best of both worlds: long-term value investing with potentially high current returns.** You can have it both ways. If your portfolio consists of carefully picked stocks of value that offer long-term growth potential, you can also generate current returns with covered call writing. Exercise is avoided with rolling techniques. When exercise does occur, you can reinvest capital in other stocks offering strong growth potential, wait for appreciation, and then include those stocks in your covered call program.

Options and Downside Risk

An essential element of using calls in down markets is the reduction of losses caused by further downside movement. Premium earned for writing covered calls reduces net basis in stock, which also helps close the gap between basis and current market value. Long puts or long calls provide profitable outcomes as long as stock prices move enough in the desired direction; the problem with long-option positions is twofold. First, time works against you when you buy options. Second, time value declines as expiration approaches, requiring far more price movement in the stock to justify the decision to go long in the option.

The Down-Market Benefits of Options

Consider the four primary down-market benefits of options in determining when to use them to manage your portfolio:

1. **Short positions reduce your basis in stock.** The first benefit worth analysis is that short options produce income, which reduces your basis in stock. This rescues a part of the paper loss during the down market; in some cases, writing short positions can completely eliminate a marginal loss position. A short position might not be exercised due to lack of movement in the stock price; or, if the position moves ITM, exercise can be avoided with rolling techniques, further reducing the paper loss and the effects of eventual exercise.

   The short position can be repeated if the option expires or loses enough value so that it can be closed profitably. In either event, you are then free to enter new short positions with richer premium. Ultimately, you recover the paper loss through the combination of improving market price levels and ongoing short-option strategies. A short position, when properly timed and when strike prices are properly selected, is programmed to ensure net profit positions and reduced overall basis in stock. If short puts are exercised, the overall, lower basis position in stock can be advanced to a secondary rescue phase such as writing covered calls, and if short covered calls are exercised, the resulting sale of stock will either produce a net profit or mitigate losses, freeing you to reinvest funds in more promising stocks.

2. **Short-put premium reduces overall basis in the event of exercise.** Writing short puts produces income and, possibly, allows you to accept exercise if the stock continues to decline. The strategy is also a feature of your long portfolio strategy. The

price depression is a buying opportunity. As long as you have confidence that prices will eventually rally, the short put either produces income to reduce the basis in your existing holdings or, if exercised, lowers your basis in the stock, often significantly. Both events speed your price recovery.

It is a mistake to view put writing as an options-only, isolated strategy. If it is performed without a logical, fundamental basis for the decision, it is not advisable. If it is performed as a strategic form of contingent purchase, it places you at an advantage because actual basis in the stock becomes the strike price minus the put premium. If the stock's support level is at or above that net basis price, short puts are a powerful method for contingent purchase. The third reason for selling puts—to reduce overall basis in the stock when the puts are exercised—can speed recovery time in a down market. As demonstrated in Chapter 6, the rescue strategy often *immediately* transforms a paper loss into a paper profit. When the short put is exercised and followed with the covered call leg of the strategy, it is entirely possible to recover all the paper loss without waiting out the market. If, in the meantime, the fundamentals of the company change for the worse, this fast recovery enables you to complete an exit strategy and still create a net gain.

3. **Repetitive covered call writing increases current income while cushioning risk range.** The most conservative strategy—writing covered calls on existing stock positions—also helps to protect against paper loss, even in a down market. The strategy can be entered repeatedly, with current positions closed at a profit, allowed to expire, or rolled forward to avoid exercise. This creates a cash cow of current income without increasing market risk. This approach assumes, of course, that if exercised, those covered calls would create a gain in stock, not a net loss. If you are close to breakeven or if you will suffer a loss in the event of exercise, covered call writing is an ill-conceived strategy under any circumstances except intentional exit due to changed fundamentals.

4. **Downside risk is also reduced with price averaging.** When a short put is exercised, you end up with reduced-basis stock. This is a positive outcome as long as you want more shares; however,

if the fundamentals of the company are weakening, this is not a conservative strategy. The inadvisability of placing more money into a poor investment makes this point. Conservative principles mandate that you cut losses as soon as the fundamental attributes of a company begin to change. This does not always require an immediate sale. Earlier in this chapter, the example was given in which a covered call was written at the same time as a long put at a lower strike price. This is a rescue strategy that protects your position in the event of a downward price movement while producing potential gains in the event of a price rally. The strategy is most practical when the long put cost and short call premium are close enough that the positions can be opened for little or no net cost.

Option Planning with Loss Carryover

One potentially troubling aspect of using options in down markets is the possible tax effect. If you create capital gains through exercise, those gains are taxable. Do you prefer reversing paper profits or deferring taxable gains? A lot of emphasis is placed on tax deferral, but in reality, you are better off accepting additional tax this year if that tax results from creating net profits.

The alternative—holding on to shares of stock whose basis is higher than current market value—affects your current investment return and, in some cases, traps you in a losing portfolio position. If you can use options to change the course of profits, you are far better off. For example, let's assume that your effective tax rate (federal and state combined) is 40 percent. All additional income you generate will be taxed at the 40-percent rate, and your after-tax profit will be the remaining 60 percent. In this condition, are you better off waiting?

If your income is high enough this year that you would prefer to take profits in the future, you can avoid creating additional profits from options. However, the outcome of that decision is zero additional profits. If you can create additional earnings on your investment portfolio, you are ahead with a net 60 percent—compared to no profit at all.

Current-year profits can also be sheltered entirely if you have a large carryover loss. With a limitation of $3,000 maximum net loss deduction per year, you may need many years to absorb your loss. One solution is to generate profits in conservative strategies this year. Another is to offset current-year gains against losses in stocks you want to dispose of without option activity. A third is to invite exercise by writing deep ITM covered calls to dispose of stock at a sure profit and to absorb a part of the carryover. In this situation, the loss of long-term status is not a concern because your purpose is to dispose of stock *and* to use up the carryover loss.

Timing: Matching Current-Year Profits and Losses

When it comes to tax ramifications, planning ahead is essential. If you face a large capital gains event this year, be careful to avoid writing ITM covered calls, which may put your long-term gain status in jeopardy. Such a consequence can be suffered unintentionally. For example, if you roll a short call forward and create an ITM situation without realizing its consequences, and then the call is exercised, you could end up with a large short-term gain instead of a long-term gain. The resulting tax liability could more than offset any option profits you earned in the strategy.

Even without options, timing is an important aspect of tax planning. If you have stocks you would like to sell and replace with more promising growth issues, time the loss to offset part of the big gain you expect to realize this year. By planning ahead, you can match gains and losses in the same year to minimize the impact of both, and if you are carrying forward a large loss, it can be used to shelter short-term gains from option trades.

A carryover loss should be viewed as an investment portfolio problem and as an opportunity. It is a problem because it represents a zero return on your investment. You can use only $3,000 per year, so if you are working with a $30,000 net loss, it will take 10 years to realize the full benefit, and a $90,000 loss would take 30 years to absorb if you had no gains in ensuing years. This situation is an advantage because you are free to realize year-to-year gains without worrying about the tax consequences. Timing of sales does not matter, because your profits will be absorbed to the extent of the loss carryover. The sooner you absorb the carryover loss, the greater the benefits. In taxation, the concept of deferring liabilities while accelerating benefits is well understood. It is similar to calculations of internal rate of return. You maximize your earnings by compounding your return, avoiding idle cash or other value (and "value" can include the benefit of sheltered gains), and seeking maximum gain without additional risk. So, a large carryover loss presents flexibility in the timing of current-year profits.

Taxes complicate the calculation of net gain. This makes it necessary to think about *all* the aspects of gain and loss on a *net* of taxes basis. A marginal gain can actually turn out to be a net loss if you do not plan ahead. With taxes and trading costs in mind, some options traders prefer to trade in blocks of options rather than in single contracts. The question of how many contracts to use is a complex one for your conservative approach to options. It depends largely on the number of shares you own and the additional number you would like to acquire. The strategies employing single contracts can be easily applied in multiples. Risks are identical as long as the relationship between the number of shares and the number of options remains the same, at least on the short position. When you consider using long options, the question of risk changes. The more contracts you buy, the greater your exposure to market risk, so you need to balance the dollar amount of risk with the potential benefits in long options—and you must understand the tax rules in any option strategy you use.

Multiple option strategies also open up a range of strategic expansion. You can use rolling techniques to incrementally increase the number of short calls. If you own 1,000 shares, you can replace a single option contract with as many rolled-up contracts as you want. This provides a credit on the transaction while effectively avoiding exercise. Conservative option strategies, when you own multiple lots of shares, also expand potential profitability and may even reduce risk. For example, you can write a series of covered calls at several strike price and expiration levels. These strategies may not save trading fees, but they do add interest and profit potential to your conservative use of options—notably to covered call strategic possibilities.

The next chapter explains conservative combination strategies involving options. These can dramatically reduce your basis in stock while creating current returns with options and without incurring added market risk.

8

COMBINATION CONSERVATIVE TECHNIQUES

The most impressive returns available using options involve combination strategies: spreads and straddles. With short straddles, you can achieve higher-than-average current returns. However, in utilizing these more advanced strategies, you need to remember two important points. First, the complex tax rules for such positions could jeopardize your long-term capital gains status. Second, the risks involved are conservative only if and when the basic assumptions continue to apply. These assumptions include your willingness to acquire more shares of stock and to accept exercise if it occurs, and your continued belief that the fundamental value of the underlying companies remains strong.

Ptions traders employ a variety of strategies, combining options in short and long positions, hoping for various forms of price movement (or lack of movement), and hedging other positions in stock, both long and short. Most of these strategies are inappropriate for your portfolio. However, some combinations can provide a valuable way to maximize your income from options without added market risk.

Many of these strategies have always been available on short-term options but considered impractical because expiration invariably occurred too soon. With the advent of Long-term Equity AnticiPation Security (LEAPS) options, the entire picture has changed. Because LEAPS options last up to 30 months, advanced strategies have moved from the realm of theory into the realm of practicality. For speculators, this means that it is possible to take greater risks and create combinations with potential for higher-than-average earnings or losses. For conservative investors, the availability of long-term options increases the current income potential with less concern for pending expiration.

In this chapter, the various types of combinations are analyzed to provide a complete background and explanation of the range of possibilities and to create examples of some interesting conservative strategies that do meet your conservative profile: the creation of higher-than-average returns without a corresponding increase in market risk.

Spread Techniques

The first popular strategy is the spread: the opening of two or more option positions on the same stock, involving different expiration dates or different strike prices. A more complex spread involves both different expiration and strike features.

The options industry has its own range of specialized terms, each used to communicate specific strategies and positions. For example, a spread can be described as vertical, horizontal, or diagonal. A vertical spread has different strike prices but the same expiration date. A horizontal spread is the opposite: It contains the same strike price but different expiration dates. A diagonal spread has different strike prices and different expirations. These three spreads are compared side by side in Figure 8-1.

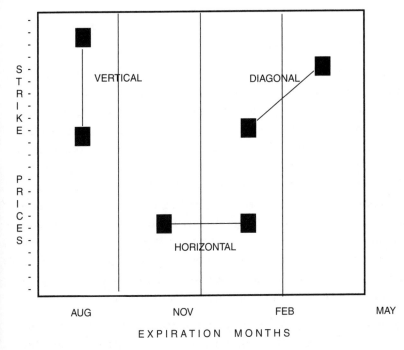

Figure 8-1 Types of spreads

By viewing the shape in each type of spread, you get an idea of how these strategies work. The spread is distinguished in other ways as well. For example, a bull spread is one designed to work out profitably if and when the value of the underlying stock rises. In comparison, a bear spread is maximized when the underlying stock's value declines. A box spread is the simultaneous opening of a bull spread and a bear spread. The use of any of these spreads depends on the direction of price movement you expect to see in the stock between the opening date and the expiration date. However, because you must spend money (for long positions) or expose yourself to market risk (for short positions), a spread—with a few exceptions—is usually not appropriate for your conservative portfolio.

The selection of long options whose premium is greater than the premium from any short options in the spread is called a debit spread (in other words, you have to pay money to open the position). The reverse situation—the use of short positions exclusively, or of short positions whose total premium receipts are higher than the cost of long positions—is called a credit spread.

Advanced Spread Terminology

The terminology is even more complex than these basic definitions. For example, a ratio calendar spread is any spread in which the long and short positions are not identical in number. As part of a complex rescue strategy, for example, you may open a series of long calls in the belief that the stock will rise, and you may offset a portion of those long calls by writing higher strike-price short calls. This reduces the overall cost but still enables you to benefit from upward price movement. A ratio calendar combination spread involves a ratio of a greater number of long and short options with a box spread. A conservative use of options rarely employs this advanced strategy. However, it is possible to end up with complex strategies by opening a series of simpler options at various times. The point is that while you are wise to know about the full range of option strategies, you probably will never use them.

One final advanced spread is called the butterfly spread. This strategy has three parts: open options within a strike-price range, offset by other options at both higher and lower strike price ranges. The purpose of the butterfly is to limit losses in exchange for limited profits. It is difficult to justify such positions, and they often result from a series of less complex decisions over a period of time and in reaction to price movement in the underlying stock. The transaction cost of opening positions with limited profit also makes complex spreads unproductive.

Straddle Techniques

Whereas the spread involves variation of strike price, expiration date, or both, the straddle by definition requires that strike price and expiration are the same. To open a straddle, you buy an equal number of calls and puts (a long straddle) or sell an equal number of calls and puts (a short straddle); in either case, the option positions would have the same strike price and expiration date.

With a long straddle, you experience a loss in the middle range, represented by a point spread on either side of the strike price, and profits either above or below that range. For example, if the total cost of opening a long spread is 11 ($1,100), then the stock must move either up or down by 11 points for you to break even. Anything beyond that range is profitable, and if the stock's price remains within the 11-point range until expiration, the position becomes an overall loss. You can close one side of the position without closing the other. For example, if the price of the underlying stock moved up enough points to make the calls profitable, it could be closed, and the puts left open. The same argument is true on the downside. Puts could be closed and calls left open. In writing a long straddle, the best possible outcome would be price movement in both directions, enough so that each side can be profitable in turn. The long straddle is highly speculative.

Short Straddles for Conservative Positions and High Rates of Return

The short straddle involves opening two short positions with the same strike price and expiration. An equal number of calls and puts produces a middle-range profit zone with potential loss zones above and below. For example, if you receive a net premium of 9 by opening a short straddle, your profit zone is 9 points on either side of the strike price; above or below that range, you face a loss. The troubling aspect of the short straddle is that you are always at the money (ATM) or in the money (ITM) on one side or the other, so exercise is an ever-present possibility. You can roll forward and up with the short call to avoid exercise, and you can roll forward and down with the short put. If you own shares of the underlying stock and you write no more than one call per 100 shares, the risks in this position are minimal, because the short call is covered. However, if you do not own 100 shares, the short straddle is a high-risk strategy, a combination of both a short call and a short put.

The short straddle with ownership of the underlying stock is one variation of the contingency strategies covered in Chapter 6, "Alternatives to Stock Purchase." It involves a contingent sale of stock you own (the covered call) with a contingent purchase of additional shares (the uncovered put). Because premium income can be substantial in this combined strategy, the short straddle can serve as a viable conservative strategy. Later in this chapter, a similar strategy with less risk is introduced, designed to maximize your returns without adding to your market risk.

Long or Short Positions

The obvious problem with advanced strategies is the high-risk attributes of each. Positions involving long calls and puts require substantial point movement; even in a net debit position (in which the cost exceeds the receipt), you must fight against time erosion. Positions with any short calls or puts involve market risk. Uncovered calls are the highest risk position possible using options—clearly inappropriate in a conservative portfolio. Short puts may or may not be appropriate either, depending on your opinion of the underlying stock, its fundamental strength, and whether you are willing to buy shares at the put's strike price.

When the mix between long and short positions is used, the possible variations of spreads and straddles present conservative possibilities. Some have already been introduced. For example, to remove the risk factor from a ratio write, you can add a long call at the top of the strategy. If you own 300 shares, you might write 4 calls with a strike of 50. You also buy a call at 55, 5 points above the strike price of the ratio, thus covering the otherwise uncovered short option in the ratio spread. The top-side long position is a form of market risk insurance; if the stock's price were to rise so that all 4 calls were exercised, you could cover 3 of them with your 300 shares; the remaining call is covered with your long 55 call. You would lose $500 on the difference between those strike prices (55 less 50 strike). However, there are two mitigating factors. First, you received premium for the overall ratio write. Second, the $500 loss is preferable to the possibility of being exercised and losing much more. This is a conservative use of options to manage a ratio write, transferring it from a potentially risky strategy to a safe one.

Mixing the Long and the Short

Another example using combinations of options is the opening of a long call and a short put in a down market. This provides multiple benefits. First, the cost of the long call should be offset by the income from writing the short put. Second, if the stock declines further in value and the short put is exercised, your basis in the stock is averaged down. The average basis consists of the average price between original purchase of shares and the strike price of newly acquired shares, minus put premium. Third, if the stock does rise, you can either close the call at a profit or exercise it and buy additional shares below market price, further reducing your average basis in the stock. This strategy—assuming you would be satisfied if and when the short put was exercised—is conservative. It involves low cost or zero cost (in some cases, even a small credit), and it is advantageous under any scenario of price movement. Even no movement would be satisfactory, considering that the combined strategy is a zero-cost one.

Using long puts to insure paper profits against the possibility of price decline is a sensible strategy by itself. But consider yet another variation combining long and short options: the long put and short call combination. In this instance, you achieve downside protection in two ways. First, the long put would match ITM intrinsic price movement dollar for dollar. That put can be exercised and shares sold above market value, or it can be closed to *take* paper profits without selling shares, a highly desirable attribute of the insurance strategy. Second, the covered call offsets all or part of the long put cost, so that you end up with free downside protection, and it may reduce your basis in the stock to the extent that the short premium of the call exceeds the long premium of the put. Remembering, too, that time works to the advantage of the short position, the covered call can be closed at a profit, allowed to expire worthless, or exercised. You can also roll forward and up to avoid exercise if the stock's price continues to rise.

These are only some examples of how you can continue to manage your portfolio on a conservative basis using options in combination, enabling you to take appropriate action in three market conditions:

1. In up markets, protecting or realizing paper profits without having to sell stock

2. In low-volatility markets, increasing current income with covered calls

3. In down markets, averaging down your basis and turning paper losses into paper profits or realized profits

Theory Versus Practice

The *concept* of using options in your long-term portfolio works as long as you structure that use within the guidelines of your conservative risk profile and consider all possible outcomes. For example, whenever you go short on calls or puts, you should fully understand the consequences of exercise.

The primary requirement for a conservative application of options is that any and all strategies should involve stock that you have qualified under your individual standards, that you either own or want to own, and that you consider an attractive long-term investment. Nonconservative option strategies tend to be overly complex and, although they may work out quite well on paper, they do not always produce the high rates of return that seem so easy. Stocks do not always move in the desired direction, or quickly enough, for high-risk strategies to become profitable. Speculators—especially inexperienced ones—often pay too much attention to the profit potential of complex option combinations and far too little to the associated high risks. In especially complex option strategies, the minimal loss is often offset by a related minimal profit. In calculating the cost of opening these positions, speculators often suffer a net loss due to trading expenses for opening *and* closing the positions.

Simplicity as a Worthy Goal

One conservative principle worth adopting is this one: *Keep it simple.* The fallback position for any options strategy is to return to the basic conservative theme: Select high-quality growth stocks, and hold for the long term, selling only if and when the fundamentals change. If any options strategy is overly complex or difficult to understand, avoid it without exception. You can use plenty of worthwhile conservative strategies to contend with short-term paper profits, offset depressed markets, and employ for contingent purchase; you do not need to extend your risk range because a particular options strategy would require it.

Risk analysis is an important and essential part of the informed options strategy. This is the process by which you determine whether a particular strategy is appropriate, given the range of risks involved. The analysis also includes evaluating the outcomes that may occur and then comparing potential return to the potential market risk and other risks (lost opportunity risk, for example).

In performing a risk analysis, the worst-case outcome has to be considered in deciding whether to proceed. Actual outcome comparisons are difficult because one involves selling stock and another does not; so the purpose of analyzing outcomes has to be to ensure that in any possible event, you are satisfied with that outcome. For example, if you are thinking about writing puts in a down market, the obvious worst-case outcome is a continued decline in the stock. Writing puts qualifies as a conservative strategy if you have already determined the following.

- The stock is a good value at current levels.
- The strike price would be attractive if the put were exercised.
- Premium income is high enough to justify the short position.
- You will accomplish an attractive averaging down of your basis if the put is exercised.
- You would like to acquire additional shares of the stock.

If any of these features is not part of your conclusion, writing puts makes no sense.

Worst-Case Outcome as a Desirable Result

The worst case has to be viewed as desirable based on the standards you set for yourself. For example, what if your choices meet all your criteria, but expiration is so far off that you are hesitant to tie up capital for that long? When you write short puts, you must have funds available in the event of exercise, and there may be a lost opportunity risk associated with leaving funds on deposit. If another buying opportunity appears that you would like to take, you cannot make a move because capital is committed to the possibility of short-put exercise. If capital is unavailable (or if expiration is so far off that you simply don't know what you will want to do in a few months), you may want to reconsider writing the puts.

The same worst-case analysis applies to writing short calls. You have to own 100 shares for each call you write (with the exception of the ratio write), or your market risks are unacceptably high. Is there a chance you will want to sell shares in the period between writing the call and expiration? That possibility will be strongest if and when the stock's market value rises, which means the call premium value would be higher as well. Using the short call makes sense only when you are willing to keep the position open until it is exercised, expires, or loses value so that it can be closed at a profit. When you close short calls at an appreciated value, the loss on the call offsets part of the profit in the stock. If time and extrinsic value have declined, this loss may be partially offset; but you should be willing to wait out the erosion of time value for as long as it takes to make the short position viable.

In your risk analysis, consider not only what might or might not take place in terms of profits in the open position, but also how the exposure and commitment to a particular strategy will affect your ability to make decisions. If you conclude that being short in options is not well timed or, more likely, that the exposure period is too long, reevaluate your strategies. You may prefer to use shorter-term options. In fact, a study of annualized returns reveals that more attractive annualized returns are achieved on options that expire sooner. In Chapter 7, "Option Strategies in Down Markets," for example, comparisons of annualized returns demonstrated this fact. The puts closest to current market value were better yielding in the shorter configuration than in the lengthier alternative. The puts further out of the money were better yielding in the shorter expiration mode. This disparity demonstrates the correlation between time to expiration and time value premium, and the importance of checking annualized returns along with proximity between current market value and strike price. The comparative value of the annualized premium has to be weighed against the exposure period; capital gain on the underlying stock in the event of exercise has to be part of the consideration as well, even though the capital gain is not part of the option profit.

Tax Problems with Combination Strategies

The complexity of combination strategies is only one of the problems you have to sort through. As a conservative investor, you may prefer simplicity, if only because basic conservative strategies involve fewer risks. The possible tax consequences may also discourage you from involvement with complex strategies.

Some forms of combinations create an unintentional wash sale, so profits or losses you intend to recognize in one particular tax year could be disallowed. Any "offsetting position" that creates a straddle could result in the loss of long-term capital gains status for long stock. The IRS definition of offsetting positions in which this could occur requires a "substantial diminution of risk of loss" for the capital gains penalty to apply. By definition, a conservative straddle makes sense only if it reduces your risk exposure, and under the tax rules, you do not have to actually cover stock to fall within the definition of having an offsetting position.

The Anti-Straddle Rule and Its Effect

The tax rules set up the potential consequence that the transaction will be negated under the 30-day wash-sale rule. You could also lose long-term capital gains status on stock sold, and the deferral of deduction for losses. If, by definition, a current-year loss is offset by a successor position (a related second side of a straddle, for example), the losses could be deferred and deducted from the basis in that successor position. This limitation applies to the loss on an option position, the expense of executing transactions, and applicable margin interest.

The so-called "anti-straddle rules" in the tax code are complex and designed to discourage the use of options to create current-year losses to offset future-year gains. However, the complexity of these rules may discourage you from considering complex straddles as a viable part in your conservative portfolio. The complexity itself is a form of risk—tax complexity risk—that makes advanced options troubling. A part of the risk to which you may be exposed is the unexpected loss of long-term gains status that, in some cases, could end up causing substantially higher tax liabilities. You can also create an "unqualified covered call" unintentionally when you roll forward to avoid exercise. If you become involved with advanced options, including ITM covered calls or straddle positions, you should first consult with a tax professional who understands the current tax rules and question whether any use of options that may complicate the tax status of long-term stock is worth the tax complexity risk. Even if you use expert help in preparing your tax return and in planning investment income each year, the special rules concerning these option transactions change everything. You may not simply be able to pick a strategy and proceed, without also knowing how it will affect your tax status.

The Ultimate High-Return Strategy

It is wise to shun any strategies that are overly complex, that are unclear as to risk levels, or that contain unintended tax consequences—which immediately disqualifies an array of possible option strategies (the distinction is clear between conservatism and outright speculation). By the same argument, there is a difference between investors who appreciate simplicity and those who are attracted to the exotic, the complex, and the difficult to understand. Some option trading takes place for the enjoyment of the complexity rather than for a specific desire to create profits.

One particular strategy is especially appealing because it creates an immediate return, it is not complicated, and market risks are not increased. A straddle involves the simultaneous opening of a call and a put with identical strike prices and expiration dates. By modifying the straddle, you can create a short position without also facing the near certainty of exercise. Instead of employing identical strike prices, this involves the use of out-of-the-money (OTM) strikes to create a short combination made up of covered calls and uncovered puts.

A Review of Your Conservative Assumptions

For the modified straddle to work, observe the following ten rules.

1. **You are willing to accept exercise of the covered call.** As with all conservative strategies involving short options, you must be prepared for exercise. If you are unwilling to face even the

remote chance that the call could be exercised, this strategy is not a good fit for your portfolio.

2. **Exercise of the call will result in a profit in the stock.** There is never a reason to open a covered call position if exercise would create a loss. Ensure that your basis in stock is lower than the strike price of the call. The further the gap between the basis and strike, the better.

3. **You are willing to accept exercise of the uncovered put.** You also need to acknowledge that the short put could be exercised. The strike price of the put should represent a desirable buy price for the stock, in your opinion. For example, if your portfolio strategy calls for purchasing more shares of the stock if the price falls adequately to become a bargain, you achieve the same outcome by selling a put that is later exercised.

4. **You have funds available to buy shares if and when the put is exercised.** Your broker requires that you have funds available to complete this transaction if the put is exercised. Even if you can complete this option position for only a portion of the possible price of the stock, you still have to leave funds on deposit.

5. **You consider the put's strike price a good price for stock.** The put's strike price should, in your opinion, be desirable. This reduces the chance of exercise; even if exercise does occur, you would expect the stock to return to its established range above that support level.

6. **The strike prices are selected with the stock's trading range in mind.** Your review of this strategy should be coordinated with a study of the stock's recent trading range history. The ideal situation is one in which the stock has demonstrated consistent, steady growth in market price within a relatively narrow trading range. While exercise of either side of this transaction would be welcomed, the best outcome allows you to manage the positions to avoid exercise and then repeat the position later.

7. **Premium income from both positions is attractive.** To justify any option position, the premium levels have to be right. In this strategy, you write two short positions. Longer exposure

increases the chance of exercise on either side of the transactions, but rolling techniques can help you to avoid exercise long enough that the positions can close at a profit.

8. **The proximity of strike prices to current market value is ideal.** The current market value of stock should ideally reside exactly halfway between the strike prices of the call and the put, or within $1 of the halfway mark. For example, if your strike prices are 45 and 55, the ideal market price of the underlying stock would be $50 per share. (For the purposes of illustration, the examples that follow are limited to strike prices about 5 points OTM.)

9. **Fundamental analysis of the underlying stock has passed your review.** It is always essential to evaluate the stock before deciding to buy shares or to continue holding shares you already own. This strategy makes sense only if it also makes sense to own the stock, based on your conservative profile.

10. **You have evaluated all possible outcomes, and you are satisfied that this strategy is worth entering.** Consider all possible outcomes, including the net portfolio value when the stock declines below the put's strike price and you end up with a paper loss. Your analysis should be comparative based on your outcome if you simply continue holding shares of the stock without writing options.

Examples of the Strategy in Practice

This combination strategy requires several steps.

Pick Your Portfolio

The model portfolio of ten stocks is used for this example. The assumption here is that all the stocks passed fundamental tests.

Pick the Expiration Dates

The comparisons are made among the model portfolio stocks assuming that expirations will occur in 9-month or 21-month periods. In practice, you can alter the expiration dates between calls and puts. There is no specific reason why identical expirations have to be applied for this strategy unless you are working from an assumed target date for final closure of the strategy.

Review the Trading Range Trends

The next step is to review the trading ranges for these stocks. The following approximate trading ranges apply over 12 months:

Stock	Trading Range
Caterpillar	22–86
IBM	69–131
Johnson & Johnson	46–73
Coca-Cola	37–59
McDonald's	46–67
3M	41–80
Altria	14–23
United Parcel Service	38–72
Wal-Mart	46–64
Exxon Mobil	56–96

Look for Available Options and Strike Prices

Next, check available options on all the issues. Based on the model portfolio, look at the 9-month and 21-month contracts for both calls and puts for each option and select those that are OTM in each instance. Limit your analysis to options that are OTM on both sides of the stock's current value.

In examining the available options, you discover a range of calls and puts meeting these criteria, summarized in Table 8-1.

Table 8-1 Stocks for Combined Call and Put Short Strategy

Stock	Symbol	Current Price	9-Month Options		21-Month Options	
			Call	Put	Call	Put
Caterpillar	CAT	32.29				
	35 call / 30 put		4.70	5.15	7.00	8.25
IBM	IBM	101.27				
	110 call / 95 put		7.90	10.00	13.43	16.10
Johnson & Johnson	JNJ	53.05				
	55 call / 50 put		3.60	4.10	6.20	7.20
Coca-Cola	KO	45.02				
	47.50 call / 42.50 put		3.05	4.30	5.10	7.00
McDonald's	MCD	56.09				
	60 call / 50 put		3.50	3.90	5.20	7.70
3M	MMM	53.81				
	55 call / 50 put		5.44	5.39	8.00	8.60
Altria	MO	16.99				
	17.50 call / 15 put		1.34	1.37	2.06	2.88
United Parcel Service	UPS	54.65				
	60 call / 50 put		3.60	5.40	6.00	8.28
Wal-Mart	WMT	50.20				
	55 call / 45 put		3.20	3.56	5.90	6.35
Exxon Mobil	XOM	66.75				
	70 call / 60 put		6.01	5.45	10.00	9.45

The information in Table 8-1 is difficult to judge comparatively for several reasons. First, it is not annualized, but you are dealing with significantly different expiration terms, price ranges, and distances between current market value and strike price. For example, compare unannualized returns for IBM, the highest-priced stock, and Altria, the lowest-priced. At first glance, IBM looks more desirable because the dollar value of options is much greater. But when you calculate the return from option premium based on current price, the picture changes:

	Unannualized Returns	
IBM	9-month	21-month
	calls	7.8%	13.3%
	puts	9.9	15.9
Altria		
	calls	9%	12.1%
	puts	8.1	17.0

The returns are comparable for both stocks; in fact, given the lower per-share cost of Altria, this selection would involve less market risk. Another factor making Altria the more desirable of the two for this strategy (which involves ownership of stock) is the difference in dividend. Whereas IBM yielded 2.0 percent, Altria's dividend at this time was 7.8 percent. This is definitely a tipping point which, when combined with the lower share price, makes Altria a better selection for the strategy. Because share prices are quite different, making comparisons solely on the basis of the dollar value in option premium is also inaccurate. For example, if your choice was between 100 shares of IBM, your basis in stock would be $10,127. If you chose instead to buy 600 shares of Altria, your basis would be $10,194 ($16.99 × 600). Dollar value of the nine-month call would be $804 for Altria (6 x 134), versus $790 for one IBM call. The nine-month puts favor IBM, with six Altria puts adding up to $822 (6 × 137), versus $1,000 for a single IBM put.

The comparison is also complicated by the potential for price movement in the stock. An analysis of the trading ranges for these two companies shows that over a 12-month period, IBM ranged between $69 and $131 per share. The trading range volatility was 89.9 percent. This is calculated by dividing the difference in the range by the low point, or (131 - 69) ÷ 69 = 89.9 percent. The same study of Altria shows a range between $14 and $23; the same volatility calculation is lower: (23 - 14) ÷ 14 = 64.3 percent.

You have to take all these factors into account when picking a stock for the short option strategy. Assuming that you like all stocks equally, consider the return from writing options, dividend yield, and historical volatility. Altria is a more favorable candidate given all these criteria. A more subtle but equally important selection criterion is the point spread betweens strikes and strike levels compared to current stock price. The wider the strike range, the more desirable. In spite of Altria's favorable return from combined options and dividend yield, it has the lowest point spread between short calls and puts—only 2.5 points. Four of the companies (Caterpillar, Johnson & Johnson, Coca-Cola, and 3M) were analyzed with 5-point spreads. Another four (McDonald's, UPS, Wal-Mart and Exxon-Mobil) used 10-point spreads. IBM had the widest margin: 15 points.

In choosing between the 9-month and 21-month alternatives, you cannot make a valid judgment until you annualize the returns and then review them side by side. Table 8-2 shows combined short call and put for each strike selection and annualizes each return. It also adds in the dividend yield to complete the overall analysis.

Table 8-2 Annualized Returns, Combined Call, and Put Short Strategy

Stock and Expiration	Combined Premium ÷ Price=	Annualize	Annualized Return		Dividend Yield	Total Return
CAT						
9-month	(9.85 ÷ 32.29)	÷ 9 × 12 =	40.7%	+	5.1% =	45.8%
21-month	(15.25 ÷ 32.29)	÷ 21 × 12 =	27.0	+	5.1 =	32.1
IBM						
9-month	(17.90 ÷ 101.27)	÷ 9 × 12 =	23.6%	+	2.0% =	25.6%
21-month	(29.53 ÷ 101.27)	÷ 21 × 12 =	16.7	+	2.0 =	18.7
JNJ						
9-month	(7.70 ÷ 53.05)	÷ 9 × 12 =	19.4%	+	3.1% =	22.5%
21-month	(13.40 ÷ 53.05)	÷ 21 × 12 =	14.4	+	3.1 =	17.5
KO						
9-month	(7.35 ÷ 45.02)	÷ 9 × 12 =	21.8%	+	3.7% =	25.5%
21-month	(12.10 ÷ 45.02)	÷ 21 × 12 =	15.4	+	3.7 =	19.1
MCD						
9-month	(7.40 ÷ 56.09)	÷ 9 × 12 =	17.6%	+	3.6% =	21.2%
21-month	(12.90 ÷ 56.09)	÷ 21 × 12 =	13.1	+	3.6 =	16.7
MMM						
9-month	(10.83 ÷ 53.81)	÷ 9 × 12 =	26.8%	+	3.8% =	30.6%
21-month	(16.60 ÷ 53.81)	÷ 21 × 12 =	17.6	+	3.8 =	21.4

Table 8-2 Continued

Stock and Expiration	Combined Premium ÷ Price=	Annualize	Annualized Return		Dividend Yield	Total Return
MO						
9-month	(2.71 ÷ 16.99) ÷ 9 × 12 =		21.3%	+	7.8% =	29.1%
21-month	(4.94 ÷ 16.99) ÷ 21 × 12 =		16.6	+	7.8 =	24.4
UPS						
9-month	(9.00 ÷ 54.65) ÷ 9 × 12 =		22.0%	+	3.4% =	25.4%
21-month	(14.28 ÷ 54.65) ÷ 21 × 12 =		14.9	+	3.4 =	18.3
WMT						
9-month	(6.76 ÷ 50.20) ÷ 9 × 12 =		18.0%	+	2.1% =	20.1%
21-month	(12.25 ÷ 50.20) ÷ 21 × 12 =		13.9	+	2.1 =	16.0
XOM						
9-month	(11.46 ÷ 66.75) ÷ 9 × 12 =		22.9%	+	2.4% =	25.3%
21-month	(19.45 ÷ 66.75) ÷ 21 × 12 =		16.7	+	2.4 =	19.1

Compare Yields

The final step before making a decision is to develop a valid comparison. If calls are exercised, you gain points between current market value and strike price. The exercised rate of annualized return is calculated based on current market value; also consider your original basis in each stock as part of the process to determine whether, in your opinion, this combined strategy is worth the exposure.

The return will also be different if either option or both options decline in value and are closed or if you replace them by rolling forward and up (calls) or forward and down (puts). These variables point out the difficulty in making accurate comparisons between stocks and between outcomes. However, if we make a few generalizations, we can compare the outcomes as reflected in Table 8-2.

This summary allows you to look at potential returns side by side between stocks and expiration dates. Even so, this analysis is only accurate on the assumption that all options expire worthless. The return will be quite different if one or both options are exercised. The point spread for the combined short position can also become quite important. With this in mind, you may further assume that you will not enter the short spread for those issues with 5 points or less; you will only consider those with either a 10-point or 15-point difference between call and put. This reduces the possible field down to 5 of the 10 stocks: IBM, McDonald's, UPS, Wal-Mart and Exxon-Mobil. Looking at the nine-month annualized returns (which are greater in each instance), the choice compares as follows:

Company	Total Return
IBM	25.6%
McDonald's	21.2
UPS	25.4
Wal-Mart	20.1
Exxon-Mobil	25.3

All these returns are impressive; all are above 20 percent annualized returns. Because dividends are included in "total return," these annualized results are truly comparative. The leader, IBM, is only 0.2 percent higher than the UPS total return. However, IBM wins in this comparison for one important reason: It has the greatest point spread between short call and short put, or 15 points. This increases the "safety zone" of the outcome on both sides. The combined premium will be 17.90 (nearly 18 points), so whether the stock rises or falls 18 points from its current price, it remains within the breakeven or profit zone. Combined, this creates a 36-point profit zone for the combined short position, while yielding 25.6 percent return. And, assuming that the criteria meet your standards, this is a conservative strategy. These criteria follow.

- You are willing to have 100 shares called away if the call is exercised.

- You are willing to buy an additional 100 shares if the put is exercised, meaning that you consider the exercise price a fair price for the stock.

- The fact that you won 100 shares makes the call side of the spread quite safe; as long as you have the same level of confidence in the put side, the strategy remains conservative.

Also remember that either short option can be rolled to avoid exercise if the stock's price rises to 110 or falls to 95; you can roll forward and up (for the call) or down (for the put) to expand your nonexercise zone.

This analysis makes IBM a favorable selection for many reasons.

- The total return is the highest in the wider-strike spread issues.
- Among those, IBM has the widest spread: 15 points.
- The total premium from writing the nine-month options is nearly 18 points, or $1,800.

The strategy, based on the current value of stock at the price of $101.27 per share, is illustrated in Figure 8-2.

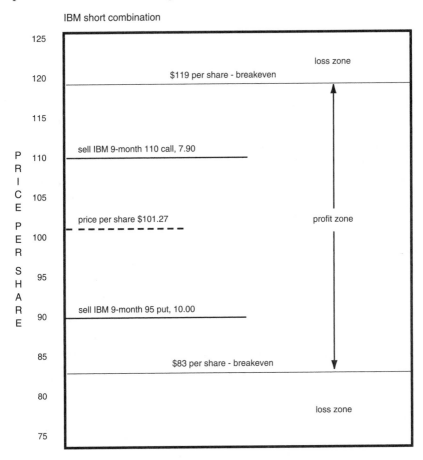

IBM short combination

Figure 8-2 Profit and loss zones, short-option combination

The profit zone is the difference between the strike prices plus the number of points received for selling the short puts. This zone is quite wide. It does not include dividend income (assuming that dividend yield comparisons were useful in comparing potential outcomes but are not part of the option-specific returns). There would no loss zone on the upside other than the lost opportunity from having stock called away; and on the downside, the loss zone represents having stock put to you above current market value. In practice, this strategy does not involve loss of value; its outcome in the worst-case scenario involves having stock called away due to the short call, or acquiring additional shares of stock due to exercise of the short put. For the total premium income in this example of $1,790, these are the risks you undertake in the short combination.

If the call were exercised, shares would be called away at the strike price of $110 per share, producing a capital gain of $8.73 per share ($100–101.27), or 8.6 percent. (If this occurred on the last day before expiration, annualized capital gain would be 11.5 percent plus 2.0 percent dividend.) If the put were exercised, your basis would be the put's strike price averaged with your original basis. If you bought shares at $101.27 and then had the put exercised for an additional 100 shares, the average basis would be $98.14 per share. However, the downside risk is reduced by 17.90 points, or down to $80.24 per share in this outcome. So as long as the stock's price remained above $80 per share, the net outcome of a put exercise (considering the combined premium from this position) would remain profitable.

If both options were exercised, you would end up with 100 shares of stock. The original 100 shares would have been called away when the call was exercised at $110 per share, and another 100 shares were put to you when the put was exercised at $95 per share. Because the original shares of stock were disposed of at a profit, the newly acquired shares represent a fresh start, with a basis of $77.10 ($95 per share new basis, minus short option premium of $17.90).

As long as you would be happy to accept exercise of either option, all the possible outcomes of this transaction are positive. In the case of the put, the assumption would be that the strike represents a fair purchase price in your opinion. Based on the IBM 12-month trading range from about $69 to $131, this does seem to be a fair conclusion.

Outcome Scenarios

Even after identifying a desirable yield, it still makes sense to go through the various possibilities to make sure that you understand what could occur and what actions, if any, you would want to take in response.

Planning Ahead for Each Outcome Scenario

You would want to consider what actions, if any, you would take in the following scenarios:

- **The trading range of the stock remains between the strike prices.** If the stock's trading range remains below the call strike price and above the put strike price, neither will be exercised. This condition occurs in one of two instances. First, the price of stock simply does not move in either direction more than the example's profit zone. In this case, you can wait for expiration or, when the value of either option or both options has declined, you can enter a closing purchase transaction and cancel the short positions. Once this is done, you are free to sell more options under the same strategy. Second, when the stock's price approaches one strike level or the other, you may roll forward to avoid exercise. This extends your period of exposure, but it also extends the future strike price (upward for calls and downward for puts). So, if the call were eventually exercised, it would be at a higher price (in the case of the call) or a lower price (in the case of the put).

  You are free to close or roll either of the short positions without changing the risk profile in the remaining segments of the position. This is only true, however, as long as you own 100 shares for each short call written. The risk profile provides great flexibility. As the trading range of the stock begins moving in one direction or the other, you can roll forward, close the position, or alter expiration dates and strike prices. The decisions about how you deal with the short call or the short put are independent of one another. They work well together due to the high returns you can earn consistently without increases in market risk; that does not mean you are limited in selection of strike prices or expiration dates.

- **Both options are exercised.** If price in the underlying stock moves enough points ITM on both sides, you could experience exercise of both options. This would require not only movement ITM, but early exercise on both sides, and you would end up where you were before entering the transaction. Upon exercise of the call, your 100 shares are sold; and upon exercise of the put, you receive 100 shares at the strike price. Because the space between strike prices is so many points, this outcome produces a gain in option exercise, plus the premium income. In the example, the total $1,790 premium is yours to keep no matter what; but if you were to sell 100 shares at $110 and acquire 100 shares at $95, you would have an additional $1,500 gain overall; this would consist of a small capital gain on the exercised call and a reduced basis in the exercised put. However, because you would end up with a net 100 shares and no open short positions, this outcome is highly desirable. Once it has occurred, you can once again write a short call and a short put.

  When both options are exercised, the most desirable sequence would be for the put to be exercised first, and then the call. The outcome then creates a situation in which you own appreciated stock. For example, if your original basis were $10,127 (the market value at the time the short positions were entered), it would be desirable to have stock purchased at $110 per share.

  This outcome is the same as if you simply bought 100 shares of stock and set a goal to buy an additional 100 shares if the stock's price falls to $95 and to sell shares if the stock's price rises to $110. The difference with the option short combination is that you express the same goals but earn a higher profit and extend the profit zone at the same time. You do not depend on price movement to reach the profit goal: The strategy produces a profit through call and put premium, no matter which direction the price moves.

- **The call is exercised but the put is not.** In this situation, your stock is called away at $110 per share (based on the preceding example), but you are not required to repurchase those shares. The short put either expires worthless or is closed through purchase. The outcome is desirable because your gain consists of

$873 on the stock plus $1,790 on the option premium. The downside of this outcome is lost opportunity. When your stock is called away, it is because that stock has appreciated in value, so you end up earning a profit, but you no longer own the stock. If you can consistently produce higher returns than the lost opportunity, it is a worthwhile trade-off.

- **The put is exercised but the call is not.** If the put is exercised, you acquire an additional 100 shares. Because the original basis is $101.27 per share, the new combined basis of 200 shares is $98.14 before considering option premium. When you deduct the $1,790 option premium, the basis is further adjusted down to $8,918.50:

($10,127 + $9,500 − $1,790) = $17,837 (200 shares)

Although the current market value of the stock in this situation would be below your net basis, you have to assume that you entered this strategy with a few important qualifications in mind: You considered $95 per share a fair price for the stock, and you are happy to acquire additional shares because this stock meets your long-term fundamental criteria. Having 200 shares may also be seen as a way to double the potential returns in writing future short positions. It is advisable, however, to wait until the price rebounds to ensure that all outcomes of short-option positions would be profitable.

- **The stock's market value falls below the put strike and remains there.** This is the worst outcome of all—whether you write short options or not. If you simply keep your 100 shares, a price decline has no mitigation. In having created a reduced basis from selling puts, you naturally hope the price returns to previous levels. Even so, this situation may require a rescue strategy, discussed in detail later in this chapter.

The Augmented Strategy: A Short Straddle

Using the previous analysis, let's see what happens if you write a straddle instead of creating a spread with its strike price gap. You do this when you would find it most desirable to have either or both options exercised. Assuming that you write a straddle as close as possible to the current market value of the stock, you could create a potentially high premium value in the options.

Looking once again at the ten stocks in the model portfolio, check the status of calls and puts with nine-month expirations, closest to current market value, as shown in Table 8-3.

Table 8-3   Stocks for Conservative Short Straddle

Company	Price	9-Month Call	Put	Total	Return	Ann'ed	Dividend	Total
Caterpillar	32.29							
30 strike		6.76	5.15	11.91	36.9%	49.2%	5.1%	54.3%
IBM	101.27							
100 strike		12.28	12.15	24.43	24.1	32.1	2.0	34.1
Johnson & Johnson	53.05							
55 strike		3.60	6.44	10.04	18.9	25.2	3.6	28.8
Coca-Cola	45.02							
45 strike		4.10	4.95	9.05	20.1	26.8	3.7	30.5
McDonald's	56.09							
55 strike		5.80	6.07	11.87	21.2	28.3	3.6	31.9
3M	53.81							
55 strike		5.44	7.60	13.04	24.2	32.3	3.8	36.1
Altria	16.99							
17.50 strike		1.34	2.58	3.92	23.1	30.8	7.8	38.6
United Parcel Service	54.76							
55 strike		8.69	5.40	14.09	25.7	34.3	3.4	37.7
Wal-Mart	50.20							
50 strike		5.50	5.45	10.95	21.8	29.1	2.1	31.2
Exxon Mobil	66.75							
65 strike		8.70	7.50	16.20	24.3	32.4	2.4	34.8

It is essential in this analysis that you emphasize annualized return rather than dollar value for the option premium. Clearly, the potential $2,442 you could receive for writing an IBM nine-month straddle is far higher than the $392 you would receive doing the same strategy on an Altria position. But the dollar values alone do not tell the whole story. In fact, the annualized return on the IBM straddle is 34.1 percent compared to 38.6 percent on Altria. Dollar values alone are deceptive. In this comparison, owning 600 shares of Altria represents approximately the same capital level as owning 100 shares of IBM, and the option premium is higher on Altria. To make the comparisons valid, you need to annualize all these returns.

How the Dollar Values Alone Can Mislead

Comparing 100 shares of IBM to 600 shares of Altria helps to clear up how this works. You need not only to annualize returns, but to make capital investment comparable.

This brief comparison demonstrates that annualized return and dividend yield are the key indicators for valid and accurate comparisons. In this sample, the higher dollar-value (IBM) spread produced only 34.1 percent annualized return while reducing stock net basis by $127 (current price of $101.27 versus strike of $100). Altria produced a 38.6 percent return and increased the stock basis of 600 shares by $51, or $306. Overall, Altria would produce a higher annualized return and a better capital gain outcome if the call side was exercised.

In the short straddle, you create consistently high current returns on an annualized basis; however, it is also quite likely that one side or the other in the short position will be exercised. If you accept the premise that exercise of either the call or the put (or both) would be desirable, this straddle example is quite impressive. The strategy works best when the short call and put strikes are as close as possible to the current market value of the underlying stock. For example, Coca-Cola's price is only 2 cents per share from the strike; and Wal-Mart is only 20 cents per share from the closest strike. In the short straddle, you will probably want to write options as close as possible to ATM. This maximizes the potential return.

For purposes of consistent comparison to the spread example, the short straddle is based on IBM, even though some of the other stocks in the model portfolio might be preferable in actual practice. The wide profit zone based on the dollar value of the premium generated by IBM options also produces the widest possible profit zone. Furthermore, it reduces the net basis in stock, assuming purchase price was $101.27 per share:

Price of stock	10,127
Short call premium	1,228
Short put premium	1,215
Net	$7,684

This outcome is shown in Figure 8-3.

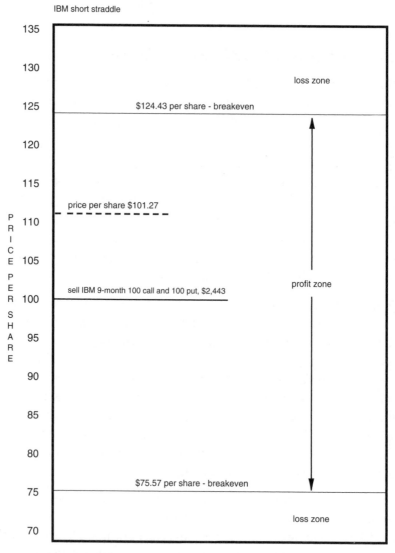

Figure 8-3 Profit and loss zone, short option straddle

The clarification of loss zone is the same as it was for the short spread: If stock price moves above or below breakeven, the loss consists of exercised options and loss of 100 shares (from exercised call) or acquisition of an additional 100 shares (from exercised put).

Maximum Advantage: Large-Point Discounts

The 34.1 percent return and discount of the net price down to $76.84 per share are impressive outcomes for this position. Referring to possible outcome scenarios, a short straddle such as this is appropriate only when you want to create exercise. It remains possible to roll out of these short positions, depending on the direction of price movement. For example, if the stock's price rises, you could close the 9-month 100 call and replace it with a 105 call expiring three months later. If the stock's price remains below the 100 put strike price, the 9-month 100 put could be replaced with a 95 put expiring three months later. In either of these events, the OTM short option loses time value and can be closed at a profit or allowed to expire. Because time and extrinsic value are quite high in this example, there is also the chance that ITM short positions could be closed at a profit due to erosion of nonintrinsic premium.

Rolling to avoid exercise extends exposure time but also increases profit potential. The short straddle is conservative as long as the usual qualifications apply: You want to keep shares of stock and add to your holdings, you have qualified the stock in fundamental terms, and you consider the put strike price (discounted by short option premium) a fair price level for the stock. In the example, the 24.43-point price discount is reasonable considering the historical trading range for IBM as of the analysis date, which ranged between $69 and $131 per share over 12 months. If you purchased 100 shares and wrote this straddle at the price shown, an exercised put would produce an average basis in the stock of the following:

Purchase price, 100 shares	$10,127
Option premium received	- 2,443
Purchase price, exercised put	9,500
Total adjusted basis, 200 shares	$17,184
Adjusted basis per share	$ 8,592

Risk is limited on the downside. Exercise of the 95 put occurring at any point between $85.92 and $9,500 per share would leave you with acquired stock at or above then-current market value (not considering trading costs). But what occurs if the value of the stock falls below $85.92 per share? If you consider the net of about $69 per share to be a low trading range for this stock, what does it mean when prices fall below the $85.92 level?

Rescue Strategies

If you write a short combination or a short straddle, it is conservative as long as you own 100 shares for each call written. This assumes that the fundamental value of the stock has been established and that you would welcome exercise. In the preceding example, a straddle on IBM produced an annualized yield of 34.1 percent and discounted the cost of stock to $76.84 per share. However, if the put were exercised, the true net cost of 200 shares (original 100 plus additional 100 shares put to you) would end up at $85.92 per share. This occurs because the 100 additional shares would be put to you at $95, bringing the net discount back up to nearly $86 per share.

If the stock's market value were to fall below $85.92 per share, you would have a net loss. Remember, if your assumed fair price level for the stock is accurate, the decline may be viewed as short term—as long as the fundamental strength of the company does not change. The price will most likely rebound above $85.92 per share at some point in the future.

Three Valuable Rescue Strategies

If necessary, you can employ one of three rescue strategies involving options and after a price decline below net basis.

1. **Sell covered calls.** The most basic rescue strategy is writing covered calls. With an increased number of shares, you can recover a paper loss and create a net profitable position, even if the calls are exercised. Referring to the previous example, if you could find a similar situation with stock at your net basis at $85.92, writing 90 calls and getting additional premium would be profitable, even if

exercised. Selling the covered calls reduces your basis below the previous net, due to the additional premium you receive.

2. **Repeat the combination or straddle. Once your previous short positions have been closed, exercised, or expired, you are free to write additional combination or straddle positions.** If you continue to believe in the fundamental value of the stock, you end up with 200 shares at a reduced basis (in the preceding example). You could write new covered calls and uncovered puts, further reducing your basis while increasing your holdings in the stock. This proposal assumes that, at reduced price per share, you remain willing to acquire more shares in the stock. With 200 shares, you may choose to keep exposure at one call and one put or, because 200 shares would be covered, you could also adjust the strategy. For example, you could sell two calls and one put or you could write two calls and one put against the position.

3. **Sell uncovered puts to reduce basis further.** Yet another alternative is to gain additional premium income by selling puts. For example, you have 200 shares, and you are willing to increase your holdings to 300. Your 200 shares have an average basis of $85.92 per share. If you write an 80 put and earn a premium of 6, or $600, it would reduce your net basis to $83.78 per share on your 200 shares. If that put were exercised, your overall basis would be $83.95 per share:

    $85.92 (2) + $80.00 = $251.84 ($83.95 per share, 300 shares)

As long as you have confidence that this adjusted basis remains a fair price for the stock, selling puts is a good form of contingent purchase *and* an effective rescue strategy. In the case of IBM, recall that the historical trading range was between $69 and $131 per share. If you use that to measure average cost, as proposed earlier, your basis remains *within a reasonable* trading range for this stock.

One final way to offset a price movement ITM on either side of the strike is to go long on a higher call or on a lower put. Based on premium levels at the time this strategy was available (with 100 strike call at 12.28 and 100 strike put at 12.15), the overall risk of exercise can be covered by purchasing a 105 call or a 95 put based on this example. You would not want to do both, but base the decision of price direction, and as an alternative to (a) rolling forward, (b) reentering the same strategy, or (c) waiting out the market. Whereas the 100 call was available at 12.28, the 105 call was priced at 9.90. This is a net difference of only 2.38, whereas the 5-point strike difference would represent a $500 loss using the long call to satisfy exercise of the short call. However, when judged against total short premium of $2,443, buying a long call is a worthwhile method for offsetting the ITM status of the short call.

Because the short position is already covered with 100 shares of stock, the need to add a long call is doubtful. It makes more sense on the short side, where a 95 put is available for 10.00. This is only 2.15 below the short premium of the 100 put; but the premium is worth considering when compared to the total short premium of $2,443. If you need to avoid exercise at $100 if and when the stock price has fallen below that level, this put purchase makes sense.

To remove all market risk from the short straddle, you can cover both short call and short put with this long put. The net credit for the position is reduced considerably:

short 100 call (covered by stock)	$1,228
short 100 put (covered by long put)	1,215
less: long 95 put	- 1,000
Net credit	$1,443

In this variation—the covered short straddle—both call and put are covered, one with underlying stock and the other with a long position. The worst-case outcome—exercise of the put—creates a $500 loss between the short and long put, reducing overall profit to $943. This is a 9.3 percent return, annualized at 12.4 percent. Considering the margin of safety accomplished with covering both short positions, many conservative investors will view this as an acceptable outcome. Without exercise of the short put, the return is 14.2 percent ($1,443 ÷ $10,127, or annualized at 18.9 percent). So without the worst-case outcome, you achieve 100 percent coverage of short option positions, and still earn a respectable annualized return.

The next chapter presents a review of sound stock selection fundamentals with option strategies in mind.

9

STOCK SELECTION AND THE OPTION CONTRACT

Selecting stocks based on your risk profile is never easy. In this chapter are conservative guidelines for smart stock selection. The worst criterion for picking a stock is basing the selection on option premium levels. By definition, high-option premiums represent greater market risk, so option premium levels are good indicators of stock market risk. This chapter proposes conservative standards, offers guidelines for managing the tax complexity of options trading, and suggests methods for using options as part of your conservative theme.

W hen all possible options strategies are considered in the context of your conservative profile, what are the criteria for determining which (if any) strategies are appropriate? A recurring theme in this book is focusing on risk profiles and remaining faithful to your original conservative investing themes, limitations, and capabilities.

No options strategy is appropriate if its use requires you to alter your risk profile. However, if you discover while investigating options that you *are* willing and able to take on higher risks than you had assumed previously, you need to reevaluate all your underlying assumptions. The process of defining risk tolerance is and should be an ever-evolving process; few investors keep the same risk profile without change over time. Risk level is determined by a broad range of other matters: knowledge and experience as an investor, personal income and capital, change of job, marriage, birth of a child, divorce, death of a family member, and changes in a family member's health.

As your personal career and life events emerge, your risk profile changes as well. This is natural and expected. The problem some investors experience is that when they suffer losses in their portfolio, they may take reckless actions, accept greater risks, and go through a transition from moderate or conservative to a more speculative profile. The intention, in many of these instances, is to gain back the losses as quickly as possible, but that is a mistake. There is wisdom in the advice to chess players: When you lose a chess piece, don't make the mistake of attacking to try to even up the score. When you are behind in points, the smart thing to do is to go on the defensive, become *more* cautious, and look for ways to protect your remaining position. If you can accomplish this *and* increase your portfolio income, you get the best of both worlds. This advice applies to most investors, especially if you define yourself as conservative. It is a mistake to try to recapture losses by taking on more risks. Everyone loses; the wise attitude is to look for ways to reduce future losses by protecting capital, insure paper profits and exploit market price swings, and seek conservative strategies that improve overall performance. All these goals are met by the thoughtful and sensible application of the options strategies explained throughout this book.

Remembering Your Conservative Profile as a Priority

Even with a thorough grounding in options and their context, you need to continually remind yourself of your personal goals, limitations, and standards. The market is a playground full of temptations, and many well-intended investors become distracted from their sensible goals and drawn to the many dangerous but exciting high-risk, exotic, and potentially profitable schemes that are so visible and so popular. Conservative, fundamentally based strategies are not terribly exciting, especially in the media-focused market environment. The media tend to emphasize index movement, substantial point change in high-profile stocks, and market rumors and news. Even fundamental news like earnings reports is focused on variation between analysts' predictions and actual outcome rather than on the value of the company as a long-term investment. This scorekeeping is the popular game on Wall Street—at the expense of less exciting but more relevant strategies based on fundamental analysis.

The market, as a media-driven "store" containing an array of products (stocks, bonds, commodities, and derivatives in many forms) is indeed a distracting place. It is very much an open market with brokers tempting buyers with promises of easy riches. Little, if any, attention is paid to the analytical, detail-oriented fundamental study of a company's financial statements and other financial information. Why should the media highlight a subtle change in a capitalization or working capital ratio? It is much easier to report a 2-cent variation between earnings and predictions or a 4-point movement in the stock's price. So, difficulty in maintaining your focus is a constant challenge in the fast-paced market. Your success, which may be defined in terms of losing less often than average, depends largely on making good decisions at the right time.

Dangers and Pitfalls in Using Options

Options, like so many aspects of the market, offer numerous temptations. The speculator is drawn to the positive aspects: leverage of capital with the potential for fast profits, often in triple digits, and the fast pace of the market. They rarely pay attention to the other attributes of risk associated with options: equally fast losses, long-position disadvantages, and the virtual impossibility of profiting from speculation consistently.

It is always tempting to go for fast and easy profits at the expense of conservative standards. However, you know that, by definition, your standards include resisting that temptation. You are aware that opportunity and risk cannot be separated and that those potentially high returns are *usually* accompanied by a similar high level of risk. Although there are exceptions within the options market, all conservative strategies have a common attribute: They are geared toward augmenting returns and protecting positions in your portfolio.

Remember how easy it is to lose sight of your original goals. You can slip out of your conservative mode, allowing risks to expand unintentionally, and become fascinated with the potential of a particular options strategy. Throughout this book, the importance of testing every strategic choice against the sound, conservative risk profile you have already established in your portfolio has served as a standard for selection.

Allocation by Risk Profile

Some people believe that a sensible way to use options is to create a base in their portfolio at some percentage of capital. For example, they may devote 80 percent of their capital to conservative investments. The remaining 20 percent is "mad money," put aside to give in to temptation and to seek high returns along with high risk. However, this is poor advice. The majority of outcomes involve losing that 20 percent. As an alternative, why not invest 100 percent of your portfolio in high-value stocks and then use options conservatively to augment returns, protect long stock positions, and take advantage of market price overreactions? It makes far more sense. You will experience consistent current yields using strategies like contingent purchase, covered calls, and short combinations (involving covered calls and uncovered puts, which is in effect a contingent purchase and a contingent sale opened at the same time). These specific uses of options do not add to market risk. Their overall theme is easily summarized: They are designed to provide conservative returns consistently over time. Of course, you will occasionally have shares of stock called away with short calls or put to you with short puts, and you may lose the opportunity to make a higher profit if you had made different choices—the value of hindsight. So, in exchange for the occasional lost opportunity, you can modify your portfolio to create option returns, a trade-off you will probably view as a good choice most of the time.

Without exception, though, these strategies (along with the use of long puts or short calls for portfolio insurance) must always conform to your long-term conservative risk profile. Your purpose is to build wealth, not to speculate recklessly; so the use of options has to be restricted to those strategies that enhance your existing long stock positions or that expose you to the purchase of stock that you desire to own—either more shares of existing issues or shares of other stocks that have been prequalified as appropriate within your portfolio.

Some people, notably those who have not examined the conservative potential in the options strategies explained in this book, may argue against the concept that options can and do augment the conservative attributes of your portfolio. One conclusion is impossible to avoid: Not only are some option strategies conservative, but not employing them puts your portfolio at greater risk. For example, when a stock's market value rises far above its normal trading range, you naturally expect a short-term correction. This is the perfect time to write covered calls. You expect the stock's value to retreat, but if strike price is properly selected with current higher-than-expected prices in mind, exercise itself would create a substantial profit. If, instead, you buy puts for insurance, you also protect paper profits by timing your decision based on a keen awareness of trading range versus current price spikes. The same observation is true when prices decline rapidly. A downward spike is a buying opportunity. The traditional method, buying additional shares, is a difficult decision to make when prices have fallen because you may be uncertain about short-term volatility and potential for further decline. An alternative is to buy calls or, even more conservatively, to sell out-of-the-money (OTM) puts. In either event, you create the potential to buy more shares and average down your basis in the stock without placing more capital at risk through purchase of shares.

Using Options to Reduce Market Risk

These are conservative strategies. The ultimate conservative approach—the short combination or short straddle explained in Chapter 8, "Combination Conservative Techniques"—creates a position in which even a drastic decline can be rescued with additional options positions. When you create a large protective range through the selection of options strategies, you *reduce* market risk rather than increase it. In many instances, just holding shares and taking no action becomes high-risk, even in a conservative portfolio. The long-term approach traditionally has shunned strategies based on reaction to short-term price movement in favor of holding onto conservative growth investments. That plan certainly works; however, *average* returns on a conservative portfolio are less than 10 percent. By definition, a conservative portfolio is unlikely to exceed market averages. Options can help you to adhere to your conservative risk profile while also beating the market consistently and substantially.

You have heard wild promises about double-digit and even triple-digit returns by applying an investing "system" of one kind or another. Experience (meaning "loss") has taught you that schemes do not work and that there are no easy or sure-fire ways to beat the market. Even the conservative use of options requires diligence, learning techniques, mastering terminology, and becoming more knowledgeable than the average investor. Some conservative investors are content to buy shares in blue chips and to place the balance of their capital in a moderate growth mutual fund. Although this traditional approach may enable you to experience average growth or even to outperform long-term averages, it is not spectacular.

Temptation to Select Most Volatile Stocks

When your conservative portfolio does not perform as you expect, what can you do? Some investors are tempted to sell lackluster stocks and go with more exciting, more volatile issues. The idea is that you can experience profits more rapidly, make up for past losses, and outperform the market. In fact, though, this approach is an abandonment of conservative principles. You need to continue to carefully select value stocks and then protect their equity value. That is the truly conservative strategy.

Investors who like the idea of using options also face danger if and when they pick stocks inappropriate for the conservative risk profile. If you shop option premiums with the idea of buying stock and then discounting your purchase price with covered calls, you are taking the wrong approach. A conservative application of options requires that you first select stocks based on fundamental analysis and comparison; that you pick stocks with lower-than-average volatility and potential for price appreciation; and that the capital structure, revenue and earnings, PE ratio, dividend history, and other indicators of your stocks are a good fit for your conservative standards. Then you use various conservative options strategies to protect equity and enhance current income. Remember, using conservative options strategies on risky, volatile stocks contradicts your standards. The first rule is to pick your stocks carefully and then identify methods for protecting their value.

Creating a List of Potential Investments

There is no shortage of high-quality stocks. By applying conservative principles, you can easily identify at least 10–20 stocks you would like to own. You might not be able to afford to buy shares of all of them, but that is not the point. Once you develop your list of potential quality-growth investments, you can buy shares in several of those companies; if a covered call strategy ends up with stock called away, that is not a complete loss. The transaction frees up capital that can be reinvested in the stock of another company on your list. As long as you continually maintain that list of strong candidates based on sound fundamentals, you should never have a shortage of good value investments that you can buy and hold, buy and cover, or apply in contingent-purchase strategies. It is a mistake to believe that only a limited number of "good" stocks are available at any given time; more likely, there will be far more issues than you can afford to own, which gives you great flexibility in moving capital from one stock to another if you need to. A long-term buy-and-hold strategy makes sense as long as fundamentals remain strong, but it does not mandate that you avoid selling stock under any circumstances. The proper selection of conservative options strategies may result in shares being called away, but as long as you experience a higher-than-average current annualized return, it is a successful transaction. In fact, application of conservative strategies can produce consistent annualized double-digit returns, as demonstrated by the many strategies explored in preceding chapters.

You gain further flexibility in options trading when you own more than 100 shares of stock. This gives you the chance to vary the use of options, to cover partial holdings, and to change the mix of short options against long stock when you roll forward and up. You can also write covered calls with a mix of expiration and strike prices, or make combinations and short straddles more flexible and interesting with a similar mix.

Creating Sensible Conservative Standards

Assuming that you accept certain options strategies as fitting within your conservative framework, it is worth asking again: What is the definition of a conservative portfolio? In other words, what are the basic standards for stock selection? You already know that picking stocks based on potential option premium levels is a mistake that should not enter into the equation.

The Five Conservative Standards for Stock Selection

There are a few well-understood conservative standards for picking stocks. These analytical topic areas should include, at the very least, the following five criteria:

1. **Revenue and earnings trends.** The quarterly and annual rate of growth in revenues and consistency in earnings is always a sound starting point in fundamental analysis. In spite of the popularity of some dot-com stocks whose companies never earned a profit, the fact remains that conservative investing is based on consistent growth in the operating statement: increasing revenues, well-controlled ratios of cost and levels of

expense, and strong earnings trends. Both revenue and earnings trends should be demonstrated over many years to establish the strength of the company.

In analyzing these trends, pay close attention to the gross profit and expenses. Gross profit should remain consistent even when revenues change significantly. Expenses should remain as constant as possible in relation to sales. You may expect some expansion in expenses as corporations diversify, acquire new lines of business, and expand geographically. But the ratio between expenses and revenues should *not* be negative. Revenues should outpace expenses, and when they do not, it is a sign of trouble. When you see sales flattening out or falling but expenses continuing to rise, that is a serious problem. Well-managed corporations should put the brakes on expenses when revenue trends slow down.

The revenue-costs-expenses-profit interaction is the essential fundamental indicator that should be the starting point in any financial review. This means that when a corporation has a net loss, there is a fundamental problem. One-time charges may explain the loss, and if that is the case, you should adjust those charges for the purpose of performing year-to-year trend analysis of the operation. However, if net losses continue from one year to the next, it is only a matter of time until capital deteriorates. Expanding net losses are a warning sign that a once-valuable investment has peaked and is on the decline.

2. **Capitalization and working capital.** The most overlooked aspect of a company's ability to remain competitive is its relative capital strength. If a company is depending increasingly on long-term debt to fund growth, an increasing portion of future earnings will have to go to debt service, leaving less capital for expanded operations and dividend payments. So a negative trend in capitalization is an alarming signal in your conservative portfolio. Tracking working capital is another method for judging a corporation's financial health. Changes may be subtle, but trends can be observed over time, and what you seek is a company that is able to anticipate cyclical change through proper planning and working capital management. A change in these

indicators is an early warning sign of a shift in long-term capital trends.

Initial review might indicate that a company is healthy in terms of working capital when that is simply not the case. For example, you may notice that a corporation maintains a strong 2-to-1 current ratio (comparison between current assets and current liabilities) from year to year, while reporting declining sales and large annual net losses. How can that be? A more detailed review may show that the corporation has been increasing its long-term debt (which is not part of the current ratio) as a means of maintaining its working capital ratio. It is a popular practice to check working capital without also reviewing the long-term debt trend. However, that trend is essential and can prove that during periods of declining sales and profits, debt is being used to bolster the balance sheet. Ultimately, the ever-growing long-term debt affects financial health, so capitalization trends, represented through the debt ratio, have to be reviewed along with the current ratio.

3. **Price-Earnings, or PE ratio trends.** The PE ratio is a perplexing indicator. It combines technical (price) and fundamental (earnings) in a single multiplier. But it is troubling because the price is current but earnings may be several months out of date. With this in mind, the PE is best reviewed as part of a trend over time. As the PE inches upward, you may conclude that investors are placing too much value in future growth potential. A more revealing form of PE than current price and latest earnings is to compare quarter-end closing prices to quarter-end earnings, and then review that version of PE over a series of fiscal quarters.

   History has demonstrated that lower PE stocks outperform higher PE stocks with remarkable consistency. But, by definition, the higher PE also indicates greater market interest in the company. Thus, this hybrid technical/fundamental indicator is a valuable meter of market sentiment. When the PE begins rising above its historical range, it may indicate that the price of stock is outpacing anticipated future growth. Because the PE reflects earnings multiples, the higher the PE, the more concern you should have regarding the long-term value of stock.

Another factor that can distort the PE is the degree of one-time adjustments needed in the reported profits of the company. If earnings per share (EPS) includes noncore items (see item 4) or one-time extraordinary adjustments, the PE is going to be inaccurate and unreliable as an indicator. You may need to adjust reported earnings to arrive at a reliable "core PE" for the purpose of trend analysis.

4. **Core-earnings-based analysis.** The need to adjust reported financial results makes all the difference in fundamental analysis. For example, if current net earnings include proceeds from the sale of a segment or other capital assets, profit from an accounting change, or pro forma earnings on invested pension assets, those items should be removed from the analysis. In many cases, core earnings adjustments can significantly change the fundamental conclusions you will reach about a particular company or about company-to-company comparisons. The intention in making core earnings adjustments is to identify the true core earnings so that comparisons from period to period or between corporations are valid.

   If you do not calculate core earnings adjustments, all other fundamental indicators are unreliable as well. For example, the PE ratio compares the stock price to earnings per share; however, if earnings per share is distorted, the PE will be distorted as well. One solution is to compute *core* earnings per share and use that in calculations of the PE. As a result, the core PE ratio becomes an indicator of the company's long-term growth trend.

5. **Dividend history and reinvestment plan.** The history of dividend payments and the current yield are important indicators. In a comparison of various options strategies, for example, you have seen that the dividend yield makes a big difference in which company you select. If you limit your selection to dividend achievers, those companies that have increased dividend payments every quarter over the past ten years, you naturally pick from among the strongest value investments available. If you also reinvest dividends in the purchase of additional shares, you achieve a compound rate of return on dividend income,

which over time adds great value. You will find plenty of conservative investments that meet these criteria, and it is an excellent method for narrowing the list of candidates.

This list is only a starting point—the bare minimum of fundamental indicators that you need. In your own conservative analysis program, you may also use any number of other indicators you find useful, including a broad range of balance sheet or income statement ratios, management indicators, or combinations of fundamental and technical trends. For example, in judging the safety of a company, the fundamentals are of paramount importance, but you may also want to examine technical volatility and implied volatility (both in stock and option price and volume trends).

Maintaining Fundamental Clarity

Investors tend to believe that good values are difficult to find. However, confusion arises in an attempt to define "value" in the market. Some investors believe they should buy stocks that double in value immediately after they purchase shares. This is simply unrealistic. But even conservative investors may end up chasing short-term profits and may conclude that it is difficult to find profits—by a double-in-value definition—with consistency.

Under a truly conservative standard, a quality investment should be defined as a strongly capitalized, well-managed, profitable, and competitive company whose stock has performed strongly and consistently, and whose fundamental and technical risks are a good match for your conservative profile. Under this definition, there are many good values to be found in the market. The argument against covered call writing—that you risk losing stock if exercised—is often premised on the idea that a particular stock, once lost, cannot be replaced. In fact, though, good values abound and can be located using fundamental criteria. Additionally, the certainty of better-than-average returns from writing covered calls more than offsets the occasions in which stock is called away. You may want to develop a list of prequalified companies. The list may be far larger than the number of stocks you can afford to own, but it broadens your strategic range, and you come to realize that having "good" shares called away is not actually a loss. As long as you can consistently earn current returns in your portfolio *and* maintain a conservative standard, there is no real lost opportunity problem. You simply replace one opportunity with another.

Distinctions: Risk Standards versus Brand Loyalty

The clarity with which you view your long-term goals has everything to do with how you manage your portfolio. Investors often develop a "brand loyalty" to the stocks they own. Closely related to this is an aversion to some companies based on noninvesting criteria. For example, some people hate Wal-Mart, Microsoft, or Halliburton to the extent that they will never buy shares in those companies. Some investors are faithful to IBM, Sears, or Kodak. These love-or-hate opinions often are not based on fundamental analysis but on some personal, social, or political opinion. To maintain clarity, it is advisable to avoid investing in companies that you either love or hate, if only because strong feelings about a particular company can cloud judgment. You can make more objective decisions about when to buy, hold, or sell a company's stock if you are neutral about its management, policies, politics, or social impact. For example, if you once owned a small retail store and you were forced out of business because Wal-Mart opened a Supercenter across the street, you may not be able to objectively evaluate the investment value of Wal-Mart stock. If you swear by Kodak products for your personal use, you may not be able to analyze the company's ability to compete in the digital camera market.

Given the large number of excellent quality investments, it makes sense to limit your analysis to those companies that you can evaluate objectively. In stock selection as well as in a decision to employ options strategies, there is plenty of fundamental analysis to be done without also struggling with personal feelings about the company itself. If you have personal conflicts about a company, avoid buying shares, and restrict your search to those companies that you do not find offensive on some noninvestment level.

Once you pick companies that qualify for your fundamental, conservative standards, you also want to maintain clarity on two other levels:

stock ownership and the use of options. Base the decision to hold or sell on consistency in fundamental indicators or on emerging changes in trends. A particular stock might be a good candidate for option strategies; this does not mean that the stock continues to qualify as part of your conservative portfolio. It makes sense to sell shares of stock as soon as the risk factors change and those factors are clear and precise, based on financial information and capital strength, not on technical aspects of option values.

The second form of clarity is the use of options. A limited number of appropriate strategies are present in your conservative portfolio, and once you have set standards limiting their use, be sure to avoid the temptation to wander from those limited, conservative applications. To review, your criteria may include the following.

- Use options only for stocks you own or want to own.
- Use short calls only if and when you are willing to accept exercise.
- Use short puts only if you are willing to buy additional shares, either through a contingent-purchase plan or when market movement presents buying opportunities.
- Premium value from writing short options should be at or greater than a minimum annualized return (for example, you might use 10 percent as a minimum in annualized standard).
- Long options should be purchased to (a) protect existing paper profits, (b) exploit unusual and temporary market movements, (c) provide cover for short option positions, and (d) average down your basis in the stock.
- Long calls may also be used as a form of contingent purchase, but only for stocks you want to buy; it is one way to leverage capital by locking in strike prices on numerous stocks, notably when using Long-term Equity AnticiPation Security (LEAPS) options.
- Writing short combinations or straddles is appropriate only when the call side is covered and when all possible outcomes have been evaluated and qualified to meet your conservative standards. To make these short positions more conservative, you can cover short put positions with lower-strike long puts, reducing overall profit but removing market risk.

The Importance of Taxes in the Option Equation

Even when you have defined clear guidelines for using options in your portfolio, you may yet face complications due to the tax rules, one of the most troubling aspects of including options as a portfolio strategy. Although everyone hopes for tax simplification, history shows that reforms in the federal tax system have invariably made matters more complex.

A seemingly innocent strategy, such as a short straddle, can cause complex tax problems. The least of these may be deferral of losses to a future period when a second leg of a straddle closes.

Five Tax Guidelines

A more significant threat than deferral of losses is the removal of long-term capital gains status in exercised stock. Some tax guidelines worth remembering include the following.

- **Limit covered calls to OTM positions.** Using OTM calls avoids the complexities that arise when writing in-the-money (ITM) calls. Additionally, the most conservative method in the market involves OTM positions, so this makes sense based on your risk profile as well.

- **Accept exposure to loss of long-term capital gains only when you have carryover losses.** Most investors are not happy to exchange a large, long-term capital gain for the higher-rate short-term gains tax. One exception is that if you have large carryover losses to absorb, you can maximize options strategies by accepting short-term gains and sheltering them by using part of the carryover loss. Net losses are limited to $3,000 per year; so a large carryover shelters current year profits.

- **Be aware of how the tax rules affect any combination strategies, especially short straddles.** This book emphasizes the strategic possibilities of taking various options positions as well as maintaining a conservative risk profile while maximizing potential profits. However, you should also be aware of how a specific strategy affects your tax liabilities.

- **Remember that rolling out of one position and into another could change the status of capital gains taxation.** If you begin with an OTM covered call and then roll forward to a later expiring ITM position, you could trigger the loss of long-term status for the underlying stock. Before picking a new position, be aware of the potential higher tax that could result.

- **Check with a qualified tax expert before you enter into trades.** The tax rules for options are complex and, in some cases, uncertain. For example, the antistraddle rule is so vague that it may even be unclear when it applies. Make sure that you and your tax expert understand the rules and the tax consequences of your decisions before executing trades.

Option Volatility to Judge Stocks

Tax rules are certainly a complication in your portfolio. Taxes alone may prevent your entering specific types of transactions. However, knowing the tax outcome in advance provides you with better information and guidelines for proceeding. For most investors, managing market risk—usually measured by degrees of volatility—is a more immediate problem.

Most investors agree that, as a technical indicator, changes in volatility also signal changes in risk. High volatility in option premium is a warning sign. Although higher-than-average option premium (caused by implied volatility) is attractive, it also tells you that buying shares of stock is a high-risk idea. It contradicts your conservative risk profile.

The temptation to buy highly volatile stocks specifically to sell covered calls is difficult to resist. But the greatest trap is to start out as a conservative investor and end up with a portfolio of inappropriate stocks. It can happen easily if your selection is based on option-specific valuation rather than on tried-and-true fundamental indicators for selection of the underlying stock. It is not necessary to stray from the conservative standard because it is not difficult to earn options-based returns through conservative strategies. This is possible using LEAPS options in short positions on conservative stocks with strong fundamentals, for example. A 16-percent annualized return using options with a conservative stock is far better than a 32-percent return from covered calls on a highly volatile stock. Compare the potential return to what you earn on average rather than on what you could earn using more volatile stocks and higher risk strategies. That is the key.

Volatility as an Early Indicator

Option volatility itself may indicate emerging fundamental problems in a company. The problems may be temporary or permanent. For example, the current quarter's earnings may be lower than expected, which creates momentary volatility. But in the long-term, bigger picture, the company's fundamentals have not changed. In other instances, perhaps a corporation has peaked and is now beginning a gradual downward earnings slide, loss of competitive position, or subtle changes in financial strength. If debt capitalization is inching upward as a percentage of total capitalization, for example, it could signal a change in fundamental strength. This ultimately affects dividends and erodes working capital; recognizing such changes early helps you to time decisions. Option volatility is not always an early indicator, but it could be. So, if option volatility changes suddenly, it is worth the effort to check fundamental trends, evaluate recent news or earnings reports, and look for any confirming signs that the financial strength and position of the company have changed.

Using the company's fundamental indicators as a means for deciding whether to buy stock is always the preferred place to start. Options should be viewed as alternative strategies that may augment the conservative portfolio strategy, provide alternatives to outright purchase, or enable you to protect or take paper profits without having to sell shares.

Option volatility can help you to coordinate your fundamental analysis with technical tests. Degrees of volatility provide potential confirming information or even signal coming changes. In addition to reviewing the fundamentals, technical tests of various types can be used—in conjunction with fundamental analysis—to augment your study of trends. Technical and fundamental volatility are closely related. For example, when a company reports consistent growth in revenues and earnings over time, you are likely to also observe a gradual increase in stock market value within a relatively narrow trading range. When the trading range is broader or erratic compared to marketwide trends, it usually signals similar volatility in the fundamentals.

With this in mind, it makes sense to test a limited number of technical indicators along with your fundamentals. These may include option premium volatility as well as trading-range trends and the stock's support and resistance levels. A comparison between fundamental and technical indicators improves your overall program and often provides greater insight than you can achieve with a program limited only to a few fundamental indicators.

The time difference between financial reports and current trends limits the isolated use of fundamentals. Because quarterly and annual reports are outdated by the time they are released, it is difficult to equate these reports to current price trends. However, you often see emerging trends in price volatility as an indicator of pending financial changes, just as current earnings reports have an immediate effect on the technical side.

It makes perfect sense to consider option volatility within a coordinated fundamental plan; this is especially true if you incorporate technical indicators into your study of a particular company. Options have no fundamentals of their own, which is why it is so important to limit your use of options to appropriately selected stocks. A conservative portfolio's overall return can be both protected and enhanced with options, and done so in a way that remains faithful to your risk profile that is so crucial to your investing success. You want to avoid the mistake of using options in ways that expose your portfolio to high risk. Thus, you want to isolate your options program to only those strategies that protect your portfolio or that provide premium returns without increasing market risk. As with any range of strategies, the *appropriate* range of possible uses of options is a short list—and it should be. Inexperienced investors are invariably surprised when they experience losses. Wiser investors know that although some losses are unavoidable, reducing the chances of loss is the key to success. Options can help achieve that while improving overall rates of return in your conservative portfolio.

Appendix

OPTION TRADING STRATEGIES

Following is a summary of the strategies presented in this book.

Strategy		Purpose/Explanation
Basic long call	a.	As a purely speculative position
	b.	Used to take advantage of price declines in stock
	c.	As a form of contingent purchase
Basic long put	a.	As a purely speculative position
	b.	Used to take advantage of price rise in stock (insurance for paper profits)
	c.	As a form of contingent sale of stock
Basic uncovered call	a.	A highly speculative position with unlimited risk
	b.	As part of a ratio write
Basic uncovered put	a.	As a form of contingent purchase
	b.	As part of a rescue strategy

Put insurance	**a.**	Buying long puts to ensure current long-stock profits
Contingent-purchase strategies	**a.**	Long calls purchased as an alternative to buying stock
	b.	Puts sold to create a credit as well as contingent purchase
	c.	The covered long call with higher strike price, shorter expiring short calls
Rolling strategies	**a.**	Rolling forward to defer expiration while creating a credit
	b.	Rolling short calls forward and up to defer or avoid expiration and to increase potential exercise price
	c.	Rolling short puts forward and down to defer or avoid expiration and to reduce potential exercise price
	d.	Rolling back—exchanging a current option position for one expiring sooner
Ratio write	**a.**	Creating partially covered positions with some degree of risk
	b.	Modified to eliminate all risk by buying high calls to offset short exposure

Rescue strategies	**a.**	Short puts to create a credit and, if exercised, to reduce average basis
	b.	Covered calls to reduce paper loss
	c.	Two-part combination of short puts and, when exercised, converting to covered calls
Forced exercise	**a.**	Intentional exercise using covered calls
Spread strategies	**a.**	Long spread, high risk requiring adequate price movement
	b.	Short spread with uncovered positions— high risk
	c.	Short spread involving covered call and uncovered put—conservative when fundamental criteria and assumptions are present
Straddle strategies	**a.**	Long straddle, high risk requiring substantial price movement
	b.	Short straddle with uncovered positions— extremely high risk
	c.	Short straddle combining covered call and uncovered put— ultimate conservative strategy with higher-than-average returns, assuming that basic fundamental criteria and assumptions are present

GLOSSARY

annualized basis   a calculation of return on an option strategy, adjusted to reflect that return as if the position had been open for one year.

at the money (**ATM**)   the status of an option when its strike price is equal to the stock's current market value.

average down   a technique for reducing net basis in stock as part of a rescue strategy; by purchasing shares at the current market price, the overall basis in the stock is reduced so that option strategies can be employed to create a net profitable outcome.

call   an option providing the buyer with the right, but not the obligation, to purchase 100 shares of a specified stock, at a specified strike price and by an expiration date, and obligating a seller to deliver 100 shares at a fixed strike price if and when the buyer exercises the contract.

closing purchase transaction   an order to close a short position through purchase at the current price or premium.

closing sale transaction   an order to close a long position through sale at the current price or premium.

combination   any strategy involving option contracts on the same underlying stock, when terms (strike price, expiration, or call versus put) are not identical.

core earnings   the earnings of a corporation based on inclusion of revenue, costs, and expenses only related to its core business, and excluding all noncore, extraordinary, or other nonrecurring items.

covered call   a strategy in which one call is sold for every 100 shares owned; considered a conservative strategy because it reduces market risk while offering exceptional return.

current market value   the value of a stock or option based on what a buyer would pay or on what a seller would receive if a transaction were executed now.

deep in or out   a condition in which an option is more than 5 points in the money (ITM) or out of the money (OTM). A call is ITM when the current market value is higher than the strike price; a put is ITM when current market value is lower than the strike price.

discount   a reduction in cost or price, creating a lower basis in stock through selling options.

dividend yield   the yield from dividends paid on stock, calculated by dividing annual dividends by the current value (current yield) of the stock or by the original cost of the stock.

downside protection   advantage gained using options to protect long positions through the purchase of an insurance put or through the sale of covered calls.

exercise   the purchase of stock under terms of a call, or the sale of stock under terms of a put; exercise takes place at the fixed strike price of the option, regardless of the stock's current market value.

expiration   the date on which an option becomes worthless.

fundamental volatility   the relative tendency of a company's operating results to be consistent from one period to another or to be erratic. The higher the inconsistency of revenue and earnings results, the higher the fundamental volatility.

implied volatility   the anticipated future value of an option based on the current market value of the stock and its proximity to strike price, the time remaining until expiration, the stock price volatility, and the transaction volume in the option.

in the money (ITM)   the condition in which the stock's current market value is higher than a call's strike price or lower than a put's strike price.

intrinsic value   the portion of option premium equal to the number of points, if any, that are in the money (ITM). When the option is at the money (ATM) or out of the money (OTM), there is no intrinsic value.

leverage a strategic utilization of capital to control more capital; for example, a contingent purchase plan involving options is a form of leverage because it locks the purchase price, but the buyer has the right to exercise or not exercise the option in the future.

listed option an option available to the general public and through public exchanges, which normally expires in 8 months or less.

lock-in price the strike price of an option, which is the purchase or sell price in the event of exercise.

long position a position in a stock or option in which the first transaction is an opening purchase, followed later by a closing sale.

Long-term Equity AnticiPation Securities (LEAPS) an option whose life lasts up to 36 months as opposed to a traditional listed option, whose life is limited to 8 months or less.

naked position any short call not covered by an offsetting stock position. A naked call is a short position in which the seller does not also own 100 shares of stock for each option written.

opening purchase transaction an order to open a long position through purchase at the current price or premium.

opening sale transaction an order to open a short position through sale at the current price or premium.

option an intangible call or put contract providing certain rights to buyers and obligations to sellers. A buyer pays a premium to acquire rights. The buyer of a call option has the right to purchase 100 shares of stock at a specified strike price and by a specified date in the future. The buyer of a put option has the right to sell 100 shares of stock at a specified strike price and by a specified date in the future. An option seller receives a premium for accepting obligations. A call seller is required to sell 100 shares of stock at a specified strike price and by a specified date in the future if and when the buyer exercises the call (calls the stock from the seller). A put seller is required to buy 100 shares of stock at a specified strike price and by a specified date in the future if and when the buyer exercises the put (puts the stock to the seller). In all cases, options exist on a specific stock and cannot be transferred.

out of the money (OTM)   a condition in which the current market value of stock is lower than a call's strike price or higher than a put's strike price.

premium   the current value of an option, which is paid by the buyer or to the seller for opening a position.

put   an option providing the buyer with the right, but not the obligation, to sell 100 shares of a specified stock, at a specified strike price and by an expiration date, and obligating a seller to purchase 100 shares at a fixed strike price if and when the buyer exercises the contract.

ratio write   a variation on the covered call strategy involving the writing of a number of calls other than one call per 100 shares of stock.

rescue strategy   an option strategy designed to offset a net decline in value of stock, using options to average down basis or to offset paper losses with option profits.

return if exercised   a calculation of overall return from a short-option strategy, based on exercise of the option and expressed on an annualized basis.

return if unchanged   a calculation of return from a short-option strategy, based on expiration of the option and expressed on an annualized basis.

roll down   replacement of one short put with another when the strike price of the replacement put is lower than the strike price of the original put.

roll forward   a replacement of one short call or put when the strike price remains the same but the current expiration date is replaced with a later one.

roll forward and up/down   a strategy in which an existing option is replaced to avoid exercise, often also creating a net credit. An existing short call is closed and replaced with another whose strike price is higher and whose expiration occurs later (roll up); an existing short put is closed and replaced with another whose strike price is lower and whose expiration occurs later (roll down).

roll up a replacement of one short call with another when the strike price of the replacement call is higher than the strike price of the original call.

short position a position in a stock or option in which the first transaction is an opening sale, followed later by a closing purchase.

speculation an investment profile accepting high risk in exchange for the opportunity to earn exceptionally high short-term profits (or to suffer high short-term losses). Speculators usually are not interested in long-term growth or in holding equity positions.

spread a strategy in which options are either purchased or sold on the same stock, with varying strike prices, expiration dates, or both.

straddle a strategy in which an identical number of calls and puts, with identical expiration dates and strike prices, are either purchased (long straddle) or sold (short straddle).

strike price the price at which options are exercised, regardless of the current market value of the underlying stock.

support level the price or price range of a stock representing the lowest likely price that buyers and sellers agree upon.

terms collectively, the contractual conditions and definitions of every option, including identification of the option as either a call or a put, the expiration date, the strike price, and the underlying security.

time value the intangible option premium, equal to all out-of-the-money (OTM) value and exceeding any intrinsic value.

total return the combined return from option strategies, including option premium, capital gain, and dividend income, all net of transaction costs.

uncovered option a short call when the seller does not own 100 shares of stock for each call written, or any short put.

underlying stock the stock on which an option is bought or sold.

volatility a measurement of safety, the degree of movement in current market value of a stock's price or of an option's premium.

INDEX

A

Altria, 5, 41, 72-76, 78, 111-113, 139, 145, 162, 203-207, 215
anti-straddle rule, 199-200
at the money, 21-22

B

Black-Scholes Model, 38-40

C

call
 buying, 93
 contingent purchase, 137-140
 contingent sale, 155-156
 covered, 108-120, 129, 140-144
 down markets, 172-175
 rescue strategy, 148-150, 218-220
 selling, 91
 strategies, 17-22
 uncovered, 64-65
 volatility, 28-30, 35-45, 105, 176-177
carryover loss, 102-103, 185-187
Caterpillar, 5, 41, 72, 75-77, 111, 138, 145, 162, 203-204, 206, 214

Chicago Board Options Exchange (CBOE), 49, 73
Coca-Cola, 5, 41, 72-73, 75-76, 111, 113, 139, 145, 162, 203-204, 206, 214
combinations, 199-200
conservative strategies, 44-45, 60-62, 87-91, 115-124, 132, 159-160, 166-170, 200-202, 223, 228-232
contingent purchase, 27, 144-147
contingent sale, 155-156
covered LEAPS, 31-32
crowd mentality, 158

D

delayed quotes, 37-38
dividend reinvestment plans (DRIPs), 81
dividend yield, 76
downside protection, 124-127, 180-182

E

effective tax rate, 103
extrinsic value, 10, 122-124
Exxon Mobil, 5, 42, 72, 75-76, 111-115, 139, 145, 162, 203-207, 214

F

fundamental indicators, 89-90,
  159-160, 232-234
fundamental volatility, 57-59

G

ground rules, 2-4

I

IBM, 5, 41, 72-76, 111-112,
  123-124, 138, 145, 162, 168-170,
  203-218
in the money, 21-22
insurance put, 24-25
intrinsic value, 10
investing standards, 94-96

J

Johnson & Johnson, 5, 41, 72,
  75-76, 111-113, 139, 145, 162,
  203-206, 214

L

LEAPS options, 5, 10, 28-32, 55,
  76, 190
long-term goals, 80-82
lost opportunity risk, 59-60

M

margin requirements, 68-70
market box, 158

market opportunities, 40-44
market risk, 58
McDonald's, 5, 41, 54-55, 72-73,
  75-76, 111-113, 139, 145, 162,
  203-208, 214
MMM, 5, 41, 72, 75-76, 111, 113,
  139, 145, 162, 203-204, 206, 214
model portfolio, 4-6

O

option
  at the money, 21-22
  Black-Scholes Model, 38-40
  combinations, 201-202
  contingent purchase, 135-140
  contracts, 8-13
  covered, 108-120, 140-144
  downside protection, 124-127,
    182-185
  examples, 202-210
  exercise, 82-84, 130-132,
    155-156
  in the money, 21-22
  inertia problem, 99-102
  LEAPS, 5, 10, 28-32, 55, 76,
    190
  leverage, 134-137, 174-175
  listed, 28-32
  long, 13-17, 161-165, 194-196
  long-term, 11
  management, 89-91
  out of the money, 21-22
  outcome scenarios, 211-213
  paper profits, 162

perceptions, 60-63
pitfalls, 224-226
planning, 185-187
profit or loss, 46-47, 86-88,
  150-151
ratio write, 151-153
rescue strategy, 96-97,
  148-150, 171-172, 176-177,
  218-220
return calculations, 70-80,
  207-210
rolling, 130-132
secondary strategy, 97-99
short, 13-17, 25-27, 63-67,
  165-170, 194-196
spread, 190-192
straddle, 192-194, 213-218
strategies, 17-27, 200-202, 222
strike, 11-12, 170-172
taxes, 47-49, 102-105,
  127-129, 235-236
terms, 19-20
theory, 198-200
time advantage, 12-13
timing, 62-63
uncovered, 64-65
valuation, 9-10
out of the money, 21-22

P

portfolio goals, 32-35
profit taking, 14-15, 92-99

put
  buying, 91, 161-165
  contingent purchase, 27,
    144-147, 176-177
  insurance cost, 24-25
  overlooked value, 23-24
  rescue strategy, 153-154,
    171-172, 218-220
  selling, 25-27, 66-67, 93,
    165-170
  strategies, 22-27
  volatility, 35-45, 105

Q

qualified covered calls, 129
quality of earnings, 45

R

ratio write, 151-153
realized profits, 92-94
rescue strategy, 96-97, 148-150,
  153-154, 218-220
return calculations, 70-80,
  169-172
risk
  allocation, 224-226
  downside, 124-127, 182-185
  evaluation, 180-182
  lost opportunity, 59-60
  market, 58, 172-175, 226
  mitigation with options,
    55-57

nature of, 52-60
net, 93
options, 181
profile, 182
realities, 90-91
short put, 66-67
short selling, 17, 66-67
standards, 233-234
volatility, 35-45, 53-55,
176-177, 226-228, 236-238
rolling forward, 130-132,
142-143

S

secondary strategy, 97-99
short sellers, 12-13
speculation, 159-160, 174-175
spread, 192-194
stock evaluation, 175-182,
227-232
straddle, 192-194, 213-218
strike price, 11-12

T

tangible book value, 65-66
time value, 10, 12-13, 122-124
trading costs, 20, 46-47

U

UPS, 5, 41, 72, 75-76, 111, 113,
139, 145, 162-164, 203-204,
206-208, 214

V

volatile markets, 28-30, 35-45,
89-90, 176-177

W

Wal-Mart, 5, 42, 72, 75-76,
78, 111-113, 139, 145, 162,
203-208, 214
wash sales, 47-48

FINANCIAL TIMES

In an increasingly competitive world, it is quality
of thinking that gives an edge—an idea that opens new
doors, a technique that solves a problem, or an insight
that simply helps make sense of it all.

We work with leading authors in the various arenas
of business and finance to bring cutting-edge thinking
and best-learning practices to a global market.

It is our goal to create world-class print publications
and electronic products that give readers
knowledge and understanding that can then be
applied, whether studying or at work.

To find out more about our business
products, you can visit us at www.ftpress.com.